THE TROUBLE WITH FARRAKHAN AND THE NATION OF ISLAM

ANOTHER MESSAGE TO THE BLACK MAN IN AMERICA

BY ELRETA DODDS
FOREWORD BY GLENN R. PLUMMER

PRESS TOWARD THE MARK PUBLICATIONS
DETROIT MICHIGAN

The Trouble with Farrakhan and The Nation of Islam

Published By Press Toward The Mark Publications
P.O. Box 02099 Detroit Michigan 48202. First Edition.
Printed and bound in the United States of America.

Library of Congress Catalog Card Number: 97-92584
ISBN 0-9660390-0-9

Edited by Noreta Dennard
Cover Design: Barb Gunia, Ypsilanti MI

THE TROUBLE WITH

FARRAKHAN

AND THE NATION OF ISLAM

ANOTHER
MESSAGE
TO THE
BLACK MAN
IN AMERICA

THIS BOOK IS DEDICATED TO
PASTOR EMERY MOSS JR.
FOUNDER AND SENIOR PASTOR OF
STRICTLY BIBLICAL BIBLE TEACHING MINISTRIES

HE IS MY PASTOR, TEACHER, AND FRIEND

ACKNOWLEDGEMENTS

Shouts of praise and a resounding "Thank you" to Jesus Christ, Lord and Saviour, who has given me the strength and fortitude to take on such an endeavor.

Special thanks to Pastor Emery Moss Jr., Senior Pastor of Strictly Biblical Bible Teaching Ministries, for his critique. Special thanks to Noreta Dennard, my beloved sister, for her critique and editorial revisions. Special thanks to Glenn R. Plummer, President of the Christian Television Network, for his Foreword. Special thanks to Charles Reed for his research. Special thanks to Paul Campbell for his transferring of computer systems data. Special thanks to all those who have supported this project.

TABLE OF CONTENTS

Foreword by Glenn R. Plummer.......i

Introduction................................iii

PART ONE

CHAPTER ONE
Christianity, Orthodox Islam, and the Nation of Islam: Do They all Really Worship the Same God?...........p. 1

CHAPTER TWO
Defending the Christian Faith: The Apologetics of it All
....p. 28

PART TWO

CHAPTER THREE
A Discussion of Farrakhan's 1995 Million Man March Speech
....p. 48

CHAPTER FOUR
A Brief Look at the Prelude to Farrakhan's 1996 Saviour's Day Speech...p. 77

A Discussion of Farrakhan's 1996 Saviour's Day Speech,
....p. 82

CHAPTER FIVE
A Discussion of Farrakhan's 1996 New Bethel Church Speech,
....p. 124

CHAPTER SIX
A Discussion of Farrakhan's 1996 Mosque Maryam Speech
....p. 145

CHAPTER SEVEN
Farrakhan: Called of God or Guided by Satan
....p. 181

THE EPILOGUE: To American Blacks
....p. 201

FOREWORD

In reading *The Trouble with Farrakhan and the Nation of Islam: Another Message to the Black Man in America,* I'm reminded of a November 1956 sermon delivered by Rev. Martin Luther King Jr. in Montgomery Alabama. During the sermon, Rev. King said "always be sure that you struggle with Christian methods and Christian weapons. Never succumb to the temptation of becoming bitter. As you press on, be sure to move with dignity and discipline, using only the weapon of love."

In this book, Elreta Dodds takes the high road of dignity and discipline. She offers a thoughtful and scholarly assessment of the trouble and dangers of Louis Farrakhan and his Nation of Islam. Although she stands in defense of the gospel of Jesus Christ, she uses among her arsenal of weapons, the weapon of love. Elreta says some tough yet necessary things, particularly during a pivotal time in the history of African Americans in this nation.

During the 1990s, the church in America has undergone a frontal attack by the followers of Islam. The black church in particular has experienced a cleverly devised strategic shift to pull it into their web of deception. Elreta clearly and effectively discusses this phenomenon.

Although Orthodox Islam does not embrace, and in fact, rejects the claims of the Nation of Islam, Orthodox Islam has, nevertheless, seen the Nation of Islam as a major foothold in impacting America with its anti-Christian beliefs.

For decades, it was common, within the African American community to hear the members of the Nation of Islam say that "the Bible was written by the white man" and that "Christianity is the white man's religion." Because of this firm position taken by the Nation of Islam, black America, by and large, rejected any serious dialogue with them. Since, the largest majority of African Americans are members of a black Christian church, the Nation of Islam's strategy had to shift in order to bring more credibility to them within the black community. Thus, Louis Farrakhan, the current leader of the Nation of Islam, began to publicly and positively affirm the teachings, parables, and name of Jesus Christ. He further began to quote from the Bible in most all of his public addresses to black audiences and ceased from quoting the Koran. A surprising thing took place: Mr. Farrakhan's following among African Americans began to significantly increase. He began to enjoy new alliances with black Christian ministers and of course, the shift of this new strategy culminated with the Million Man March.

Foreword

In order to balance the growing concerns among members of the Nation of Islam regarding this new, positive affirmation of Jesus Christ and the Bible, Mr. Farrakhan began to define for the Black Muslim who this "Jesus" really is that he was quoting so frequently. Interestingly, as he defined this *real* Jesus, he cleverly did it away from any black Christian audience. It has since been nationally noted, in public forums, that Mr. Farrakhan believes that he himself is Messiah, Saviour, deliverer, and in fact, Jesus. This is the epitome of modern-day blasphemy. He unwittingly did not expect this damnable antichrist doctrine to be disclosed to a national black Christian audience.

It is time for Christians to involve themselves in the great issues of our day. We should be unafraid and unashamed to fight with heart and passion, with intelligence and integrity, for the things we hold most dear. Elreta Dodds, without apology, is standing up for what she stands for while at the same time saying what she will not stand for. I am pleased to say that the church of Jesus Christ is fortunate to have her as a defender of the faith once delivered to the saints.

--Glenn R. Plummer

INTRODUCTION

In the year 1619 an event took place in America that would forever effect its economy, politics, social functioning, reputation, race relations, and spirituality: the first African slaves, twenty of them in all, were sold to English colonists in Jamestown Virginia. Ultimately, slavery in America was abolished in 1865 but not without the intense fighting and massive bloodshed of the Civil War whose end included the assassination of President Abraham Lincoln, a man loved by the North and hated by the South.

America endorsed many of the atrocities committed against Africans and African-Americans during its two hundred and forty-six year reign of slavery. Even after slavery became illegal, injustices against blacks continued into the twentieth century, which spurred the fight for civil rights. Historically, the ill-treatment of blacks in America has not only included slavery but has also involved separation of the family, beatings, rapes, public floggings, lynchings, civil rights infractions, discriminatory practices, and the list goes on.

It is therefore no wonder that, even today, African-Americans are still emotionally effected by the lingering stench of a once all prevailing brutal slavery system and a bloody civil rights struggle that the American government refuses to offer so much as a mere apology for.

Race relations between blacks and whites in America continue to be strained. Institutional racism against minorities indeed exists. However, the government as well as some whites deny its reality. The Rodney King tragedy as well as the Mark Fuhrman fiasco along with countless similar unrecorded incidences, continues to spawn distrust in the black community toward the police and the "white establishment." However, in recent years nothing seemed to bring more attention to how damaging the detachment is between blacks and whites as did the reactions to the verdict of the O.J. Simpson double murder trial. Most blacks were elated with the verdict while the majority of whites were devastated. With this, many whites began to realize that the problem of race relations in the United States is much more serious than they had suspected, which is what blacks had been trying to say all along.

There is no question about it: the racial divide in America continues to expose itself and recurrently rears its ugly head out of hibernation with a bang. If the sixties was the landmark era for civil rights then the nineties has become the land mine era waiting to explode in the face of civil rights injustices. It is plain to see that the issues of discrimination, hatred, and oppression continue to be predominant in today's American society. Appearing in the midst of the madness is

Introduction

Louis Farrakhan (a man who has positioned himself to be thought of by many as a prominent leader of black Americans) whose 1995 organization and administration of a Million Man March to Washington catapulted him to fame, stardom, and a dangerous position of authority within the American black community. Farrakhan is the present day leader of the Nation of Islam. He believes and supports the teachings of Wallace Fard and the writings of Elijah Muhammad. The Nation of Islam began with Wallace Fard in the 1930s and continued with Elijah Muhammad in the sixties. It is a religion that is a cult of Orthodox Islam. Orthodox Islam does not follow the teachings of either Wallace Fard, Elijah Muhammad, or Farrakhan.

In his 1965 book, *Message to the BlackMan in America*, Elijah Muhammad basically taught that white people are devils, that black people are superior beings, and that Christianity is the "white man's" religion. I have another message to give to the black man in America; a message that tells the truth. Despite his flowery speeches and grand mastery of the art of expression, Farrakhan's main goal is to convert black people to the Nation of Islam and to pave the way for separation between America's black and white communities. This goal is his hidden agenda. In his book, *The Black Muslims in America*, Eric Lincoln quotes Gordon Allport as saying, "The Black Muslim believes that the day of the white man has passed or soon will. Peaceful integration is not the Negro's goal, for 'why integrate with a dying man?' What the Negro requires is a new morale, economic self-sufficiency, a high code of personal morals, and a return to the pristine glory of his race. He needs to free himself from all remnants of slave mentality and from Christianity which has too long kept him doped in subservience to the white man. These are the underlying propositions upon which the movement rests."

Many black people in America are mad. They are hurting and often times ponder how a government could have sanctioned such a disgraceful and deplorable system of slavery as did the American government. No answers have been given. As a result, those same blacks are bitter towards whites. Since the government is a majority white rule then anger against the government filters into feelings about white people as a whole. Consequently, blacks who are bitter, see all white people as their enemy, and it is these blacks, Christian and non-Christian alike, who are the most easily influenced by the likes of Farrakhan and his rhetoric.

This book speaks to everyone, but it especially speaks to black people in America and more specifically to Christian blacks who insist on supporting and following Farrakhan. The purpose of this book is to 1) challenge the modern-day fallacy that Christianity and Islam are compatible, 2) reveal, in detail, the true agenda of Farrakhan, and 3) expose Farrakhan for who he really is: an antichrist and a false prophet steered by racist views.

Part One of this book will include Chapters One and Two. Chapter One will discuss the differences between Christianity, Orthodox Islam, and the Nation of Islam (the Black Muslims) with a specific focus on the question as to whether or not the three religions worship the same God. A comparative analysis between the three doctrines will be made.

Chapter Two will present arguments in defense of the Christian faith. Some of these arguments will be compared with arguments that defend Islam and the Nation of Islam. Without hesitation, Christianity is emphasized as being the only righteous religion.

Part Two of this book will include Chapters Three through Seven and the Epilogue. Chapters Three, Four, Five, and Six will consecutively discuss, in detail, excerpts from the following speeches: Farrakhan's 1995 Million Man March speech, Farrakhan's 1996 Saviour's Day speech, Farrakhan's 1996 speech delivered at Detroit's New Bethel Church and Farrakhan's 1996 speech delivered at Chicago's Mosque Maryam. Excerpts taken from Farrakhan's speeches will be in bold print. The focus here is to expose the mentality behind the man in an effort to prove that Farrakhan has other motives besides merely bringing black people into a better state of unity.

Chapter Seven answers the question as to whether or not Farrakhan is called of God or guided by Satan, and also summarizes the diabolical strategies being used in this particular demonic spiritual attack against blacks in America.

Farrakhan is propagating Islam under the guise of black unity. He wants to convince blacks that Islam is the "natural religion of the black man." Again, Farrakhan's goal and hidden agenda is to convert blacks, particularly Christian blacks to Islam. If enough Christian blacks are converted, then the influence of the Nation of Islam will become very powerful in the black community and Farrakhan would be closer to his secondary goal of racial separatism. This agenda is real whether he acknowledges it or not. It is through God's directive placed in my heart that I feel burdened to expose the heretical and racist teachings of the Nation of Islam, as well as expose Farrakhan for who he really is and for what he actually represents.

PART ONE

CHAPTER ONE

CHRISTIANITY, ORTHODOX ISLAM, AND THE NATION OF ISLAM: DO THEY ALL REALLY WORSHIP THE SAME GOD?

Since Farrakhan (who frequently speaks of both Islam and Christianity) is a Black Muslim and primary spokesman for the Nation of Islam, it is important to get a grasp of what all three religions (Christianity, Orthodox Islam, and the Nation of Islam) teach.

There are many differences between the three religions. The Nation of Islam is a cult of Orthodox Islam. The members of the Nation of Islam are also known as the Black Muslims. Orthodox Muslims are quick to state that they do not agree with the teachings of the Nation of Islam and that they do not want to be identified with the Black Muslims. However, Farrakhan's recent association with khadafy may have softened their position somewhat. Christianity does not agree with either Orthodox Islam nor the Nation of Islam and considers both to be false religions. Neither of the three religions worship the same God, as Farrakhan would like us to believe. This fact, as well as other facts that point out the differences between the three religions will be discussed in this chapter in a question and answer fashion.

Questions and Answers

To which teaching does each religion ascribe itself?

Christians believe that the Bible is the unadulterated, infallible Word of God. The Bible contains sixty-six books that were written by God's prophets and the apostles of Jesus Christ over a time span of 1500 years between 1400 B.C. and 100 A.D. The sixty-six books from Genesis to Revelation are inspired by God and there is evidence of this divine inspiration. Any other books besides these sixty-six, that are said to be biblical, are spurious and do not coincide with the prophetic teachings and gospels of the sixty-six book text. Catholics, who are considered Christians, include fourteen of these spurious books into the Bible. They are called the Apocrypha. Orthodox Christians believe that the Apocrypha are documents that should not be included in the Bible because the Apocrypha books contradict many of the teachings of the prophets and the apostles. The Apocrypha is analogous to an unauthorized biography. Why read something unauthorized when you can read the authorized version?

Other illegitimate "biblical" books are referred to as the Lost Books of the Bible. These "lost books" are called Pseudo-Pigrapha: meaning false books. The Pseudo-Pigrapha is believed to have been mostly written by heretics of that day. They can not be lost books of the Bible if they were never part of the Bible to begin with.

Black Muslims and Orthodox Muslims ascribe to the Koran, which is a book of religious writings that was written by Muhammad about 600 years after the death and resurrection of Jesus Christ. This Muhammad was born in 570 A.D. in the land of Mecca which is located in Western Arabia. The Black Muslims are also considered by some to be influenced by the early teachings of Noble Drew Ali. Orthodox Muslims view the Nation of Islam as a cult of Orthodox Islam.

The Black Muslims regard two other books to be just as "holy" as the Koran. They are "The Supreme Wisdom: Solution to the So-Called Negroes' Problems" and "Message To The Blackman in America" both of which were written by Elijah Muhammad in the years 1957 and 1965 respectively.

You said that the Black Muslims are heavily influenced by the early teachings of Noble Drew Ali. Who was this man and what were his teachings?

Noble Drew Ali was born as Timothy Drew in 1866. When he was forty-seven years old he began a religious organization which he called the Moorish Science Temple. As this movement grew it infiltrated many American mid-western cities including Detroit Michigan. Drew had been greatly influenced by Oriental religious philosophies and noticed that these philosophies contained no mention of race nor did they contain any race-focused doctrines. Drew felt that blacks in America could benefit by identifying with a people whose religious philosophies were void of race consciousness. Because of this, he began to teach that all black Americans were to be referred to or considered as Asiatic (coming from Asia) with the term "Moor" acting as a better specific descriptive rendering. Drew felt that these were the only terms that should have been used to identify black Americans. He felt that salvation for black people in America was impossible unless black people discovered the origin of their heritage and believed that self realization and proclamation as an Asiatic black man was what was needed to gain spiritual awakening. According to Drew's way of thinking, race and ethnicity for the most part, superseded spirituality.

Drew considered Jesus, Muhammad, Buddha, and Confucius to be prophets and believed they were all divine. However, he believed in "Allah" as being God and identified with the teachings of the Koran.

Those blacks that followed Drew during his time called themselves Moors and were asked to carry identification cards as a means to identify themselves as a part of Drew's organization. It was Drew's belief as well as his follower's belief that the white race would soon perish and the Asiatic non-whites would take over. The "Moors" began to flaunt their religious beliefs publicly in front of whites. Additionally, they considered Drew to be their prophet and felt that Drew had freed them from what they deemed as European white oppression.

Eventually there was a struggle for power within Drew's movement and Drew was killed. The identity of his murderer has remained a mystery. After Drew's death the Moors split into different sects. However, each of the sects maintained its belief that the "Holy Koran of the Moorish Temple Society" was the only legitimate sacred book. According to Muslim scholar C. Eric Lincoln, the Koran of the Black Muslims is different from the Quran of Orthodox Islam. Lincoln surmised that the Koran is actually the Moorish Temple book of Drew and that the name of the book diminished over the years to just the "Koran" or "Holy Koran." However, this is the only reference to this possible distinction that this author was able to find. Therefore, for the purposes of our discussion, no distinction will be made between the Koran and the Quran and the title "Koran" will be used generically.

Drew was one of the first influential black men of America to propagate the notion that there should be religious separatism of the races. He believed that each race should have their own religion. The Moors therefore felt that Christianity was the religion of the white man and that Islam was the religion of the Asians.

Many Black Muslims claim that the Nation of Islam has not been influenced by the teachings of Noble Drew Ali. However, several similarities between Drew's teachings and the teachings of the Nation of Islam are revealed throughout the pages of this book. The high incident of similarities makes the claim of non-influence suspect and questionable.

So, what's the history behind the Nation of Islam and how did it come into being?

In order to understand how the Nation of Islam came into being, we not only have to speak of Drew but of Marcus Garvey as well. During Drew's reign until his death, Garvey began a movement in America. This movement had a great influence among the black masses. Garvey, a Jamaican, began the Universal Negro Improvement Association (U.N.I.A.) in 1916. This organization was the first call in America for black unity. Garvey conducted speeches on street corners and coined the phrase "the so-called Negro" which Elijah Muhammad would eventually use repeatedly in his writings. Blacks in America were defined as "the so-called Negro" in order to emphasize the point that the word "Negro" was not a term that black people had voluntarily used to describe themselves but instead, were "so-called" by whites.

Garvey despised white people to the point where he felt that biracial blacks could not be trusted because they had too much white in them. Although misguided by his own racist views, Garvey's main purpose behind his movement was to discourage racial injustices and eliminate white rule over many parts of Africa. In August of 1920, Garvey held the First International Convention of the U.N.I.A. It was held in New York and was attended by twenty-five thousand blacks which was an unprecedented number for that time. Also present were representatives of twenty-five countries worldwide. From this convention, a flag was produced for the movement which is symbolic of "black pride" for many African Americans today. It is the red, black, and green flag. Initially, the color red stood for the blood that has been shed by those blacks who have fought and continue to fight for civil and human rights. The color black stood for pride in the fact that one's skin is black (similar to Drew's focus on nationality) and the color green stood for the hope and promise of blacks acquiring a more prosperous and meaningful life in Africa.

It was Garvey's dream that every black person in America would go back to Africa (the "motherland"). Millions of blacks poured money into this vision. Garvey had planned to take four hundred million blacks with him to Africa and begin colonization in Liberia. However, the French and the British pressured the Liberian government into opposing the move. Consequently, the land that the Liberian government promised to Garvey was leased to the Firestone Rubber Corporation. The "Back to Africa Movement" was never able to resurface itself.

The fact that Garvey did not trust whites and felt that all black Americans should have gone back to Africa indicates that he too, like Drew had separatist views. Segregation of the races was a strong message that he indirectly pushed. This spilled over into his religious philosophies.

Garvey also felt that Christianity was the spoken word of a God who was only the God of the white man. He felt this way because during his time, Jesus was depicted as white with blue eyes and blond hair. Instead of realizing that whites may have depicted God (Jesus) as white because of their own prejudices at the time (the Bible does not specifically say what color Jesus is), Garvey embraced the notion of the Christian white God and convinced his followers that a white God could not serve a black people thereby deciding that only a black God could serve a black people. Because of this, Garvey began to promote the idea of a black Christ and a black Madonna while at the same time encouraging blacks all across America to destroy any replicas they possessed of a white Jesus and replace them with replicas of a black Jesus. Interestingly, Garvey never saw himself as behaving in the same dogmatic manner with regards to his "black Jesus" as did many whites at the time with regard to their "white Jesus."

Eventually, the National Association for the Advancement of Colored People (N.A.A.C.P) and the Urban League spoke against Garvey and his way of thinking. Garvey was convicted in 1925 of mail fraud and served five years in a federal prison. His sentence was commuted in 1927 and he was deported. Garvey died in 1940. His movement had faded long before his death but not without adding more fuel to the notion of racial religious separatism that Drew had created. Conditions were ripe for a movement with the likes of the Nation of Islam. Drew and Garvey had paved the way.

In 1930, when the depression was growing, a certain peddler roamed the streets of Detroit. He went from black home to black home selling raincoats, silks, and talking to those blacks in the community about their heritage. Many blacks at that time had not had the opportunity to learn anything of their historic past and graciously welcomed this stranger. This peddler called himself W.D. Fard. He has also been referred to as Farrad Muhammad, F. Muhummad Ali, Professor Ford, Wallace Fard, and Wali Fard. Many blacks whom he spoke to considered him a prophet.

Wallace Fard assured the blacks he spoke with that they would be healed from their ailments if they lived as those in the "home country." He also told them that their true religion was not Christianity but instead Islam, and encouraged them to read the Koran, while at the same time attacking biblical doctrine. This was Garveyism taken a step further.

Eventually, the number of blacks attending Fard's house to house meetings became too large and a hall was rented out in order to obtain more adequate space. This meeting place was named the Temple of Islam. Fard was the first to refer to white people as "blue eyed devils." He emphasized African and Asiatic non-white history as well and continued to spread his concept that the black race was the greater race while also planting his notion that whites were somehow inferior to blacks.

Fard eventually labeled himself as the Supreme Ruler of the Universe thereby inferring divine status. Fard was able to convince some of his followers that he was a god. Fard taught that God's name is "Allah." He wrote two manuals, one of which was entitled "The Secret Ritual of the Nation of Islam" and the other called "Teaching for the Lost Found Nation of Islam in a Mathematical Way." Fard also began an elementary and secondary school which he named "The University of Islam." From Fard's teachings and influence, the Nation of Islam was born and its convert count grew fast and steady in the black community.

What is the history of Christianity and how did it come into being?

The first five books of the Bible (Genesis, Exodus, Leviticus, Numbers, Deuteronomy) comprise what is called the Pentateuch. Most Christian theologians agree that Moses wrote a major portion of the Pentateuch if not all of it. Moses was the Old Testament God-ordained leader of the Israelites. He led them out of bondage from Egypt into the Promised Land. We have evidence, from the Bible itself, that Moses wrote much of the Pentateuch and that God commanded him to do so:

> 9So Moses wrote down this law and gave it to the priests, the sons of Levi, who carried the Ark of the Covenant of the Lord, and to all the elders of Israel. (Deuteronomy 31:9)

> 1Here are the stages in the journey of the Israelites when they came out of Egypt by divisions under the leadership of Moses and Aaron.
> 2At the Lord's command Moses recorded the stages in their journey. This is their journey by stages: (Numbers 33:1-2)

The Pentateuch teaches about God as creator, what he created, the beginning of sin, God's judgments, God's laws, God's promises and God's deliverance. The Pentateuch is contained in the writings of the Old Testament. The Old Testament contains the books of the Bible that were written before the coming of Jesus Christ. The thirty-nine books of the Old Testament were written by prophets of God. These prophets predicted the coming of the Messiah (Jesus Christ) as well as predicted world and national events during their time and times to come. The books written after Christ's coming (twenty-seven books in all) make up the New Testament. The New Testament contains the four gospels (the books of Matthew, Mark, Luke, and John) as well as the other apostolic writings. The books of Matthew, Mark, Luke, and John are considered the gospels because they specifically include exact quotes from Jesus. The apostles were mainly responsible for the writings of the New Testament.

Do They All Really Worship The Same God?

The Bible tells us that in the beginning God created the heavens and the earth. God went on to create Adam and Eve who lived in the Garden of Eden. They sinned against God by being tempted of the devil who appeared to them as a serpent. The world was initially populated by the children of Adam and Eve. Eventually the people of the world began to sin in excess. Because of this, God decided to destroy the human race except for Noah who was righteous under the eyes of God as the scripture below attests to.

> 5The Lord saw how great man's
> wickedness of the earth had become, and
> that every inclination of the thoughts of his
> heart was only evil all the time. 6The Lord was
> grieved that he had made man on the earth,
> and his heart was filled with pain. 7So the
> Lord said, "I will wipe mankind, whom I have
> created, from the face of the earth--men and
> animals, and creatures that move along the
> ground, and birds of the air--for I am grieved
> that I have made them." 8But Noah found
> favor in the eyes of the Lord.
>
> 9This is the account of Noah.
> Noah was a righteous man, blameless among the people of his time, and he walked with God. (Genesis 6:9)

Noah found favor with God because he was a righteous man. Therefore, Noah and his immediate family were spared from the flood. God destroyed that particular wicked generation of people by means of flooding the entire earth with water. Noah had three sons named Ham, Shem, and Japheth. Christian theologians indicate that from these three sons came the races of the present day world.

From the beginning of creation, God had a relationship with man (the word "man" is used generically and includes women as well). God conversed with Adam and gave him rules and regulations (Genesis Chapters 2 and 3) to live by just as he has done throughout time and as he does with us today. He is a reachable and approachable God.

The books of Isaiah and Jeremiah document God's intense desire that man should worship him and no other god (small "g" indicates a false god). When speaking of the God whom the Bible speaks of (Yahweh) we will simply use the word "God" with a capital "G." It should be stressed that when Moses asked God to identify himself by name (Exodus 3:13-14), God responded by saying: "I AM THAT I AM."

The Hebrew name for God was YHWH. The written Hebrew language had no vowels, only consonants. However, the spoken Hebrew language had vowels. Consequently, a person who read the Hebrew language during those times, would have to cognitively include the vowels. Most theologians have assessed and agree that the vowels for YHWH were "a" and "e" respectively, making the name look like this: Yahweh. Since the Hebrews felt the name was too reverent for the written or spoken word, they replaced it with the word "Adonai," meaning "Lord." The English translation capitalizes "LORD" when referring to Yahweh. The Latin translation for "Adonai" is "Jehovah."

There were many nations (including the Israelites) of that time and of times past who insisted on worshipping man-created gods (idols) and would turn their heads from God himself. The Bible indicates that God has always been grieved when man decides to worship other (false) gods.

The prophets of the Old Testament prophesied about the coming of the Messiah (the "anointed one"). This Messiah would atone for man's sin by offering himself as the supreme sacrifice thereby becoming a ransom for many who are lost (those who do not know God). To atone means to make amends for. During Old Testament times God required certain animals to be sacrificed for the atonement of man's sin. The coming of the Messiah would therefore eliminate the need to continue animal sacrifices. The prophets also predicted that this Messiah would be resurrected after being crucified on a cross. A place in God's kingdom was guaranteed by a confession of faith in this Messiah. Jesus Christ fit the profile of the coming Messiah that was prophesied about and is therefore considered by Christians to be the Messiah who had indeed been spoken of. No other person in the history of man has ever fit the biblical Messianic profile.

What is the history of Orthodox Islam and how did it come into being?

As the Introduction stated, the writings contained within the Koran are based on the visions of Muhammad who was born in Mecca in the year 570 A.D. Mecca was the main city in Western Arabia where merchant trading took place. Mecca also housed a building known as "The House of Allah." The site where the building sat was known as the Ka'aba. Many Arabs believe that Abraham and his son Ishmael rebuilt The House of Allah after it was destroyed earlier by a flood. Islam is mainly identified with the culture of Arabia during the seventh century. It's religion encompasses quite a bit of this early Arab culture.

The word "Allah" is the Arabic translation of the word "God." Although the Arabs of ancient times considered Allah to be preeminent, they also worshipped other lesser "gods." The Ka'aba contained many statues and paintings of these other gods. Therefore, when the Arabs went to trade their wares at Mecca, they would also make certain to involve themselves in religious ceremonies in and around the Ka'aba.

Muhammad was a descendant of the Quraish tribe. This Quraish tribe was responsible for the construction of the Ka'aba many years earlier. Muhammad was orphaned when he was six years old and was raised by his uncle who taught him about his past. At age twenty-five Muhammad married a wealthy widow from Mecca. As a result of his marriage to her, coupled with his good business sense, Muhammad adopted a high position of power and prestige in Mecca.

During Muhammad's time, it was a common practice to go to the caves and "seek God." Muhammad would often involve himself in this type of "meditation." In 610 A.D., during one particular such adventure, according to Muhammad, the angel Gabriel appeared to him during a dream and instructed Muhammad to recite what the angel told him. Muhammad claimed that the angel Gabriel brought revelations to him either through a vision, a dream, or in audible form. Sometimes these "revelations" came to Muhammad through his own thoughts. Muhammad would often suffer from seizures when experiencing these "revelations." Since Muhammad was illiterate, he would recite the messages that he claimed to have gotten and others would document what he said. After Muhammad's death, these written recitations were collected and put together in a book called the Koran, of which the Arabic for is "Quran" which means "recitation." Muhammad was convinced that the messages of his recitations came from God and that no-one else but him was chosen of God to recite these messages. Those who followed Muhammad were called Muslims. They also believed that what Muhammad recited came from God.

I've got a general idea of how Jesus fits into Christianity and how Muhammad fits into Islam, but how does Elijah Muhammad and Farrakhan fit into the Nation of Islam?

Elijah Muhammad was born as Elijah Poole on October 7, 1897 in Sandersville Georgia. He was the son of a Baptist preacher and came from a sibling count of thirteen. Both of his parents had been slaves. Poole married in his twenties and moved to Detroit with his wife and two children in 1923. In the early 1930s, Elijah became one of Fard's students. The two became very close. Poole ran errands for Fard and gave Fard a place of refuge when he was being pursued by police because of his high profile.

In 1932, Poole established his own mosque which was based in Chicago. By this time his name had been changed by Fard twice. Fard, at first, gave Poole the name Elijah Karriem but later re-named him Elijah Muhammad. The second re-naming of Poole indicated to his followers that Fard had great respect for Poole because the name "Muhammad" means "worthy of praise." It was apparent that Fard was grooming Elijah Muhammad to be his successor.

Fard disappeared in 1934 without a trace. Elijah Muhammad then took it upon himself to take over where Fard had left off. He declared his mosque in Chicago to be the new headquarters of the movement. Elijah Muhammad designated himself as the only person who could relay the meaning of Fard's teachings to blacks.

Elijah Muhammad is considered by the Nation of Islam to be a prophet, messenger of Allah, the original spiritual leader of the Nation of Islam, and a type of Messiah. Elijah Muhammad was schooled by Fard. Fard is considered to be God. Therefore, Elijah is considered to be "The one who knew God." In later years, Elijah Muhammad adopted a chief aid to assist him with his work; his name: Malcolm X Shabazz.

Born in 1925, Malcolm, like Elijah, was also the son of a Baptist preacher. As a small child Malcolm moved with his family to Lansing Michigan. When Malcolm was six years old the Ku Klux Klan torched the family home. The fire department came and did nothing to extinguish the flames. Consequently, Malcolm's home burned to the ground. This incident fueled Malcolm's impending bitterness towards whites. Later, his father was found murdered. During Malcolm's teenage years, he became a prominent figure in the Harlem drug and numbers world. Eventually, he was arrested and jailed. While in prison Malcolm met a Black Muslim from the Detroit temple and was greatly influenced by him. After being released from prison, Malcolm joined the movement. His skill as an administrator and leader did not go unnoticed by Elijah Muhammad who indoctrinated Malcolm as his apprentice. Malcolm became Elijah Muhammad's principle student just as Elijah was Wallace Fard's principle student.

Eventually, dissention grew between Elijah Muhammad and Malcolm X. In 1963, during a meeting in New York, Malcolm made an offensive public statement regarding the assassination of President Kennedy. Elijah Muhammad, in return, took punitive measures against Malcolm and suspended him from his duties within the organization for a period of three months. The following year, Malcolm left the Black Muslim Movement and began his own conglomerate under which were two separate but non-mutually exclusive functional organizations which he named "The Muslim Mosque Inc.," and "The Organization of Afro-American Unity." Malcolm also traveled to Africa and the Middle East.

He made a pilgrimage to Mecca and began to change his thinking about white people. Malcolm no longer saw them as "blue-eyed devils" and began to embrace Orthodox Islam; a religion that is not color-conscious. During this time, Malcolm also publicly spoke against Elijah Muhammad, revealing Elijah's sexual exploits with women. Malcolm X was assassinated in 1965.

Before his death, Malcolm X had recruited Louis Farrakhan into the Black Muslim religion in the early 1950's. Farrakhan was born on May 11, 1933. His birth name was Louis Eugene Walcott. Farrakhan grew up in a Christian home. His father was also a preacher as Elijah Muhammad's father had been. After being recruited into the Nation of Islam as a young man, Farrakhan was eventually appointed as the Nation of Islam's national minister and became its national spokesman as well. Farrakhan was not in favor of Malcolm's split with the Nation and had no problem saying so. Some believe that Farrakhan may have had something to do with Malcolm's murder.

After Malcolm's death, a large number of Black Muslims fell away from the Nation of Islam. However, Farrakhan rebuilt the Nation and re-instituted many of the teachings of Elijah Muhammad.

The Nation of Islam has been accused of incorporating racist doctrine and ideology. Why have they been accused of this?

In his book, "MESSAGE TO THE BLACKMAN IN AMERICA," Elijah Muhammad taught that the white race is inherently evil. The Nation of Islam teaches that blacks and whites should live separately, independent of one another and should not marry interracially. Black Muslims believe that every black person is a Muslim by nature. Any black person who does not confess a belief in "Allah" and follow the doctrine of the Koran and Elijah Muhammad is berated by the Nation.

What is their reasoning behind this?

Elijah Muhammad wrote that black people (which he called "the so-called Negroes") are Asian blacks and descendants of the tribe of Shabazz. He believed that this tribe originated on earth sixty-six trillion years ago resulting from an earthly explosion that divided the world into two parts: the earth and the moon. The explosion is attributed to the unsuccessful attempt of a god-scientist whose purpose was to kill all of mankind. Elijah goes on to say that the blacks of that time ended up living in Egypt, Mecca and Arabia which he depicted as the best part of the world during that era. Allah is described as the "first and smartest" scientist who decided to exalt the black man above all others. However, Elijah reasoned that black people are not aware of this heightened status. He went on to write that black skin was the best skin and taught that blacks should not marry whites.

Elijah believed that Islam is the religion of the black man and accused whites of turning blacks away from their "true religion." He wrote that all members of the white race are devils and that at the beginning of all existence these "devils" caused mischief in heaven. He continued by saying that as a punitive measure, God dismissed these devils from heaven and they had to suffer among the wild beasts of the earth. As a matter of fact, Elijah wrote that the "devils" became beasts themselves and wound up walking on all fours just as a dog would. Muhammad wrote that eventually the whites ("devils") migrated to Asia and America.

The Bible tells us that the devil (Satan) and his demons are actual angelic beings that were cast out of heaven because they revolted against God. No color nor race is attributed to them and they are not described as human, even though the Bible tells us that they are able to possess human beings. A more in-depth discussion on this is presented in Chapter Seven.

Elijah believed that there were twenty-four black god-scientists (one of which was Allah) and that the birth of these scientists dated back sixty-six trillion years (spoken of earlier). Elijah believed that Yakub was born six thousand years ago and that he (Yakub) was the last of the scientists. Elijah believed that Yakub created the white race six thousand years ago with the specific purpose to rule over black people. Here, we have a contradiction in Elijah's own teaching. Remember, Elijah taught that white people existed from the very beginning, sixty-six trillion years ago, and that they lived in heaven but were really devils who were eventually cast out of heaven for being mischievous. Elijah Muhammad also taught that white people were not created until approximately 6,000 years ago by a god-scientist named Yakub. Now which is it? Did white people exist as devils in heaven sixty-six trillion years ago, or were they created by the god-scientist Yakub as recently as 6,000 years ago? Of course it is neither, but one can clearly see a contradiction here. Apparently Elijah got tangled up in his own absurdities. Elijah further believed that after six thousand years Allah would be born and be known as the "Supreme Being" who would eventually destroy the entire white race.

Earlier you said that the Nation of Islam considers Fard to be God and now you are saying that they consider Allah to be God. Which is it?

The Nation of Islam teaches that Fard and Allah are one in the same. They believe that Allah came to them in the person of Fard.

They also believe that God is a black man. When the Nation of Islam makes reference to Allah, they are in actuality making reference to Fard.

Is this the same Allah that Orthodox Muslims worship?

No. Black Muslims say that Allah is Fard Muhammad incarnate, while Orthodox Muslims say that Allah is the same God that Christians worship.

Is Allah the same God that Christians worship?

No.

What's the difference?

Jesus taught (John 4:24) that "God is spirit, and his worshippers must worship in spirit and in truth." However, Orthodox Muslims don't believe that God is a spirit.

The Bible teaches that there is one God who represents himself in three persons, those being: The Father, the Son, and the Holy Spirit. Lets look at some Biblical scriptures that convey this teaching.

> 26Then God said, "Let us make man in our image, in our likeness, and let them rule over the fish of the sea and the birds of the air, over the livestock, over all the earth, and over all the creatures that move along the ground." (Genesis 1:26)
>
> 22And the Lord God said, "The man has now become like one of us, knowing good and evil. He must not be allowed to reach out his hand and take also from the tree of life and eat, and live forever." (Genesis 3:22)
>
> 19Therefore go and make disciples of all nations, baptizing them in the name of the Father and of the Son and of the Holy Spirit. (Matthew 28:19)
>
> 16Beyond all question, the mystery of
> godliness is great:
> He appeared in a body,

was vindicated by the Spirit,
was seen by angels,
was preached among the nations,
was believed on in the world,
was taken up in glory.
(1Timothy 3:16)

In the first and second scripture references above we see that God (singular) refers to himself as "us" (plural) thereby indicating that there are multiple personages of God equal to one another. The third scripture reference identifies these personages and the fourth reference renders more detailed information concerning the trinity of God by informing us that Godliness (The Father) appeared in a body (The Son, Jesus Christ) and was vindicated by the spirit (The Holy Spirit).

Orthodox Islam does not teach that God is the Father, the Son, and the Holy Spirit. They do not believe in the Trinity (three persons of one God). Orthodox Muslims believe that it is irreverent to attribute human qualities to God and therefore consider it blasphemy to say that Jesus is God incarnate.

Many Muslims as well as Christians have stated that Muslims and Christians worship the same God and that the only difference between the two religions is the name each religion attributes to God himself. However, when we look further into the matter there is clear indication to the contrary. If Christians say that God is the Father, the Son and the Holy Ghost and Muslims say he is not (which they do) then logic says that Christians and Muslims do not worship the same God.

The name "Allah" originated from an ancient pagan cult of pre-Islamic Arabia whose members worshipped a moon god that they named Allah. On the other hand there are several names for the God of the Bible, none of which include the name "Allah." El-Shaddai was used mostly in the books of Genesis and Job and means "The God Almighty." Reference to El-Elyon is found in the books of Numbers, Samuel, and Psalms and means "The Most High God." El-Olam is found in Genesis, Isaiah, and Psalms and means "God the Everlasting One." El-Berith translates into "God of the Covenant" and is found in the book of Judges. El-Roi means "God of Vision" and is used in the book of Genesis. As stated before, the very personal name for God (Exodus 3:13-14) that the Jews considered the most reverent in the days of the Old Testament was "Yahweh," which translates into "He who is." These biblical names for God do not appear in the Arabic language of the Koran. There is no Arabic translation of Yahweh, El-Shaddai, and so forth. It is reasonable to conclude that if Muslims worship the same God as Christians that there would be at least one instance in the Koran whereby the name of God translates into at least one of the biblical names for God. However, this is not so. On the other hand, God is never referred to as "Allah" in the Bible. We can therefore conclude that Christians, Muslims, and the Black Muslims do not worship the same God.

What did Elijah Muhammad say about Jesus?

Elijah Muhammad said that Jesus was no more than a dead prophet. He also stated that Jesus can not hear our prayers because he is dead. In saying these things he has denied the Lordship of Jesus Christ. Not only did Elijah Muhammad embrace the Koran but he also embraced, as do most Orthodox Muslims and Black Muslims alike, the Hadith, which is another book of "sacred writings" that Muslims put on the same level as the Koran. The Hadith says that Jesus was a white man with straight hair (Vol. 9, Hadith # 242). Consequently, not only do the Black Muslims believe that Jesus is nothing more than a dead prophet but by their own belief system they have no other choice but to also regard him as a devil. Elijah also taught that Jesus did not pay the price for our sins and that the resurrection does not make any sense. He denied that there is any salvation through Jesus Christ.

What is salvation?

Salvation is an action whereby one is saved from impending danger. It is the act of rescuing another. Religiously speaking, as a noun, salvation is that which one possesses when he or she has been "saved" from an afterlife of eternal damnation. To be "saved" is to be spared from entering hell at the point of death. One is saved from hell and instead, enters into heaven.

What does the Bible say about salvation?

The Bible tells us that belief in Jesus Christ is the only road to salvation. Through the blood of Jesus our sins are atoned for. Jesus was crucified on the cross and became the ultimate sacrifice for the sins of the world. Jesus gave his life as a ransom by which men could be saved. The following scriptures give testimony to this.

> 10Then know this, you and all the people of
> Israel: It is by the name of Jesus Christ of
> Nazareth, whom you crucified but whom God
> raised from the dead, that this man stands
> before you healed. 11He is

"'the stone you builders rejected,
which has become the capstone.'

[12]Salvation is found in no one else, for there is no other name under heaven given to men by which we must be saved.
(Acts 4:10-12)

[32]Whoever acknowledges me before men, I will also acknowledge him before my Father in heaven. [33]But whoever disowns me before men, I will disown him before my Father in heaven. (Matthew 10:32-33, Jesus is speaking here)

[16]For God so loved the world that he gave his one and only son, that whoever believes in him shall not perish but have eternal life.
[17]For God did not send his Son into the world to condemn the world, but to save the world through him. [18]Whoever believes in him is not condemned, but whoever does not believe stands condemned already because he has not believed in the name of God's one and only Son. (John 3:16-18)

[9]That if you confess with your mouth, "Jesus is Lord" and believe in your heart that God raised him from the dead, you will be saved. [10]For it is with your heart that you believe and are justified, and it is with your mouth that you confess and are saved. [11]As the Scripture says, "Anyone who trusts in him will never be put to shame." [12]For there is no difference between Jew and Gentile--the same Lord is Lord of all and richly blesses all who call on him, [13]for, "Everyone who calls on the name of the Lord will be saved." (Romans 10:-13)

[9]We accept man's testimony, but God's testimony is greater because it is the testimony of God, which he has given about

> his Son. [10]Anyone who believes in the Son of God has this testimony in his heart. Anyone who does not believe God has made him out to be a liar, because he has not believed the testimony God has given about his Son.
> [11]And this is the testimony: God has given us eternal life, and this life is in his Son. [12]He who has the Son has life; he who does not have the Son of God does not have life. (1 John 5:9-12)

The testimony that God has given about Jesus also includes the fact that Jesus came as God incarnate (God in the flesh) and was sent to redeem the world. Evidence of this is discussed in detail in the following chapter.

The Bible is very clear in its teaching as to how one is guaranteed a place in heaven. The only way to get into heaven (God's eternal kingdom) is to confess a heart felt belief in Jesus Christ as Lord and Saviour and believe that he has risen from the grave. Those who worship Jesus must do so in spirit and in truth.

What do Orthodox Muslims say about salvation?

Orthodox Muslims believe there will be a resurrection of the dead. They believe that some time in the future a trumpet will sound from one of God's angels and everyone in heaven and earth will die. A second trumpet will sound and the dead will be resurrected. They go on to say that those who have believed in Allah, have done good deeds and have followed his commandments (which include the Islamic five pillars of faith: prayers, fasting, almsgiving, pilgrimage to Mecca and Holy war) will go to heaven, while all others go to hell. Orthodox Muslims believe that there is no Saviour and that one must save himself through his own good deeds and devotion to Allah.

What does the Nation of Islam say about salvation?

The Nation of Islam believes in a resurrection of the dead, but not a bodily resurrection. Instead they believe in a mental resurrection of black people. They feel that blacks are superior to whites and need a mental awakening in order to accept this claim. They feel that the Bible is basically accurate but has been misinterpreted throughout the years. Consequently, they apply their own misinterpretations to the scriptures. It is questionable whether or not they believe in afterlife. But, they do not believe in a heaven or a hell. This forces them to concentrate on an earthly life and may be the underlying reason behind their belief that the black man is destined to rule in power over the white man. If there is no heaven then one may feel the need to make his or her heaven here on earth. To do so, the desires of one's heart must be manifested. Some desire money, others desire fame. The Nation of Islam desires power.

You spoke earlier about the Hadith. Can you go into more detail about it?

The Hadith is another sacred writing of Islam that both the Nation of Islam and Orthodox Islam ascribe to. The writings in the Hadith contain further teachings of Muhammad (sixth century Muhummad) which were recorded by family members. These extra teachings are not generally found in the Koran. Not only does the Hadith teach that Jesus was white but it also gives reference to Muhammad as being a white man.

What does the Nation of Islam have to say about the Hadith referring to Muhammad as a white man?

Not much. Members of the Nation of Islam do not talk much about the Hadith publicly. However, they do not shun the teachings of the Hadith and basically accept the writings contained in its pages as divinely inspired.

Where are the references found in the Hadith that describe Muhammad as white?

In volume 1, Hadith # 63, Muhummad is described by others as being a white man. In volume 2 Hadith #141 Muhammad's armpits are described as being white. In volume 1 Hadith #367 Muhammad is said to have a white penis.

How do the Black Muslims justify the teachings of Muhammad while at the same time calling white people devils? According to the Hadith, Muhammad was white. Wouldn't that make Muhammad a devil too?

The Black Muslims don't speak much about this particular teaching in the Hadith, at least not publicly. However, if confronted, it would seem that they would have no alternative but to admit that the Hadith does indeed say these things.

What about Wallace Fard? Didn't you say he was white? And if he was white, wouldn't that make him (according to the Nation of Islam's own teachings) a devil too?

Some of those who met Fard in person, said he was a white man. Others say he may have been of Arab descent. If indeed he was white, then the Black Muslims worship a "white god" since they consider Fard to be Allah. If, by their own logic, white people are devils and Allah (Fard) is white, then Allah is a devil.

With all this brought to light, wouldn't it be more appropriate for the Black Muslims to label their own religion as the "white man's religion" since Fard may have been white and the Hadith describes Muhammad as white?

Looks that way.

They'd probably think it would be silly to do this, wouldn't they?

Yes, and it would be.

Isn't it just as silly to label Christianity as the "white man's religion?"

Yes.

Is there anything in the Bible that would make one think that Christianity is the "white man's religion" or that salvation through Jesus is only available to a specific race of people?

No. Lets take a look at the scriptures that challenge Garvey's "white man's religion" accusation against Christianity.

> 12For there is no difference between Jew
> and Gentile--the same Lord is Lord of all and
> richly blesses all who call on him, 13for,
> "Everyone who calls on the name of the Lord
> will be saved." (Romans 10:12-13)

> 5Put to death, therefore, whatever belongs
> to your earthly nature: sexual immorality,
> impurity, lust, evil desires and greed, which is
> idolatry. 6Because of these, the wrath of God
> is coming. 7You used to walk in these ways, in

> the life you once lived. [8]But now you must rid yourselves of all such things as these: anger, rage, malice, slander, and filthy language from your lips. [9]Do not lie to each other, since you have taken off your old self with its practices [10]and have put on the new self, which is being renewed in knowledge in the image of its Creator. [11]Here there is no Greek or Jew, circumcised or uncircumcised, barbarian, Scythian, slave or free, but Christ is all, and is in all. (Colossians 3:5-11, Paul is speaking to those who have come to Christ and are saved)
>
> Anyone who does wrong will be repaid for his wrong, and there is no favoritism. (Colossians 3:25)

The above scriptures unquestionably teach that God does not focus on race when it comes to salvation. Race consciousness is clearly a human flaw. Jews and Gentiles (those who are not Jews) alike can call on the name of the Lord and be saved.

Does Orthodox Islam embrace any racist views?

Although publicly they will say they do not, they embrace the Koran which says that at the day of Resurrection those going to heaven will have faces that turn white and those going to hell will have faces that turn black. Let's take a look:

And be ye not like those who have formed divisions, and fallen to variance after the clear proofs have come to them. These! a terrible chastisement doth await them,

On the Day when faces shall turn white, and faces shall turn black! And as to those whose faces shall have turned black"....What! after your belief have ye become infidels? Taste the chastisement, for that ye have been unbelievers."

And as to those whose faces shall have become white, they shall be within the mercy of God: therein shall they abide for ever. (Sura 3: 102-104, The Koran)

Those who have faces that turn black are described as infidels. Not only this, but to have a black face at the time of judgment is seen as punishment. The Koran teaches that only the faces that turn white will have mercy from God and see heaven. Muslims could arguably say that the reference is symbolic and not literal. It seems as if it would be symbolic. However, as we will see, Muhammad, the very author of the Koran, did not think well of black people. Consequently, the symbolism of this particular Sura reference is questionable.

Along with this, Arab Muslims have had a long history of enslaving Africans and great pains were taken in the Hadith to emphasize that Muhammad was white.

What did Elijah Muhammad say about Christianity?

Elijah Muhammad stated that Christianity is not God's religion and called it a "black-slave-making religion."

Is Christianity a black-slave-making religion?

No. However, many blacks believe the myth that the Bible says that blacks are cursed to be slaves. The problem has been with the interpretation of Genesis 9:18-27. Let's look at it:

> 18The sons of Noah who came out of the
> ark were Shem, Ham and Japheth. (Ham was
> the father of Canaan.) 19These were the three
> sons of Noah, and from them came the
> people who were scattered over the earth.
> 20Noah, a man of the soil, proceeded to
> plant a vineyard. 21When he drank some of its
> wine, he became drunk and lay uncovered
> inside his tent. 22Ham, the father of Canaan,
> saw his father's nakedness and told his two
> brothers outside. 23But Shem and Japheth
> took a garment and laid it across their
> shoulders; then they walked in backward and
> covered their father's nakedness. Their faces
> were turned the other way so they would not
> see their father's nakedness.
> 24 When Noah awoke from his wine and
> found out what his youngest son had done to
> him, 25he said,
>
> "Cursed be Canaan!
> The lowest of slaves
> will he be to his brothers."
> 26He also said,

"Blessed be the Lord, the God of Shem!
May Canaan be the slave of Shem.
27May God extend the territory of Japheth;
may Japheth live in the tents of Shem,
and may Canaan be his slave.

Theologians have deciphered that the name "Ham" in Hebrew means black. The Jews had a custom in which they named their offspring according to the offspring's attributes or characteristics. Therefore, since the word "Ham" means "black" then it follows that Ham was probably black.

From reading the scripture reference above we are informed that Noah drank too much wine one night, became drunk, and fell asleep, naked. Ham discovered his father in his naked condition and ran to tell his brothers. By doing so, Ham disrespected his father, because he did not attempt to cover him. Shem and Japheth did not run into Noah's tent to look at his nakedness but instead took a large piece of cloth, walked into Noah's tent backwards and covered him. Shem and Japheth probably told Noah that Ham had been disrespectful towards him. Noah became angry and cursed Ham's son, Canaan. Canaan, as well as Canaan's descendants, would be slaves.

Interestingly enough, Noah used slavery to punish Ham by cursing his children and his children's children. This in itself indicates that the Bible portrays slavery as a negative condition. At any rate, early whites who wanted to justify enslaving blacks concluded that since Ham was black and Canaan was black (he'd have to be if Ham was black) and the nation of Canaan was cursed, then all blacks were cursed. That would be the same as saying that if Ham had big feet and Canaan had big feet, and Canaan was cursed, then all the people in the world with big feet would be cursed. The latter analogy is presented to emphasize the illogical conclusion of what has been deemed to be the biblical black curse.

The Canaanites were a nation of people. There is a difference between a nation of people and a race of people. A nation of people can include many races. The Canaanites were not the only nation of people that were comprised of black people. There were many other nations that were comprised of black people. To say that all blacks were cursed because Canaan was cursed would be the same as saying that all nations comprised mainly of black people were cursed. This simply was not the case and there is no biblical indication of various other nations being cursed as a result of the Canaanites being cursed.

To take it a step further, let's say for instance, America was cursed (which it is not). Then could we say that all Asians are cursed worldwide since there would be Asians in America under the curse? Of course not. Could we say that all Hispanics are cursed worldwide since there would be Hispanics in America under the curse? Of Course not. Could we say that all white people are cursed worldwide since there would be white people in America under the curse? Of course not. Could we say that all blacks are cursed worldwide since there would be black people in America under the curse? Of course not. America is a nation, not a race. If she were to be cursed then all *Americans* would be cursed. Get the point? So it is with the curse of the Canaanites. However, during the American antebellum era, this rebuttal regarding the curse of the Canaanites was overlooked by those who were pro-slavery.

To bring the point home even further, Ham had four sons, those being: Cush (Ethiopia), Mizraim (Egypt), Phut (Libya), and Canaan. Canaan is his only descendent that is extinct as a nation today. The curse of Canaan died with the death of the nation itself.

The Bible has been sorely misrepresented and misinterpreted in regards to the Canaanite curse and has consequently gotten a "bad rep" when it comes to its stance on the issue of slavery. Apparently Elijah Muhammad fed into this myth of the "biblical black slave curse."

Well, what does the Bible say about slavery in general?

Although the Bible does not say that slavery in and of itself is a sin, it most certainly gives reference to scriptures that indicate slavery in America was. The following Biblical scriptures inform us that slave-trading as well as the kidnapping and selling of a man (which in essence is slave-trading) was a sin punishable by death.

> 9We also know that law is made not for the righteous but for lawbreakers and rebels, the ungodly and sinful, the unholy and irreligious; for those who kill their fathers or mothers, for murderers,
> 10for adulterers and perverts, for slave traders and liars and perjurers--and for whatever else is contrary to the sound doctrine 11that conforms to the glorious gospel of the blessed God, which he entrusted to me. (1Timothy 1:9-11)
>
> 16Anyone who kidnaps another and either sells him or still has him when he is caught must be put to death. (Exodus 21:16)

As we can clearly see, the Bible considered slave-trading to be synonymous with murder. Slavery (Jews were allowed to sell themselves into slavery) was allowed, but not slave-trading because along with it came kidnapping and the selling of those who were kidnapped. Africans were kidnapped, brought to this country (America) and sold. From a biblical standpoint, God was clearly against this. Furthermore, there is no indication in the Bible that blacks were targeted specifically for enslavement. Apparently Elijah Muhammad had not done his homework when he called Christianity a "Black-slave-making religion."

Despite the fact that slave-trading was a sin, the act of one man enslaving another was common during biblical times. Jews could sell themselves into slavery as a means to support themselves and many times God allowed one nation to be enslaved by another as punishment for turning against him. One of the most misunderstood Biblical references in the American black community concerning slavery is contained in following scriptures:

> 5Slaves, obey your earthly masters with
> respect and fear, and with sincerity of heart,
> just as you would obey Christ. 6Obey them not
> only to win their favor when their eye is on you,
> but like slaves of Christ, doing the will of God
> from your heart. 7Serve wholeheartedly, as if
> you were serving the Lord, not men, 8because
> you know that the Lord will reward everyone
> for whatever good he does, whether he is
> slave or free.
>
> 9And masters, treat your slaves in the same
> way. Do not threaten them, since you know
> that he who is both their Master and yours is in
> heaven, and there is no favoritism with him.
> (Ephesians 6:5-9)

Verse 5 says that slaves should obey their masters as they would obey Christ. It does not say that the masters were equal to Christ but was attempting to emphasize the great amount of respect a slave should have for his or her master. The scripture goes on to say that the slave should serve his master as if he were serving the Lord. It does not say that the slave master is equal to the Lord. Basically, these scriptures are instructing the slave to be careful of his attitude toward his master.

Do They All Really Worship The Same God?

For a black person living in America, these words are difficult to swallow. However, during the American Antebellum years, pro-slavery whites focused on what the Bible says about how slaves were to treat their masters but not how masters were to treat their slaves. When reading further we encounter verse 9 which tells us that slave masters were to treat their slaves in the same way that slaves were to treat their masters. Consequently, if slaves were to serve their masters as if they were serving the Lord, then slave masters would have to treat their slaves as they would want the Lord to treat them. If slaves were to be careful of their attitude toward their masters then masters would have to be careful of their attitude toward the slave. The scripture warns the master against threatening his slave and goes on to inform the master that God does not favor the master over the slave and that both the master and the slave have the same Master in heaven making them equal to one another in the eyes of God.

Didn't the Muhammad of Orthodox Islam have slaves?

Yes. Muhammad was the slave master of many black slaves. Moreover, he did not think very much of black people. Muhammad referred to black people as "raisin heads" in vol. 1, # 662 and vol 9, # 256 of the Hadith. The Hadith also tells us (vol. 9 # 162-163) that Muhammad labeled any black woman, who was dreamt about by anyone, an evil omen of a future outbreak of disease.

What does the Koran and the Hadith say about slavery?

The doctrine of the Koran does not deem slavery in and of itself to be a sin. There were certain regulations set forth in the Koran regarding slavery just as there were in the Bible. There is indication in the Koran that slaves were to be treated fairly. However, the Hadith (the Koran's companion book) supports the concept of the Jihad which is more commonly known today as the "Holy war." The Hadith instructs Muslims to force others into Islam by the sword if necessary. Many Christians and Jews in Africa have been slain by Muslims who declared a "Holy War" against them. Presently, slavery exists in Arab countries where Muslims are enslaving many Christian Africans. In addition to this, women employed in Saudi Arabia who do not identify themselves as Islamic are often times enslaved, beaten, and raped all in the name of Allah by order of the Jihad which the Hadith teaches and supports.

How can Elijah Muhammad accuse Christianity of being a

"black-slave-making" religion when the Hadith to which he ascribed, tells of Muhammad (a white man) enslaving black men and calling them raisin-heads while at the same time regarding black women as "evil omens?"

Beats me.

What did Elijah Muhammad say about the Bible?

Elijah Muhammad taught that the Bible was corrupted by whites and Jews therefore making it unreliable. He wrote that God is not the author of the Bible. By saying this, he denied that the Bible is the inspired Word of God. His book, "MESSAGE TO THE BLACKMAN IN AMERICA," has as one of its main focuses, the goal of attempting to discredit the Bible. Elijah Muhammad considered the Bible to be a book that has been purposely incorrectly translated by whites.

Isn't there some truth to that? What about the 16ll King James Version of the Bible? Hasn't it been corrupted?

This is another fallacy believed on by many non-Christian American blacks. The Bible is the inspired Word of God and has not been inappropriately translated. The minimal errors that are found apply to certain misspelling of words and do not, in any way, effect the actual messages (doctrine) that the Bible gives. This concern will be discussed in detail in the following chapter.

SUMMING UP THE MATTER

When taking into account all that has been presented in this chapter, no room is left for any notion that supports the belief that Christians and Muslims worship the same God. It is clear that they do not. The Nation of Islam is a cult of Orthodox Islam which means that they claim to be Islamic when they actually teach something different from Islam. Orthodox Muslims do not consider Black Muslims to be of the Islamic faith and are generally irritated by the Black Muslim's identification with Orthodox Islam. However, Orthodox Muslims may become more tolerant because of Khadafy's association with Farrakhan. We must remember that Farrakhan is a Black Muslim and is the present day leader of the Nation of Islam. Farrakhan publicly identifies Allah, not Yahweh, as God. Remember, the Nation of Islam believes that Wallace Fard is God incarnate. This can not be overlooked no matter how many times Farrakhan refers to the Bible.

Do They All Really Worship The Same God?

Farrakhan does not worship the God of Christianity and does not believe in the Lordship of Jesus Christ. More evidence of this will be presented as we go along. However, before looking at some of Farrakhan's speeches in detail, it is essential that a discussion regarding the translation of the Bible be presented in order for issues to be clarified surrounding the question of its authenticity. The following chapter does just that.

CHAPTER TWO

DEFENDING THE CHRISTIAN FAITH: THE APOLOGETICS OF IT ALL

The word "apology" originated from the Greek term "apologia" deriving from the verb "apologeisthai" which means to defend with words. Apologetics is the art of speaking in behalf of something or someone by using logical arguments. It is the method of putting "two and two together" in order to come up with a valid conclusion. Because there are so many evidences that give credibility to the Bible as being the Word of God, Christian Apologetics has become a tool of great importance to the church when encountering skepticism surrounding biblical doctrine. There are many facets of Christian Apologetics. History, archaeology, and the laws of probability all play a part. This chapter will present some of the arguments that are used to defend the Christian faith and make a comparative analysis between those arguments and the arguments used to defend Islam and the Nation of Islam.

DEFENSE OF THE WRITTEN BIBLICAL WORD

Clearing up the misunderstanding behind the 1611 King James Translation of the Bible

In the non-Christian African-American community, there is great skepticism as to the reliability of the Bible. Many blacks are convinced that the Bible has been tampered with and that the "white man" has been the one doing the tampering. There is wide-spread doubt, resulting from the dissemination of misinformation propagated mostly by those who believe that the Bible is the "white man's religion," as to the validity of the 1611 King James version of the Bible.

First of all, the King James Version of the Bible is simply an English translation of the Bible. Initially, the Bible was written in Hebrew and Greek. There is also some Aramaic text. Since most people who speak English do not speak Hebrew, Greek, or Aramaic, it stands to reason that an English translation is needed.

There are many black people who insist that King James actually translated the King James version of the Bible. This is simply not true. King James authorized a *new* translation of the Bible (not a *different* one) at the urging of the Puritan ministers at the time. He appointed approximately fifty theological scholars to take on the task of the translation.

King James VI was King of Scotland from 1567 to 1625. When Queen Elisabeth of England died in 1603 she had no heirs. Therefore, King James was the closest political leader to take over her throne. King James served as king of England from 1603 to 1625, thereby presiding as king over both Scotland and England simultaneously for twenty-two years. When serving as King of England, King James' title was changed from King James VI to King James I since he was the first to reign as king over the United Kingdom.

When King James came into power over England, he inherited the problems that Queen Elisabeth had. One of the main problems, at the time, was the dispute between the Puritans, the Presbyterians, and the Brownists. The Brownists were a Puritan sect who promoted the idea of church government autonomy (congregationalism). During these times in England, the church organized itself in an Episcopal manner. They appointed Bishops over priests and other clergy. The Bishops were given a great deal of power in the church and were deemed as a supreme authority, much as the Pope is deemed as having supreme authority in the Catholic church today. However, it should be noted that this way of church administration is not biblical.

During Old Testament times, priests were given certain responsibilities by God that he gave no other men. However, when Jesus came, he fulfilled the law thereby making many of the Old Testament laws unnecessary. Priests were no longer needed since everyone could go to God his or herself through Jesus. At any rate, the Puritans realized that governing the church in an Episcopal way (a Priestly way) was not biblical. Because of this, they came against the Episcopal organization of the church. Despite their correctness, the Puritans decided that they would settle for moderate reform and were willing to compromise a little. However, the Presbyterians were not willing to compromise and wanted to do away with the episcopacy altogether. The Puritans also wanted everything excluded from their current translation of the Bible at the time that was not in the original Greek and Hebrew manuscripts.

Before continuing, a brief history of biblical translation must be given. As stated before, the Bible was originally written in Hebrew (Old Testament), Greek (New testament), and Aramaic (very few sections of the New Testament). The Old Testament was translated into Greek by seventy ancient Jewish scholars. This Greek translation is called the Septuagint. Later, in the Fifth century, Jerome translated the Old Testament directly from its original Hebrew language into Latin. This translation is called the Vulgate. In the seventh century a monk named

Caedmon was the first to translate parts of the Old and New Testament from the Vulgate into English. Other English translations of the Bible during the eighth and ninth centuries were made by Bede and Alfred the Great. These early English translations were also made from the Vulgate (the Latin text).

The first scholar to translate the entire Bible into the English language was John Wycliffe who did so during the fifteenth century. Wycliffe also used the Vulgate as the basis for his translation. Scholars did not begin to read the New Testament in its original Greek language until the1500s.

In 1516, a scholar named Erasmus produced the first printed copy of the English Bible. Before that, everything was written by hand. Erasmus also took on the task of translating the Bible into English. He was the first to use Greek manuscripts in the process. However, he only had a few manuscripts available to him and had to rely on the Vulgate. The Greek manuscripts that Erasmus used dated between the tenth and thirteenth centuries and were copies of the originals. Erasmus' translation corrected Jerome's earlier Latin translation which had errors in it that did not go along with the Greek. Erasmus' translation of the Bible became known as the Textus Recepticus.

Other translations came about using the Textus Recepticus as their base. William Tyndale studied Hebrew and Greek and in 1525 was the first to translate the entire Bible into English from Hebrew and Greek instead of just from Greek and Latin. However, he was heavily persecuted and eventually executed in England for his translations because England wanted to hold on to their earlier traditional translations. Other translations came about using the Textus Recepticus as their base including the Coverdales version of 1537, the Thomas Matthew Version of 1537, the Geneval Bible and the Bishop's Bible. These latter translations contained footnotes (commentaries) from the scholars who translated them.

During the 1600's the Puritans felt that the Bible should have no footnotes at all and should remain void of any scholarly commentary. Between them and the Presbyterians, they had the loudest voice and were causing the greatest uproar. One thousand Puritan Ministers petitioned King James demanding permission to create a new translation of the scriptures that would not include any footnotes. King James basically supported the Episcopal church and was against the Presbyterian cause. Since the request for a more accurate translation came from the Puritans, King James agreed to their demands and appointed a group of fifty theological scholars who were to begin work on the translation. The translation was completed in 1611 and is known as the 1611 King James Version of the Bible. It's translation was based on the Textus Recepticus.

Ironically, King James is responsible for attempting to do what many blacks say he didn't do, and that was to institute a more precise and correct translation. King James did not wake up one and day and suddenly decide to appoint scholars the task of translating another English version of the Bible but instead did so in response to the request of a very influential Christian religious denomination. King James did not at all assist in the actual translation of the 1611 version. He couldn't have. He knew no Greek, Hebrew, or Latin. The fact that King James was a homosexual is further proof that he did not have a hand in the actual translation because the Bible vehemently speaks against homosexuality. If it had been King James' intent to translate the Bible according to his own likes and dislikes, and not according to earlier manuscripts, then it would seem as though he would have made certain to delete any scriptures which spoke of homosexuality as a sin. However, as clearly indicated by the eighteenth chapter of book of Leviticus, as well as other scriptural passages in the Bible, none of the doctrine surrounding the issue of homosexuality was eliminated.

King James simply opted for a better English translation of the Bible void of the opinions and commentaries of men. The reason why the 1611 English translation is called the King James Version is because King James was the King at the time of its translation. The scholars gave the translation its particular name out of respect for the King and nothing else.

Greek/Hebrew Manuscripts and the Dead Sea Scrolls

The original Greek and Hebrew manuscripts of the Bible have not yet been found. Translations are based on copies of the originals. At the time when the 1611 King James Version of the Bible was printed, the earliest copies of the original Greek and Hebrew manuscripts dated back no earlier than the tenth century. Skeptics of the Bible were constantly attacking the validity of any translation since the time span between the original writings of the Bible and the available copies of the original was approximately a thousand years. Then, in 1947, skepticism declined due to the finding of the Dead Sea scrolls. The Dead Sea scrolls are Greek and Hebrew texts of the Bible that date back to the second and third century. Now, instead of a thousand years between the original biblical writings and the most recent copies of the original, the gap decreased to two hundred years. Therefore, there is almost a thousand year difference between the dead sea scrolls and the texts used to translate the 1611 version of the Bible. Despite this, there are no remarkable differences in the documents. When scholars investigated both the second century texts and the tenth century texts they discovered that there were no errors of significance between the two texts. The only errors may have been the misspelling of a word or two, but there were absolutely no contradictions between the two texts as to the doctrine (the message) of the Bible. This discovery gives indication that translators of the Bible took great care in correctly transcribing the text from year to year and gives even greater indication that the Bible we have today is indeed representative of the original Bible written between 1400 B.C. and 100 A.D. No other book in antiquity, except for Homer's Illiad, has such stagnating evidence as to its original writings being kept in place as does the Bible. The Koran can not even make this claim.

The History of the Koran's Translation

Around 610 A.D. Muhammad, at the age of forty, stated that the angel Gabriel came to him as he slept. Muhammad went on to say that Gabriel commanded Muhammad to recite all that Gabriel told him. During the following two years Muhammad claimed that Gabriel often appeared in his dreams giving him more revelations. Muhammad was illiterate and therefore not able to write the things that he said the angel told him to write. Consequently, the Koran was developed by others who wrote what Muhammad recited.

The Koran was initially written in the Quraish dialect of the Arab language and was first translated into Western Language by a twelfth century English scholar named Robertus Retenensis. In the 1500s, a medieval Latin version was published. This version had been edited by Theodor Bibliander of Zurich and contained many inaccuracies and misinterpretations. Bibliander's version served as a foundation for early European translations. In the 1700s a French translation of the Koran by Sieur Du Ryer was published of which the first English translation derived. A man named Alexander Ross was responsible for this first English translation of the Koran. However, he stated that the Koran was full of contradictions, blasphemies, and fabrications. In the latter part of the 1700's, a man named Abraham Hinckelmann printed the Koran in its original Arabic text. George Sale used Hinckelmann's Arabic translation to replace Ross' English translation. Sale's translation was used by most English speaking persons until the end of the nineteenth century. However, in 1861, J.M. Rodwell rendered another English translation in which he arranged the Suras (synonymous to what is called *scripture* in the Bible). Rodwell's translation is regarded as the standard English version. Interestingly, Rodwell did not believe that the Koran was God-inspired but believed instead that it was the product of a man (Muhammad) who suffered from delusions. It must be noted that none of the early translators of biblical text doubted that the Bible was God-inspired.

Most of the historicity of the translation of the Koran comes from the Hadith. The Hadith tells us that the Koran was written in accordance to how Muhammad recited is dreams and "revelations" to his friends and family. There was no actual book of the Koran before the death of Muhammad. After his death, those close to him who had heard his recitations collected the leaves, rock, and bones that the recitations had been written on and put them together to form the Koran. The Hadith (vol.1, 63) tells us that a man named Caliph Uthman gathered all of the recited writings together and put them into book form (the Koran) and then proceeded to send them to far away lands. Some of the recitations conflicted with one another. The Hadith states that Uthman attempted to destroy those recitations which conflicted with one another (vol 6 #510).

Not only were there conflicts in Muhammad's own recitations but the Quran is said to be missing certain verses. Furthermore, the Hadith indicates that Muhammad himself claimed that at times the visions he saw and the revelations he recited were from demonic sources (Hadith vol. 4 # 400, 490).

When looking at the history of the Koran's translation, everything Muhammad said and did is called into question due to the fact that, at times, Muhammad claimed to be inspired by the Devil. Therefore, it makes no difference as to whether or not the Koran has been translated properly since, according to Muhammad himself, much of the text is demonic.

The Bible as God Inspired

> 16All scripture is God-breathed and is useful for teaching, rebuking, correcting and training in righteousness, 17so that the man of God may be thoroughly equipped for every good work. (2 Timothy 3:16-17)

The book of 2nd Timothy tells us that God breathed his Word into those who wrote the scriptures and that all biblical scripture is spirit breathed. In other words, it is inspired by God. None of the authors of the books of the Bible were ever said to be inspired by Satan in their writings as was said of Muhammad by the Hadith.

There are many evidences that give indication that the Bible is the inspired Word of God. One such evidence is the way in which it was written. The Bible was written in three different languages (Greek, Hebrew, and Aramaic). It is believed that the Old Testament (written in Hebrew) was written between 1400 B.C. and 450 B.C. and the New Testament (written in Greek) was written between 60 A.D. and 100

A.D. The prophets and apostles, totaling over forty authors, wrote the different books of the Bible. Many of them never met one another. Not only was the Bible written by forty different authors in three different languages over a time span of hundreds of years but it was also written on three different continents: Africa, Asia, and Europe. When looking at this, it is nothing short of a miracle that the books of the Bible never doctrinally contradict one another. This gives evidence that proves that the Bible must be God-inspired. There is no other explanation for the miracle behind its development.

When looking at the development of the Koran it is apparent that no miracle lies behind its creation. One man alone was responsible for it. Muhammad recited the words of the Koran to his friends and family who in turn wrote down his words and passed it on. Anyone could have done that.

Archaeology also plays a big part in proving that the Bible is the Word of God. At one time it was thought that the art of writing was not present during the time of Moses and therefore all of the writings of Moses were said to be erroneous. However, in 1968, archaeologists uncovered the Elba Tablets in Northern Syria dating back a thousand years before the writings of Moses. The tablets were writings telling of the Elba Kingdom which had a population of two-hundred and sixty thousand people in 2300 B.C. The Elba Kingdom was eventually destroyed in 2250 B.C. by Sargon the Great.

Another archaeological proof that attests to the Bible's authenticity has to do with the walls of Jericho. The Bible says that the walls of Jericho fell flat which means they fell outwards. During the excavations of Jericho in the 1930's the walls of Jericho were found to have indeed fallen outward. The reason why this information is deemed special is because city walls, when they fall, fall inward. Once again, archaeology proved what the Bible had already said was true.

The Bible also speaks of the nation of the Hittites and Amalakites which were said never to have existed. However, archaeology has uncovered evidence that these nations did indeed exist. The Bible is the only book that speaks of these nations of people.

Not only are there archaeological findings that give proof that the Bible must be the Word of God, but historical data indicates that biblical prophecy has reigned true throughout the ages which also gives profound evidence in favor of the argument that the Bible is indeed the Word of God. In Ezekiel 26:7-14 the prophet Ezekiel predicted that the ancient city of Tyre would be destroyed by Nebuchadnezzar. Three years after the prophecy, Nebuchazdnezzar destroyed the city. Ezekiel also predicted that Tyre would never be rebuilt. In other words, it would never again rise to the commercial center it once was. Ezekiel 26:5-6 says of Tyre that "out in the sea she will become a place to spread fishnets, for I have spoken, declares the sovereign Lord. She will become plunder for the nations, and her settlements on the mainland will be ravaged by the sword. Then they will know that I am the Lord." Today Tyre has indeed been reduced to a small fishing village where fishermen cast their nets daily against the rocks. The prophecy was, without question, fulfilled. History reveals that biblical predictions of the following ancient cities all came to past: Sidon,Samaria,Gaza-Ashkelon,Moab-Ammon, Petgra-Edom, Thesbes-Memphis,Ninevah,Babylon,Chorazin-Bethsaida-Capernaum, and Palestine. No other book can claim the prophetic value that the Bible has.

We have only scratched the surface of prophetic evidences that give indication that the Bible is indeed the Word of God. To cite all of the evidences would constitute a book in itself.

DEFENSE OF JESUS AS GOD INCARNATE

Biblical accounts of the Deity of Christ

The Bible informs us that Jesus came to the earth as God in human form and gave himself as a living sacrifice for the redemption of our sins. During Old Testament times, before the coming of Christ, an unblemished lamb was one of the animals that God instructed his people to offer to him as a living sacrifice for their sins. When Jesus came, he took the place of the actual unblemished lamb and became the figurative unblemished lamb of God. Animal sacrifice was a shadow of things to come. After the coming of Jesus there was no more need for animal sacrifices for the redemption of sin. Jesus became our sin offering. He became our sacrifice and is the lamb of God. The following scripture clarifies this:

> [18]For you know that it was not with perishable things such as silver or gold that you were redeemed from the empty way of life handed down to you from your forefathers, [19]but with the precious blood of Christ, a lamb without blemish or defect. [20]He was chosen before the creation of the world, but was revealed in these last times for your sake. [21]Through him you believe in God, who raised him from the dead and glorified him, and so your faith and hope are in God. (1Peter 1:18-21)

There are many scriptures in the Bible that teach on the deity of Christ. Let's look at some.

> [1]In the beginning was the Word, and the Word was with God, and the Word was God. [2]He was with God in the beginning.
> [3]Through him all things were made; without him nothing was made that has been made. (John 1:1-3)

> [14]The Word became flesh and made his dwelling among us. We have seen his glory, the glory of the One and Only, who came from the Father, full of grace and truth. (John 1:14)

Jesus is the Word that the above scriptures speak of. The Word was God. The Word was with God in the beginning and became flesh. Jesus is the only person spoken of in the Bible as God in the flesh. Therefore, Jesus is part of the Godhead (Father, Son, and Holy Ghost) and was with God in the beginning.

> [16]Beyond all question, the mystery of godliness is great:
>
> He appeared in a body,
>   was vindicated by the Spirit,
> was seen by angels,
>   was preached among the nations,
> was believed on in the world,
>   was taken up in glory. (1 Timothy 3:16)

John and Timothy both bear witness that Jesus appeared in human bodily form. Jesus was God in human form and now sits on the right hand side of the Father as part of the Godhead. In the scriptures below, Jesus refers to himself as God. Let's take a look.

> [8]Philip said, "Lord, show us the Father and that will be enough for us."
> [9]Jesus answered: Don't you know me, Philip, even after I have been among you such a long time? Anyone who has seen

> me has seen the Father. How can you say, 'Show us the Father'? (John 14:8-9)

In the following scripture reference (verse 8), God refers to Jesus as God.

> In the past God spoke to our forefathers
> through the prophets at many times and in
> various ways, [2]but in these last days he
> has spoken to us by his Son, whom he
> appointed heir of all things, and through
> whom he made the universe. [3]The Son is
> the radiance of God's glory and the exact
> representation of his being, sustaining all
> things by his powerful word. After he had
> provided purification for sins, he sat down
> at the right hand of the Majesty in heaven.
> [4]So he became as much superior to the
> angels as the name he has inherited is
> superior to theirs.
> [5]For to which of the angels did God ever
> say,
>
> "You are my Son;
> today I have become your Father"?
>
> Or again,
>
> "I will be his Father,
> and he will be my Son"?
> [6]And again, when God brings his firstborn
> into the world, he says,
>
> "Let all God's angels worship him."
>
> [7]In speaking of the angels he says,
>
> "He makes his angels winds,
> his servants flames of fire."
> [8]But about the Son he says,
>
> "Your throne, O God, will last for ever and ever,

> and righteousness will be the scepter of your kingdom. (Hebrews 1:1-8)

The ultimate confirmation of the deity of Christ is his resurrection. The resurrection of Christ is the basis on which the Christian faith rests. As revealed in the following scripture, Jesus predicted his own death and resurrection.

> 18Then the Jews demanded of him, "What miraculous sign can you show us to prove your authority to do all this?"
> 19Jesus answered them, "Destroy this temple, and I will raise it again in three days."
> 20The Jews replied, "It has taken forty-six years to build this temple, and you are going to raise it in three days?" 21But the temple he had spoken of was his body.
> 22After he was raised from the dead, his disciples recalled what he had said. Then they believed the Scripture and the words that Jesus had spoken. (John 2:18-22)

God appeared to many (including the apostles) in his resurrected body. The following scripture reference gives account of this. Let's take a look:

> 24Now Thomas (called Didymus), one of the Twelve, was not with the disciples
> when Jesus came. 25So the other disciples told him, "We have seen the Lord!"
> But he said to them, "Unless I see the nail marks in his hands and put my finger where the nails were, and put my hand into his side, I will not believe it."
> 26A week later his disciples were in the house again, and Thomas was with them. Though the doors were locked, Jesus came and stood among them and said,
> "Peace be with you!" 27Then he said to Thomas, "Put your finger here; see my hands. Reach out your hand and put it into my side. Stop doubting and believe."

> [28]Thomas said to him, "My Lord and my God!"
> [29]Then Jesus told him, "Because you have seen me, you have believed; blessed are those who have not seen and yet have believed."
> [30]Jesus did many other miraculous signs in the presence of his disciples, which are not recorded in this book. [31]But these are written that you may believe that Jesus is the Christ, the Son of God, and that by believing you may have life in his name. (John 20:24-31)

Evidences of the Deity of Christ

The Old Testament Prophets gave over three hundred predictions about the coming Messiah. At the time they gave their predictions, the Messiah (Jesus) had not come yet. There are sixty-one very distinctive Old Testament Messianic prophecies. God gave the prophets their knowledge concerning the coming Messiah in order that they may impart to others those factors that would identify him. We will look at several of these prophecies.

Isaiah 7:14 prophesied that the Messiah would be born of a virgin. It says: "Therefore the Lord himself will give you a sign: The virgin will be with child and will give birth to a son, and will call him Immanuel." The name "Immanuel" means "God with us." Matthew 1:18-24 reveals that the prophecy was fulfilled. It says:

> [18]This is how the birth of Jesus Christ came about: His mother Mary was pledged to be married to Joseph, but before they came together, she was found to be with child through the Holy Spirit. [19]Because Joseph her husband was a righteous man and did not want to expose her to public disgrace, he had in mind to divorce her quietly.
> [20]But after he had considered this, an angel of the Lord appeared to him in a dream and said, "Joseph son of David, do not be afraid to take Mary home as your wife, because what is conceived in her is from the Holy Spirit. [21]She will give birth to

> a son, and you are to give him the name
> Jesus, because he will save his people
> from their sins."
> 22All this took place to fulfill what the
> Lord had said through the prophet: 23"The
> virgin will be with child and will give birth to
> a son, and they will call him Immanuel"
> which means, "God with us."
> 24When Joseph woke up, he did what
> the angel of the Lord had commanded him
> and took Mary home as his wife. But he
> had no union with her until she gave birth
> to a son. And he gave him the name
> Jesus. (Matthew 1:18-24)

The name "Jesus" is the Greek version of the Hebrew name "Joshua" which means "Yahweh delivered." "Yahweh" is the most revered Hebrew name for God.

Micah 5:2 predicted that the Messiah would be born in Bethlehem. It says, "But you, Bethlehem Ephrathah, though you are small among the clans of Judah, out of you will come for me one who will be ruler over Israel, whose origins are from of old, from ancient times." Matthew 2:1 reveals that the prophecy was fulfilled. It says, "After Jesus was born in Bethlehem in Judea, during the time of King Herod, Magi from the east came to Jerusalem and asked, "Where is the one who has been born king of the Jews? We saw his star in the east and have come to worship him."

Deuteronomy 18:18 predicted that the Messiah would not only be God but would be a prophet as well. It says, [God speaking] "I will raise up for them a prophet like you from among their brothers; I will put my words in his mouth, and he will tell them everything I command him." Matthew 21:11 reveals that the prophecy was fulfilled. It says, "The crowds answered, "This is Jesus, the prophet from Nazareth in Galilee."

Psalms 110:4 predicted that the Messiah would be a priest. It says, "The Lord has sworn and will not change his mind: You are a priest forever, in the order of Melchizedek." Hebrews 5:4-6 reveals that this prophecy was fulfilled. It says:

> 4No one takes this honor upon himself;
> he must be called by God, just as Aaron
> was. 5 So Christ also did not take upon
> himself the glory of becoming a high priest.
> But God said to him,

> "You are my Son;
> today I have become your Father.

[6] And he says in another place,

> "You are a priest forever,
> in the order of Melchizedek."

Isaiah 40:3 predicted that the coming of the Messiah would be preceded by a messenger who would tell of him. It says, "The voice of him that crieth in the wilderness, Prepare ye the way of the Lord, make straight in the desert a highway for our God." Matthew 3:1-3 reveals that this prophecy was fulfilled. It says,

> [1]In those days John the Baptist came, preaching in the Desert of Judea [2]and saying "Repent, for the kingdom of heaven is near." [3]This is he who was spoken of through the prophet Isaiah:
>
> "A voice of one calling in the desert,
> 'Prepare the way for the Lord,
> make straight paths for him.'"

Isaiah 35:4-6 prophesied that Jesus would perform many miracles. It says, "say to those with fearful hearts, 'Be strong, do not fear; your God will come, he will come with vengeance; with divine retribution he will come to save you.' Then will the eyes of the blind be opened and the ears of he deaf unstopped." Matthew 9:35 reveals that this prophecy was fulfilled. It says, "Jesus went through all the towns and villages, teaching in their synagogues, preaching the good news of the kingdom and healing every disease and sickness."

Psalms 16:9-10 predicts the resurrection of Christ. It says, "Therefore my heart is glad and my tongue rejoices; my body also will rest secure, because you will not abandon me to the grave, nor will you let your Holy One see decay." In this psalm, David was speaking to God. Not only does David (the psalmist) predict the resurrection of Christ but Jesus predicted his own death and resurrection in John 2:18-22, which says:

> [18]Then the Jews demanded of him, "What miraculous sign can you show us to prove your authority to do all this?"

> 19Jesus answered them, "Destroy this temple, and I will raise it again in three days."
> 20The Jews replied, "It has taken forty-six years to build this temple, and you are going to raise it in three days?" But the temple he had spoken of was his body. 22After he was raised from the dead, his disciples recalled what he had said. Then they believed the Scripture and the words that Jesus had spoken.

Luke 24:1-8 speaks more on the fulfilling of the resurrection prophecy. It says:

> 1On the first day of the week, very early in the morning, the women took the spices they had prepared and went to the tomb. 2They found the stone rolled away from the tomb, 3but when they entered, they did not find the body of the Lord Jesus. 4 While they were wondering about this, suddenly two men in clothes that gleamed like lightning stood beside them. 5In their fright the women bowed down with their faces to the ground, but the men said to them, "Why do you look for the living among the dead? 6He is not here; he has risen! Remember how he told you, while he was still with you in Galilee: 7'The Son of Man must be delivered into the hands of sinful men, be crucified and on the third day be raised again.'" 8Then they remembered his words.

Just as the psalmist predicted, the body of Jesus never saw decay.

The prophecies that have been spoken of in depth here only scratch the surface of the number of messianic prophecies contained in the Old Testament. Some of the other prophecies include: That the Messiah would have a ministry in Galilee, preach to many, be rejected by Jews and Gentiles alike, be betrayed by a friend (Judas Iscariot), be sold for thirty pieces of silver, endure humiliation and torture in the form of whippings, be crucified, be pierced by the sword, be buried in a rich man's tomb, and the list goes on.

Neither Muhammad, nor Wallace Fard, nor Elijah Muhammad has fulfilled at least one of these Old Testament Messianic prophecies. As a matter of fact, no one other than Jesus Christ has fulfilled all of the prophecies. This is an historical fact. The probability of one man fulfilling only forty-eight of the prophecies is one in ten to the one hundred and fifty seventh power. This number is so large that there are no words to describe it. Between Jesus, Muhammad and Wallace Fard it is unquestionably more likely, when looking at the fulfillment of messianic prophecy, that Jesus was God incarnate and is our Messiah, our Lord and our Saviour, not Muhammad, Wallace Fard, or anybody else for that matter.

More on the Resurrection

Jesus performed many miracles. He performed more miracles than anyone has ever performed before or since. Jesus made the blind see, made the lame walk, gave increase of food when food was scarce, and even raised people from the dead. However, Jesus' greatest miracle was his own resurrection from the grave, which he predicted he would do. As Paul so eloquently expresses in his letter to the Corinthian church, The resurrection of Jesus Christ is the basis for the Christian faith. Let's see what Paul says:

> 12But if it is preached that Christ has
> been raised from the dead, how can some
> of you say that there is no resurrection of
> the dead? 13If there is no resurrection of
> the dead, then not even Christ has been
> raised. 14And if Christ has not been
> raised, our preaching is useless and so is
> your faith. 15More than that, we are then
> found to be false witnesses about God, for
> we have testified about God that he raised
> Christ from the dead. But he did not raise
> him if in fact the dead are not raised. 16For
> if the dead are not raised, then Christ has
> not been raised either. 17And if Christ has
> not been raised, your faith is futile; you
> are still in your sins. 18Then those also
> who have fallen asleep in Christ are lost.
> 19If only for this life we have hope in
> Christ, we are to be pitied more than all
> men.

> [20]But Christ has indeed been raised
> from the dead, the firstfruits of those who
> have fallen asleep. [21]For since death
> came through a man, the resurrection of
> the dead comes also through a man. [22]For
> as in Adam all die, so in Christ all will be
> made alive. (1 Corinthians 15:12-22)

Although many have tried, no-one has ever been able to disprove the resurrection of Jesus Christ. There are simply too many evidences upholding the fact that Jesus was resurrected. One thing's for sure: Muhammad and Elijah Muhammad died and were buried. They were never resurrected. Wallace Fard disappeared without a trace. Jesus did not disappear without a trace. He was crucified, he died, was resurrected and ascended into heaven (Acts 1:9) where he now sits on the right hand side of the Father (Hebrews 1:3).

Evidences of the Resurrection of Christ

There were many people who saw Jesus alive three days after his death on the cross. Not only does the Bible prophecy about, and describe his torturous death, but all of history does. Jesus Christ indeed lived and was crucified. To deny this is the same as denying that other major events in history happened, like the holocaust. When looking at the resurrection of Jesus Christ the question becomes: why would so many people lie about what they saw? The apostles (the special group of twelve disciples initially called of Jesus to follow him, to witness his miracles, and to spread the gospel) as well as hundreds of disciples (followers of Jesus Christ) bore witness to the resurrection of Jesus and preached the gospel of Christ even under threat of death and persecution.

It is said, by some skeptics, that the apostles stole Jesus' body from the tomb. However, the Bible (Matthew 27:62-66) tells us that the chief priests and Pharisees feared this very thing. They felt that the apostles would steal the body in order to make it look as though Jesus had been resurrected. Pontius Pilate (the Roman governor of Judea at the time) listened to these concerns and consequently placed the Roman guard at Jesus' burial site in an effort to discourage any robbers. The Roman guard consisted of many military men. They were to guard the tomb with their lives. It is logical that Pontius Pilate would place security at the tomb since he was the one who gave the order for Jesus' crucifixion. He gave the order when succumbing to the pressure put upon him by the people of that time who accused Jesus of blasphemy and desired to see him crucified. Therefore, when critics say that someone stole the body, they are also indirectly saying that Pilate did not have enough sense to place security at the tomb, or that the thieves who supposedly stole the body were strong enough to get through an army of men as well as a huge boulder that was placed at the door of the tomb with the Roman seal affixed.

There is no question that the tomb of Jesus Christ was disrupted. Even those who claim that the body was stolen are inadvertently admitting that the tomb was empty after three days. However, any attempt at stealing the body would have been a virtual suicide mission. Ironically, in Pilate's attempt to assure that there was no foul play, he created the very situation that gives rise to the probability that the resurrection did, in fact, occur. With the guard being placed at the tomb site and the stone placed at its entrance, the tomb was impenetrable, at least, by man. However, God is all-powerful and can penetrate anything. The following scripture reference tell us of the account.

> 2There was a violent earthquake, for an angel of the Lord came down from heaven and, going to the tomb, rolled back the stone and sat on it. 3His appearance was like lightning, and his clothes were white as snow. 4The guards were so afraid of him that they shook and became like dead men.
>
> 5The angel said to the women, "Do not be afraid, for I know that you are looking for Jesus, who was crucified. 6He is not here; he has risen, just as he said. Come and see the place where he lay. 7Then go quickly and tell his disciples: 'He has risen from the dead and is going ahead of you into Galilee. There you will see him.' Now I have told you." (Matthew 28:2-7)

Mary Magdalene and Mary, mother of Jesus, are the women spoken of who went to the tomb. They were the first to discover that Jesus had indeed been resurrected. God had parted the earth and sent an angel to remove the huge stone over the tomb in order to make way for Jesus' tomb site departure after his resurrection. The guards were petrified to the point where they became as dead men at the presence of God's angel. In other words, they fainted. Only an act of God could have shocked these men to the level where they failed in their mission thereby putting their very lives on the line. In order to cover up the fact that Jesus had indeed rose from the grave, the chief priests and elders bribed the guards into saying that the disciples stole the body during the night while the guards slept. Let's take a look at this:

> [11]While the women were on their way, some of the guards went into the city and reported to the chief priests everything that had happened.
> [12]When the chief priests had met with the elders and devised a plan, they gave the soldiers a large sum of money, [13]telling them, "You are to say, 'His disciples came during the night and stole him away while we were asleep.' [14] If this report gets to the governor, we will satisfy him and keep you out of trouble." [15]So the soldiers took the money and did as they were instructed. And this story has been widely circulated among the Jews to this very day. (Matthew 28:11-15)

Amazingly enough, the guards were paid to say that the disciples stole the body. The Bible specifically says that this was a concocted lie. However, the lie lived then and it still lives today. Normally, all of the men who comprised the Roman guard would have probably been executed for their inability to successfully guard the tomb. But without them, there would be no credible source for the lie. Therefore, they were allowed to live and were well compensated for their deception.

SUMMING UP THE MATTER

When comparing the Bible and the Koran it is quite evident that the historical, archaeological, scientific, and prophetic proofs as well as proofs governing the laws of probability, support the Bible's truthfulness. Such proofs are basically non-existent when it comes to the Koran. There can only be one Word of God. 1st Corinthians tells us that "God is not the author of confusion." Therefore, he would not inspire the writing of the Koran, which is distinctly different from the Bible, only to say that the Koran and the Bible are the same when they are so dissimilar from one another in context. To do so would create confusion.

In looking at all the apologetic arguments of the Christian faith (there are many more than the ones presented in this chapter), there is no question that the Bible is truly the Word of God.

The Apologetics of it All

Now that we have taken care of the preliminaries, we are ready to take an in-depth look at the teachings of Louis Farrakhan: Black Muslim and present day leader of the Nation of Islam.

PART TWO

CHAPTER THREE

A DISCUSSION OF FARRAKHAN'S 1995 MILLION MAN MARCH SPEECH

In the year 1995 Louis Farrakhan, self-proclaimed leader of the Nation of Islam, organized a March on Washington in which he asked all of the black men in America who could, to join the March. On October 16th, of that same year, thousands upon thousands (Farrakhan boasts of a million in attendance) of American black men met Farrakhan at the Nation's capital and listened to Farrakhan's Million Man March speech.

During the speech which he delivered on October 16, 1995 at the Million Man March Event held on the steps of the Nation's Capital in Washington D.C., Farrakhan said.........

In the name of Allah, the beneficent, the merciful, we thank him for his prophets and the scriptures which they brought. We thank him for Moses and the Torah. We thank him for Jesus and the Gospel. We thank him for Muhammad and the Koran. Peace be upon these worthy servants of Allah.

These were the first words Farrakhan spoke at the March after thanking the crowd. Farrakhan thanks Allah. He uses the phrase "in the name of Allah," while Christians use the phrase, "in the name of Jesus." No where in the Bible are Christians instructed to do anything in the name of Allah. Farrakhan is quick in his attempt to lump Judaism (Moses and the Torah) Christianity (Jesus and the Gospel) and Islam (Muhammad and the Koran) together. However, these are three totally different religions and can not be lumped together. Orthodox Jews do not believe the Messiah has yet come. They do not adhere to the New Testament (which testifies of the Messiah) but only to the Old. Christians believe that the Messiah has come in the person of Jesus Christ and that Jesus Christ is God incarnate who was resurrected from the dead. Those from the Nation of Islam believe that Jesus was no more than a prophet and that Fard, not Jesus, is God incarnate. With this in mind, it is impossible to ethically lump the three religions together as if they were one in the same. Farrakhan thanks Jesus for the gospel and thanks Muhammad for the Koran, but, one contradicts the other. Therefore, we can not thank God for both, as if to say God ordained both, because God would not inspire two different books that contradict one another. God can only be the author of one. The one that he is the author of is the gospel of Jesus Christ, which is given to us through the Bible. God has authorized no other book.

Farrakhan indicates that he would like peace to be upon "these servants of Allah." However, the prophets, Moses, and Jesus (which he includes as servants of Allah) were never servants of Allah but were instead servants of YAHWEH. To say otherwise is a misrepresentation of what the Bible says.

I am so grateful to Allah for his intervention in our affairs in the person of Master Fard Muhammad, the great Mahdi who came among us and raised from among us a divine leader, teacher, and guide, his messenger to us, the most honorable Elijah Muhammad. I greet all of you my dear and wonderful brothers with greeting words of peace. We say it in the Arabic language, As-salaam-alaikum (the audience replied, 'wa-alaikum salaam').

The words Farrakhan used to open his speech do nothing more than introduce Black Muslim Theology. Notice, Farrakhan presents this theology within the first minute. It is no mistake that he does this. Farrakhan says that Allah (Islam's name for God) came in the person of Fard Muhammad. He is referring to Wallace Fard. By saying this, Farrakhan has revealed that he believes Fard to be God. "Mahdi" is the word that Muslims use for "Messiah." In the above excerpt, Farrakhan describes Fard Muhammad as the great "Mahdi" thereby revealing his belief that Fard is the Messiah, God incarnate. The Bible contradicts this view and instead declares Jesus Christ to be the Messiah, God incarnate.

All thanks, all praise, all honor, all glory belongs to God. For this is the day the Lord has made. So we are here rejoicing on this day.

Farrakhan was careful to use the word "God" instead of Allah. He doesn't want to completely alienate the Christian blacks in the audience. However, when Farrakhan uses the word "God" he is referring to Allah, the false god of the Koran. He is not referring to the one and only true God of the Bible.

Farrakhan is good at using biblical scripture to further his purpose, but, he always misinterprets it, as is evident here when he says, "this is the day that the Lord has made. So we are here rejoicing on this day." The day that Farrakhan is speaking of is the day of the Million

Man March. However, the scripture that he quotes from is found in Psalms 118:22-24, and reads:

> 22The stone which the builders refused is become the head stone of the corner.
> 23This is the Lord's doing; it is marvelous in our eyes.
> 24This is the day which the Lord hath made; we will rejoice and be glad in it.

"The day which the Lord has made" is the day that Christ was resurrected from the grave, not the day of the Million Man March, as Farrakhan would like us to think. We know that the above scripture must be referring to the resurrection because Jesus is the stone that the "builders" refused until he was resurrected from the grave. When Jesus was resurrected from the grave, he became the "head stone of the corner" (verse 22). Therefore, we should rejoice and be glad in the day of Christ's resurrection, not in the day of the Million Man March. The stone that the scripture is referring to is Jesus Christ. Jesus was the rejected stone, but then was accepted as the head cornerstone after his resurrection. The day Jesus rose from the grave is "the day which the Lord has made" because it was the day in which proof of Jesus' divine status was given to us by God. Farrakhan is subtle in his approach and indirectly suggests that the day of the Million Man March can be likened to the day of the resurrection of Christ.

To all of the members of the Nation of Islam, to all of the ministers, captains and secretaries and sister captains. To all of the foot soldiers........

Farrakhan thanked all of these people. He thanked the Nation of Islam first. Farrakhan has made sure to brand the minds of the audience with the words "Nation of Islam" so that those who are impressed by Farrakhan will, in turn, be impressed by the "Nation." Farrakhan and the Nation of Islam go hand in hand and it is important to Farrakhan that black people remain mindful of the association. By doing so, those blacks who are vulnerable to Farrakhan's teachings also become vulnerable to the teachings of the Nation of Islam.

There's still two Americas, one Black, one White, separate and unequal.

Farrakhan begins early at picking the festering sore that many blacks have when it comes to racial issues. By focusing on the racial divide, he reminds blacks of the many injustices black people have had to endure over the years. Farrakhan fancies himself as one who has come to aid in the healing of the black man's festering sore. It's easier for blacks to follow Farrakhan when the discussion of issues surrounding discrimination and injustices become part of his appeal. Many blacks, Christian and non-Christian alike, are drawn to Farrakhan because of this appeal.

Here we stand in the Capital of America and the layout of this great city, laid out by a black man, Benjamin Banneker. This is all placed and based in a secret Masonic ritual and the core of the secret of that ritual is the Black man.

At this point, Farrakhan introduces the Masonic order into the minds of his audience. Apparently Farrakhan has great respect for the Masonic Order. However, the Masons accept and teach secret religious philosophies, most of which contradict the Word of God. Despite this, Farrakhan is aware that many black people are drawn to the Order and consequently adds to his own appeal when speaking of a secret Masonic ritual whose core, he says, is the black man. As before, what looks appealing is only a seductive lure.

Why did you come here today? You came not at the call of Louis Farrakhan, but you have gathered here at the call of God. For it is only the call of almighty God, no matter through whom that call came, that could generate this kind of outpouring.

There are a vast number of black men who did not participate in the Million Man March and do not follow Farrakhan because of who Farrakhan is and what he represents. A great many black people in America are Christians and some of them refuse to follow Farrakhan because they realize that they can not allow any ill feelings they may have concerning racial injustices to triumph over their responsibility as a Christian. They realize that they can not endorse the leadership of a man who promotes false doctrine.

Farrakhan realizes that many Christian blacks feel this way and therefore attempts to convince everyone that the Million Man March was God's idea, not his. He alludes to a certain innocence in the whole matter. Is it his fault that God called him? Of course not. This is his reasoning. He then attempts to strengthen his argument by saying that only a call of God could generate such "an outpouring" of people. But there have been many men throughout history who have had the magnetism and charisma to generate a following beyond the number of those who followed Farrakhan to Washington. As history teaches us, large numbers of people following a man does not automatically give positive credibility to the man they are following: Hitler proved that. The question becomes: why would God call upon a man who worships Allah to lead a people? Furthermore, why would God call a man to lead a people whom he knows will promote Black Muslim theology and misrepresent the Bible? The answer is, he wouldn't. But Farrakhan would like us to believe that he would.

Although the call was made through me, many have tried to distance the beauty of this idea [the Million man March] from the person through who the idea and the call was made. Some have done it mistakenly and others have done it in a malicious and vicious manner.

There are many blacks, Christian blacks in particular, who, because of Farrakhan's emphasis on black unity, say they can separate the "message from the messenger." They are willing to overlook the latter for the former. They disregard Farrakhan's religious beliefs even though they know he promotes false doctrine. They are willing to compromise because to do so might ease the pain of their "festering sore." Furthermore, many blacks either don't realize, or refuse to accept, that Farrakhan's black unity message is tainted with racist overtones and separatist ideas.

Ironically, Farrakhan does not want us to separate the messenger from the message. If one separates the messenger from the message then the messenger looses a portion of his influence. If people accept the message then they usually accept the messenger and if people accept the messenger then they are more prone to accept other things that the messenger has to say, other things being: Black Muslim theology.

Farrakhan states that those who have attempted to separate him from the message he gave during the March are doing so either mistakenly, viciously, or with malicious intent. In saying this, Farrakhan implies that one should not consciously attempt to separate him from his black unity message. Farrakhan realizes that his mission to promote Black Muslim Theology would be thwarted if enough blacks separate him from his message. So, he cleverly labels any conscious attempt to do so as malicious and vicious. This tends to silence those blacks who would otherwise speak out boldly against Farrakhan's rhetoric. No one wants to be thought of as malicious or vicious.

So today, whether you like it or not, God brought the idea through me, and he didn't bring it through me because my heart was dark with hatred and anti-semitism. He didn't bring it through me

because my heart was dark and I'm filled with hatred for white people and for the human family of the planet. If my heart were that dark, how is the message, how is the message so bright, the message so clear, the response so magnificent?

Farrakhan disputes the notion that he hates whites and the notion that he his anti-semitic by arguing that God would not bring the idea of the Million Man March to a man who's heart is so dark (since the message of the Million Man March is so "bright and clear"). However, what Farrakhan fails to tell his audience is that he abides by the teachings of Elijah Muhammad who literally looked at all white people as devils. If there is no hatred for white people, then why call them devils?

To call white people devils is a racist remark no matter how you slice it. Sure, there are some white people who have done "devilish" things just as there are some black people who have done "devilish" things, but that doesn't make them devils. We, who are Christians, know this all to well which is another reason why we can not listen to the message and turn a blind eye to the messenger. If we, who are Christians, embrace this man then we, by our actions, influence others to embrace him as well.

God is now calling upon the despised and the rejected to become the corner stone and the builders of a new world.

Farrakhan is a master at manipulating words to make powerful subliminal suggestions. The despised and the rejected that Farrakhan is referring to is the black man. He never really says it, however, it is implied. But he goes further than that and states that these despised and rejected people would become the cornerstone and builders of a new world. Again, Farrakhan uses the same biblical language that identifies Jesus, to identify the black man. The Bible uses the words "despised and rejected" to described how Jesus was treated at the hands of others. Not only that, but in the Bible, the words "corner stone" are used to describe Jesus, not to describe the black man, as Farrakhan has inferred. Let's look at scripture:

> 18For through him we both have access by one Spirit unto the Father.
>
> 19Now therefore ye are no more strangers and foreigners, but fellow-citizens with the saints, and of the household of God;

> [20]And are built upon the foundation of the apostles and prophets, Jesus Christ himself being the chief corner stone;
> [21]In whom all the building fitly framed together groweth unto an holy temple in the Lord:
> [22]In whom ye also are builded together for an habitation of God through the Spirit. (Ephesians 2:18-22)

Farrakhan said that God is, in this day, calling upon the rejected (whom Farrakhan infers is the black man) to become the corner stone and build a new world. But, according to the above scripture reference, God has already called Jesus for that purpose, not the black race. As verse 20 tells us, the household of God is built upon the foundation that the prophets and apostles laid through Christ. Those who believe in the deity of Christ are the ones who make up the household of God and are framed together, holy unto the Lord. Believers in Christ come in all races, not just black. Farrakhan goes on to say that the new corner stone will build a new world. Since he believes that blacks are the corner stone, then he must believe that blacks will build the new world. However, the Bible is very clear about who the corner stone is and who is doing all the building. The household of God is what the corner stone builds, and as we will see in the following chapter, it is Jesus Christ who will build and rule the new world (new Jerusalem). The Bible does not say that black people will build a new world.

Remember, Black Muslim theology does not endorse the resurrection of Christ, but instead endorses the resurrection of the black man's mind. Well, if the resurrection (a very divine occurrence) is to be attributed to the black man, then Farrakhan must somehow suggest that the black man is divine. He attempts to do this by describing him (the black man) as the corner stone (a divine description).

We are gathered here to collect ourselves for a responsibility that God is placing on our shoulders to move this nation towards a more perfect union.

Which "Nation" is Farrakhan referring to? The nation of America, the Nation of Islam, or both? If he is speaking about the American Nation, then there will be little harmony without race relations improvement. There is no question that there needs to be a more perfect union between the races in America, but this is not really the doctrine of the Nation of Islam. As we saw in Chapter One, Nation of

Islam theology teaches separation of the races. However, Farrakhan must give the illusion that he upholds racial harmony, even though the teachings that he adheres to says differently. Clearly then, he is operating in deceit when he gives his audience the impression that he is willing for black people to integrate and come into a more perfect union with all people in America.

Of course, Farrakhan may have intentionally minced words when talking about bringing the inhabitants of the nation of America into a more perfect union with one another. He may have actually been referring to the Nation of Islam. If so, then once again, he has made a "play on words," which is his forte. Beware.

Everything that is created is in harmony with the law of evolution.

The theory of evolution flatly goes against the biblical account of creation. The theory of evolution was developed in the early 1800's. The basic thought behind it is that man was not created but evolved from a single cell which was present in the cosmos millions of light years ago. However, Genesis 1:1 tells us that God created the heavens and the earth, Genesis 1:25 tells us that God made the beasts of the earth, and Genesis 1:27 tells us that God created man.

It is baffling that Farrakhan would give credence to the theory of evolution when in fact, neither the Koran nor Elijah Muhammad condoned it. Remember, the Nation of Islam believes that twenty-four scientists created the world and man.

What, therefore, would be the purpose of Farrakhan bringing up evolution? Maybe it has to do with Herbert Spencer's "survival of the fittest" which Charles Darwin included in his theory of evolution. This idea or theory proposes that anything that survives extinction does so because it is more innately fit to survive. It says that what survives is stronger and has the greater will to survive over what doesn't survive. Spencer applied his theory to the human race and believed that those who survive are the ones who are fit to survive because they have the genetic ability to survive. This comes dangerously close to saying that certain "survivors" are genetically superior to non-survivors. A person could take the idea of "survival of the fittest" and apply it not just to the human race, but to the races within the human race. If we ask Farrakhan: who is the fittest? He would say, "the black man." A skinhead would say, "the white man." You see the problem?

The word for this evolutionary changing effecting stage after stage until we reach perfection in Arabic it is called Raab and from the word Raab you get the word Rabi or teacher: one who

nourishes a people from one stage and brings them to another stage.

Farrakhan is inferring that black people, as a race, will reach perfection through the process of evolution. Then he defines the role of a Rabbi as a person who brings people, stage by stage, to that perfection. It appears that Farrakhan is indirectly speaking of himself as this Rabbi (although the word Rabbi generally refers to a Jewish Religious leader) whose mission is to bring the black man to this evolutionary state of perfection. Sounds like *survival of the fittest*, don't you think?

There can be no nation of perfection without the Lord who created the law of evolution and is the master of the changes.

Here's that talk of evolution again. There is nothing in the Bible that supports Darwin's theory (which Farrakhan calls a law). Therefore, the Lord Jesus Christ did not create the "law of evolution." Farrakhan must be referring to a different "Lord." However, the Bible tells us that there is only "One Lord, one faith, one baptism" (Ephesians 4:5). If we know that the Lord the Bible is speaking of is Jesus Christ, the question then becomes: what "Lord" is Farrakhan speaking of?

Now brothers and sisters, the day of atonement is established by God to help us achieve a closer tie with the source of wisdom, knowledge, understanding, and power....... The basic reason that this [The Million Man March] was called was for atonement and reconciliation. So it is necessary for me, in as short a time as possible, to give as full an explanation of atonement as possible.

To atone means to make amends for, or to reconcile with. The Word of God (the Bible) uses the word "atonement" when speaking of sacrifice for sin. In the Old Testament, an unblemished animal (lamb, goat, et cetera) was often times sacrificed, at God's command, to restore one's fellowship with God (to atone). Atonement is what was accomplished when animal sacrifices were offered to God for forgiveness of sin. The book of Leviticus informs us that God directed Moses to instruct the Israelites to establish a day of atonement on the tenth day of the seventh month. This day was to be a holy gathering whereby the Israelites would fast, offer up sacrifices to God, and refrain from working. Yom Kippur is the present name for this Jewish holiday.

According to the teachings of the New Testament, the ultimate sacrifice that was made for our sins and transgressions was Jesus

Christ. He was the unblemished sacrificial lamb of God. By belief in Jesus and through the shedding of his blood, we are reconciled to God, if we confess a belief in Christ's divine status and resurrection. The blood of Christ atones for our sins. Black men can not, nor can any other group of people, atone for one another's sins by participating in a March. They can ask each other for forgiveness, make amends, and pledge promises, but they can not atone for one another's sins. Only the blood of Jesus Christ atones for sins. However, one can not reap the benefit of that atonement unless one believes and confesses a belief in Jesus and in who he really is.

Farrakhan's use of the word "atonement" is improper. He does not apply the word in the biblical sense, although there are some similarities of his use of the term when compared to the Bible's use of it.

Farrakhan says there are eight stages of atonement. There is little question that when Farrakhan speaks of atonement he is speaking of it as a tool to help the members of the American black community make amends with one another.

Farrakhan says that the first stage of atonement is to point to one's own wrong or to the wrong of others. The second stage is to acknowledge one's wrong. The third stage is to confess the wrong. In saying this, Farrakhan means that blacks are to confess their wrongs or sins to one another. To confess a fault is a good thing. However, we should first confess our faults to Christ and ask him to forgive us. Farrakhan does not use this mode of repentance in his atonement formula, instead, he has managed to create his own formula of atonement. His formula does not include Jesus.

While explaining his "third stage" Farrakhan remarks that "the Bible says confession is good for the soul." Once again, Farrakhan misquotes the Bible. It's a habit of his. Let's see what the Bible actually says about confession.

> 8But what saith it? The word is nigh thee, even in thy mouth, and in thy heart: that is, the word of faith, which we preach;
>
> 9That if thou shalt confess with thy mouth the Lord Jesus, and shalt believe in thine heart that God hath raised him from the dead, thou shalt be saved.
>
> 10For with the heart man believeth unto righteousness; and with the mouth confession is made unto salvation. (Romans 10:8-10)

According to the Bible, we repent of our sins and confess our belief. When we confess, we confirm our belief but not necessarily our repentance. Criminals often times confess their misdeeds without feeling remorse. With this analogy in mind, we can see that both repentance and confession require sincerity of heart to make it worthy. Confession is more than just good for the soul. Confession is crucial to the soul. But the confession which is crucial is not the confession of one's sins (as important as that may be), but confession that Jesus Christ is Lord and has risen from the grave. However, the Nation of Islam does not believe in the resurrection of Jesus Christ but instead believes in the resurrection of the black man's mind. Therefore, Farrakhan's idea of confession doesn't coincide with God's.

The fourth stage in Farrakhan's eight stage atonement hierarchy is repentance, the fifth: correcting one's evil deeds, the sixth: forgiveness, the seventh: reconciliation and restoration, and the eighth: perfect union.

The question becomes: perfect union for whom? For blacks and whites together? No. Perfect union between the races is not what Farrakhan is really speaking of. He is speaking of perfect union among blacks. Farrakhan believes that we as blacks should have a perfect union amongst ourselves. Let's look at it this way: it would be a good idea for twenty people who live in a house together to have a "perfect union" with one another since they all live with one another. However, if only five people in the house form a "perfect union" and leave the others out, then friction will develop in the house. If we look at the land in which we live (America) as a big house, then it stands to reason that we should all try to live together more peacefully (in perfect union, as Farrakhan puts it), otherwise, there will be friction in the house. With this in mind, the question becomes: why hasn't Farrakhan included all American people in his quest toward a more perfect union? The answer is: because he follows the teachings of Elijah Muhammad and the philosophies of Marcus Garvey who both supported and believed in separation of the races.

Power and wealth has made America spiritually blind.

America has defined itself as a Christian nation. It is not a perfect Christian nation and there are certainly many policies and laws that need to be changed. However, to say that America is spiritually blind is to indirectly attack its choice of religious identification: Christianity.

Racism will cause you to reject salvation if it comes in the skin of a black person.

Farrakhan feels that those who are bigoted against blacks will reject the message of salvation if they hear it being preached from the lips of a black man. Again, Farrakhan is making large statements in indirect ways and is really saying this: Many white people will reject him (Farrakhan) as being able to offer salvation to people since his (Farrakhan's) skin is black. Farrakhan is misguided in his perceptions. White America is rejecting his message because it is full of racist overtones, not because his skin is black. Furthermore, Farrakhan does not properly instruct anyone on how to obtain salvation because salvation only comes through Jesus Christ, not through Louis Farrakhan. Farrakhan does not preach the gospel of Christ.

Whenever a nation is involved in sin to the point that God intends to judge and destroy that nation, he always sends someone to make that nation or people know their sins, to reflect on it, to acknowledge, to confess, to repent, and to atone that they might find forgiveness with God.

Farrakhan believes that God will destroy America and that God has sent him to encourage America to repent of her sins. He has also gathered together thousands upon thousands of black men in order that they may "atone" for their transgressions against one another. There is no question, therefore, Farrakhan considers himself as one whom God has sent to aid black people in recognizing and repenting of their sins. Once again, by implying that God has sent him so that others would "atone that they might find forgiveness with God," Farrakhan is likening himself to Jesus. Jesus was the one who was sent by God to atone for sins, not Farrakhan. God is not sending anyone else to atone for sins. He did it once, it does not have to be done again.

From this beautiful White House have come commands to kill the prophets. Garvey's trouble came from this house [the White House]. Martin Luther King's trouble came from this house. Malcolm's trouble came from this house. W.E.B. Dubois' trouble came from this house. And from this house you stoned and killed the prophets of God that would have liberated black people.

Farrakhan accuses the government of stoning and killing prophets of God that would have "liberated black people." Which prophets is Farrakhan referring to? He doesn't specifically name any. Interestingly enough, there is great speculation in the Black community that members of the Nation of Islam, not the government, had Malcolm killed. Malcolm X exposed his displeasure (during a news interview on national television in the sixties) of Elijah Muhammad's fathering of many babies by many different women. The "Nation" was not pleased with this. However, the "Nation" had, at one time, considered Malcolm a prophet of God. The question becomes: How can Farrakhan accuse the government of killing prophets when it appears that the "Nation" killed one of their own "prophets?" Even if America were guilty of killing prophets, is it wrong for the nation of America to kill a "prophet" and right for the Nation of Islam?

Farrakhan is making severe statements against the government (which he often does). Although it is my belief that racial tensions would heal better if the Government were to publicly apologize to blacks for historically allowing certain atrocities and injustices to take place against blacks; it is against God's will for people to go against those in authority unless those in authority are demanding ungodly things of those under their authority. The following scripture reference supports this.

> 13Submit yourselves to every ordinance of
> man for the Lord's sake: whether it be to the
> king as supreme;
> 14Or to governors, as unto them that are
> sent by him for the punishment of evildoers,
> and for the praise of them that do well.
> (1 Peter 2:13-14)

And so here we are, four hundred years, fulfilling Abraham's prophecy.

It has been roughly four hundred years since the first Africans were kidnapped and brought to America as slaves. Therefore, the "we" that Farrakhan speaks of are black people. Farrakhan feels that blacks are fulfilling the prophecy of Abraham. However, the Bible speaks more of a promise than a prophecy when it comes to Abraham. And black people (as a race) were not the one's chosen to fulfill it, the Jews (as a nation) were. Let's briefly take a look at this:

> 1And it came to pass after these things,
> that God did tempt Abraham, and said unto
> him, Abraham: and he said, Behold, here I
> am.
> 2And he said, Take now thy son, thine only
> son Isaac, whom thou lovest, and get thee
> into the land of Moriah; and offer him there for

a burnt offering upon one of the mountains
which I will tell thee of. (Genesis 22:1-2)

9And they came to the place which God
had told him of; and Abraham built an altar
there, and laid the wood in order, and bound
Isaac his son, and laid him on the altar upon
the wood.
10And Abraham stretched forth his hand,
and took the knife to slay his son.
11And the angel of the Lord called unto him
out of heaven, and said, Abraham, Abraham:
and he said, Here am I.
12And he said, Lay not thine hand upon the
lad, neither do thou any thing unto him: for
now I know that thou fearest God, seeing thou
has not withheld thy son, thine only son from
me.
13And Abraham lifted up his eyes, and
looked, and behold behind him a ram caught
in a thicket by his horns: and Abraham went
and took the ram, and offered him up for a
burnt offering in the stead of his son.
14And Abraham called the name of that
place Jehovah jireh: as it is said to this day, In
the mount of the Lord it shall be seen.
15And the angel of the Lord called unto
Abraham out of heaven the second time,
16And said, By myself have I sworn, saith
the Lord, for because thou hast done this
thing, and hast not withheld thy son, thine
only son:
17That in blessing I will bless thee, and in
multiplying I will multiply thy seed as the stars
of the heaven, and as the sand which is upon
the sea shore; and thy seed shall possess the
gate of his enemies;
18And in thy seed shall all the nations of
the earth be blessed; because thou hast
obeyed my voice. (Genesis 22:9-18)

God tested Abraham by tempting him to rebel against him. Abraham did not rebel against God, but instead, purposed to sacrifice his only son, as God had ordered him. God had never intended for

Abraham to sacrifice his son. Because of Abraham's obedience, God blessed Abraham by greatly multiplying his seed (the generations of children that would come forth from him). As we will see, this nation of people that were to be multiplied and posses the gate of their enemies is Israel: the Jews. Let's look further.

> 10And Jacob went out from Beersheba, and went toward Haran.
> 11And he lighted upon a certain place, and tarried there all night, because the sun was set; and he took of the stones of that place, and put them for his pillows, and lay down in that place to sleep.
> 12And he dreamed, and behold a ladder set up on the earth, and the top of it reached to heaven: and behold the angels of God ascending and descending on it.
> 13And, behold, the Lord stood above it, and said, I am the Lord God of Abraham thy father, and the God of Isaac: the land whereon thou liest, to thee will I give it, and to thy seed;
> 14And thy seed shall be as the dust of the earth, and thou shalt spread abroad to the west, and to the east, and to the north, and to the south: and in thee and in thy seed shall all the families of the earth be blessed.
> 15And behold, I am with thee, and will keep thee in all places whither thou goest, and will bring thee again into this land; for I will not leave thee, until I have done that which I have spoken to thee of. (Genesis 28:12-15)

Isaac was the son on Abraham. Isaac and his wife Rebecka had twins named: Jacob and Esau. Esau was the firstborn of the two. At a time when Jacob and Esau were adults, Jacob actually tricked Isaac into believing that he was Esau. Because of this trickery, Isaac gave the birthright blessings to Jacob instead of Esau. When Isaac discovered that he had been fooled, it was too late, he had already blessed Jacob. The 27th chapter of Genesis gives this account.

Jacob knew he had mistreated Esau, and ran from him in fear of his life. During a time when he rested while on his way to Haran, Jacob fell asleep and had a dream. God kept his promise to bless Abraham's seed by blessing the seed of his son Jacob. In the dream, God promised him land (verse 13) He also told Jacob that he would produce nations of people who would vastly number the earth. God also told Jacob that through his seed (through the generations of his children) "shall all the families of the earth be blessed." (verse 14)

All the families of he earth would be blessed through Jacob's seed because Jesus Christ was born into the nation of Israel through the tribe of Judah. Jacob was Israel. God changed Jacob's name to Israel:

> 9And God appeared to Jacob again, when he came out of Padanaram, and blessed him.
> 10And God said unto him, Thy name is Jacob: thy name shall not be called any more Jacob, but Israel shall be thy name: and he called his name Israel. (Genesis 35:9-10)

Jacob and Israel are the same person. Remember, God promised to multiply Abraham's seed. He also told Abraham that the families of the earth would be blessed through his seed. Abraham had Isaac who had Jacob. Both Isaac and Jacob are seeds of Abraham. God gave Jacob a dream. In the dream God informed Jacob that his seed would be blessed, that he would be blessed with land, and that all the families of the earth would be blessed through his seed. God changed Jacob's name to Israel. Israel became a nation of people. It is the original nation of the Jews. Jesus came from the line of the tribe of Judah. Judah was one of the twelve tribes of ancient Israel. Israel was promised a land flowing with milk and honey:

> 7And the Lord said, I have surely seen the affliction of my people which are in Egypt, and have heard their cry by reason of their taskmasters; for I know their sorrows;
> 8And I am come down to deliver them out of the hand of the Egyptians, and to bring them up out of that land unto a good land and a large, unto a land flowing with milk and honey; unto the place of the Canaanites, and the Hittites, and the Amorites, and the Perizzites, and the Hivites, and the Jebusites. (Exodus 3:7-8)

When Farrakhan speaks of fulfilling Abraham's prophecy, he is actually referring to the fulfillment of God's promise to multiply Abraham's seed and produce a vast nation of people. A land flowing with milk and honey was also promised to the descendant's of Abraham. These descendant's are the people of Israel: the Jews. However, Farrakhan believes that black people will fulfill the prophecy.

Atonement for the children of Israel pre-figured our [blacks] suffering here in America.

Farrakhan uses the word "pre-figured" the same way the Bible uses the phrase "shadow of things to come." In order to explain this phrase, let's briefly look at what the Bible says about the Sabbath: The ten commandments that God gave Moses to give to the Jews included a Sabbath day (seventh day of the week) of rest. However, the Sabbath day was a shadow of things to come. Jesus did not rest on the Sabbath day but treated it like any other day. He ministered on the Sabbath, thereby teaching people that every day is the same. The Sabbath, as it once was, became a shadow of what now is. In Old Testament times, following the law of Moses was the only way one could obtain salvation, but now, the grace of God through a belief in Jesus Christ guarantees salvation. The following scripture reference clarifies this.

> 16Let no man therefore judge you in meat, or
> in drink, or in respect of an holyday, or of the
> new moon, or of the sabbath days:
> 17Which are a shadow of things to come; but
> the body is of Christ. (Colossians 2:16-17)

Farrakhan is saying that atonement for the children of Israel (the blood of Jesus) is a shadow of what he thinks the current situation is: the atonement of black people with one another. However, the scriptures neither say nor imply any such thing.

Farrakhan is comparing black people with the children of Israel. He constantly suggests that black people are the one's with the promise, not the Jews. However, the Bible teaches that the Jews (Israelites) are the people who are direct descendants of Abraham. The Jews are the children of the promise. The Jews are a dispersed nation of people. Blacks are a race of people. There is a difference. This is not to say that there are no black Jews. But if there are, then their ancestors would be from Israel as well as Africa. Furthermore, the Bible tells us that one may become a spiritual "Jew" by believing in Jesus Christ as their Lord and Saviour. Therefore, anyone can become a Jew and be included on God's list as a child of the promise. Let's take a look:

> 28For he is not a Jew, which is one
> outwardly; neither is that circumcision, which
> is outward in the flesh:
> 29But he is a Jew which is one inwardly;
> and circumcision is that of the heart, in the

> spirit, and not in the letter; whose praise is not of men, but of God. (Romans 2:28-29)

God made a covenant with Abraham, that he (Abraham) would be the father of many nations (Abraham is the father of the Jews). This covenant included God's mandate that every infant boy be circumcised (removal of the male genitalia foreskin) on the eighth day after birth. The mandate was fulfilled by the coming of Jesus. Therefore, instead of a physical circumcision, the New Testament speaks of a spiritual circumcision: The circumcision of one's heart. When one praises God instead of men, the foreskin of one's heart is lifted. To praise God is to accept Jesus as Lord and Saviour. The scriptures cited above teach us that a real Jew is one who is a Jew in spirit. Therefore, as far as God is concerned, a physical Jew who has not accepted Christ is not a real Jew. However, a person who has no Jewish ancestry but does accept Christ, is. Race and nationality do not play a role in one's salvation, as Farrakhan would like us to think.

God is sending his decision. I can't help it if I've got to make the decision known.

Finally, Farrakhan labels himself as the man of the hour by claiming that God is speaking through him about decisions to be made in the black community. He is strategic in building his credibility.

And so my children, I've caused you to suffer in the furnace of affliction so that I might purify you and resurrect you from a grave of death and ignorance. I, God put in your soul, not a law written on stone but I have written the law on the tablets of your heart. So, I'm going to make a new covenant with you, oh Black man!

Farrakhan is speaking as though he is quoting God. But he is not quoting God. God has not said that he will make a new covenant (promise) with the black man. God has already made a covenant. He made a covenant with Abraham and is seed: the Jews. He made a covenant with the gentiles, and with anyone that will accept Jesus Christ as Lord and saviour. The Bible does not tell us of any other covenant. The Bible does not indicate that God ever made a covenant with any race of people. Some would say that God made a covenant with a race of people because he promised to give the Jews Jerusalem. However, we must remember that the Jews are a nation of people composed of many races from generations ago. In the above quote Farrakhan fancies himself speaking for God by speaking in the person of God. Farrakhan is essentially telling us that God is going to make a new covenant with the black man. Again, there is no biblical indication of this, however, all spiritual Jews are promised the land of the New Jerusalem (discussed more in Chapter Four).

God wants to purify you [black people] and lift you up that you may call America and the world to repentance.

Jesus is the only man that was designated by God to call the world to repentance. There is nothing in the Bible that indicates that black people are to call the world to repentance. Furthermore, Jesus did not need to repent of anything because he was sinless and therefore was qualified to call the world to repentance. When Farrakhan says that black people will call the world to repentance then he is essentially saying that blacks have nothing to repent of and everybody else does. By saying that God wants to lift blacks up so that they can call the world to repentance, Farrakhan is essentially saying that God wants to make blacks superior over others. This is racist ideology and should not be tolerated in the church or anywhere else. God is the superior being, none other.

The name for the one god in ancient Egypt...Aton, the one god. Nineteen rays. Look at your scripture, a woman, remember the nine? Means somebody's pregnant with an idea.

Aton was the name of the false sun god that the people of ancient Egypt worshipped. Farrakhan, with just a few words, ties this false god into the number 19, the number 9, and biblical scripture. Black Muslims believe that the "revelations" given in the Koran are mathematically coded based on the number 19.

But in this case it's a woman pregnant with a male child destined to rule the nations with a rod of iron. God is standing over her womb and this child will be like the day sun and he will say, "I am the light of the world", hand coming out of that sun, come unto me all ye that are heavy laden. I'm going to give you rest, but I'm going to give you life because I am the resurrection and the life and if you believe in me though you were dead, yet shall you live again. You're dead, black man.

Jesus described himself as the light of the world. Jesus told those who were heavy laden to come to him and he would give them rest (Matthew 11:28). Jesus proclaimed to be "the resurrection and the life" and said that if we believe in him, even though we were dead, we will live (St. John 11:25). As we have seen, Farrakhan believes that it is his duty to resurrect the black man's mind. In the excerpt above, Farrakhan accuses the black man of being spiritually dead and alludes to himself, not Jesus, as the resurrection and the life.

One should also note, that in the midst of quoting some of Jesus' teachings, Farrakhan adds that the "hand was coming out of that *sun*." What did Farrakhan mean by this? Remember, Aton was the Egyptian *sun*-god. Farrakhan cleverly uses the word "sun" when repeating Jesus' teachings about himself thereby subliminally associating the sun-god, Aton, with Jesus.

But if you believe in the God who created this son/sun of truth and of light with nineteen rays, meaning he's pregnant with God's spirit, God's life, God's wisdom.....Abraham Lincoln's statue, nineteen feet high, nineteen feet wide. Jefferson, nineteen feet high, sixteen [feet wide] and a third president, nineteen [feet high] standing on the steps of the capital in the light of the sun, offering life to a people who are dead.

Farrakhan names the first two presidents (Lincoln and Jefferson) but not the third. However, the man standing on the steps of the Nation's Capital that day was Farrakhan. He was standing there in the light of the "sun" (there's that word again). Earlier, Farrakhan exclaimed, "you're dead, black man!" Then he speaks of a third president standing on the steps of the capital offering life to a people who are dead. The "dead" people whom Farrakhan refers to are the black people that he spoke of earlier. Could Farrakhan be speaking of himself as this third president that is offering life to a dead people? There is no question in my mind that he is.

Black man, the Aton represents the one god. In the Koran Muhammad is called a life giving sun. So if you look at the Aton, add a "e" to it and separate [it] from the next four letters and you get the word "atone."

Farrakhan equates Aton with a god, then states that the Koran considers Muhammad as a life giving sun. As stated earlier, Aton was the name of the false *sun*-god the Egyptians worshipped. Therefore, by saying Aton is a sun-god and that Muhammad is as a life giving sun, Farrakhan has given Muhammad a divine status because he has equated the two. Farrakhan goes even further. He tells his audience to add an "e" to Aton. By doing that we get the word "atone." Farrakhan describes his Million Man March as a day of atonement (black people making amends to one another). By telling his audience to add the letter "e" to the word Aton, Farrakhan equates "Aton" with "atone."

Million Man March

Farrakhan said earlier that he organized the Million Man March for a day of "atonement and reconciliation." By saying this, he gives himself credit as one whom God has used to bring people to a place of atonement for sins. Therefore, if Farrakhan is to bring people to a place of atonement, then he is equating himself with Aton, a god. Now we have the word "atone" equated with the false god Aton, Muhammad, and Farrakhan. Has Farrakahn indirectly said that he is a god? Maybe. Is Farrakhan a god? No. God is God and there is only one God: I AM THAT I AM which represents himself in three persons: The Father, The Son, and The Holy Ghost.

We've got to move on to something else higher and better. So, my beloved brothers and sisters, here's what we'd like you to do. Everyone of you my dear brothers, when you go home, here's what I want you to do...we must belong to some organization that is working for and in the interest of the uplift and the liberation of our people. Go back, join the NAACP if you want to. Join the Urban League. Join the All African People's Revolutionary Party. Join us. Join the Nation of Islam. Join P.U.S.H. Join the Congress of Racial equality. Join S.C.L.C., the Southern Christian Leadership Conference.

In this particular excerpt, Farrakhan tells his audience to "Join us. Join the Nation of Islam." It is the only religion he actually names. All the other groups he mentions are organizations. This is just more evidence that Farrakhan wants to recruit black people into the Nation of Islam.

We must continue to reach out for those that have condemned this and make them to see that this [the Million Man March] was not evil. It was not intended for evil. It was intended for good.

Farrakhan says that the Million Man March was not intended for evil. However, many parts of the Message that he delivered at the March go against biblical doctrine and can therefore be considered evil. During the speech, Farrakhan introduces Black Muslim theology. He praises Allah, not the biblical God. It is evil to praise any other god but the true God: God the Father, the Son, and the Holy Ghost. Farrakhan speaks of Fard Muhammad, not Jesus, as being God incarnate. It is evil to speak of anyone else besides Jesus Christ as being God incarnate. Farrakhan uses the phrase "in the name of Allah" instead of "in the name of Jesus." It is blasphemous not to consider Jesus to be God. Blasphemy is evil. Farrakhan alludes to Masonic teachings. These teachings are contrary to the Bible, which makes the teachings evil. Farrakhan indirectly call blacks the cornerstone and builders of a new world. Jesus is the cornerstone and will rule a new world during the millenium. To attribute these things to anyone else is evil. Farrakhan says that the Lord created the law of evolution. This goes completely against biblical doctrine. The Bible does not support the theory of evolution. To say that the Lord created the law of evolution is heresy. It is evil. The Bible speaks of creation, not evolution. Farrakhan speaks of the Million Man March as the day of atonement. This is heresy. The day Jesus died on the cross is the day of atonement. Farrakhan says that the Million Man March was not intended for evil, however, if he insists on describing it as a day of atonement then it is evil because the March then becomes a counterfeit day of atonement.

Farrakhan's effort to discourage blacks from violence and the like is notable. However, it is interesting that he did so in such a public manner. When I clean my house, it is a private matter. I don't invite the neighbors in while I'm cleaning, only afterwards. Farrakhan says he was attempting to clean up some things within the black community. But why March to Washington for a public display of a private matter? What is the purpose of the entire nation being privy to what Farrakhan had to say? It is my estimation that there was more to Farrakhan's agenda than just encouraging blacks to be more unified. He wanted to promote the Nation of Islam, and in order to do so, he needs an audience.

Everyone of you must go back home and join some church, synagogue, temple, or mosque that is teaching spiritual and moral uplift. I want you brothers--there's no men in the church and the mosque--the men are in the streets and we've got to get back to the houses of God.

Once again Farrakhan lumps Christianity (the church/temples), Judaism (the synagogue), and Islam (the mosque) together as if the three are teaching the same thing. He calls these the houses of God. But all of these houses can not be the houses of God when they all teach totally different things about God. The Bible speaks of the Christian church as the house of God. Let's take a look at what the scriptures say.

> 13And the Jews' passover was at hand, and Jesus went up to Jerusalem,
> 14And found in the temple those that sold oxen and sheep and doves, and the changers of money sitting:

> [15]And when he had made a scourge of small cords, he drove them all out of the temple, and the sheep, and the oxen; and poured out the changers' money, and overthrew the tables;
> [16]And said unto them that sold doves, Take these things hence; make not my Father's house an house of merchandise. (John 2:13-16)

> [17]For the time is come that judgment must begin at the house of God: and if it first begin at us, what shall the end be of them that obey not the gospel of God? (1 Peter 4: 17)

Verse 15 tells us that Jesus became angry at certain Jews who treated the temple (church) like a flea market. These Jews had accepted Christ and knew better. The emphasis here is that Jesus referred to the temple as his Father's house (the house of God). The 17th verse of Peter 4 also refers to the church as the house of God. As we can see, Farrakhan has minced words again in his effort to convince unsuspecting blacks that Islam and Christianity is basically the same, which they are not. The physical church that teaches orthodox Christianity is the "house of God." God does not include the mosque when speaking of the house of God. However, Farrakhan does.

We [black people] must be prepared to help them [the people in the White House, the American government] if they're with us or to punish them if they're against us. And when they're against us, I'm not talking about color, I'm talking about an agenda that's in the best interest of the black, the poor, and the vulnerable in this country.

Farrakhan doesn't say how he plans to punish the government if they don't go along with what he has in mind for blacks, the poor, and the vulnerable.

Farrakhan went on to define his agenda by saying that he wanted to develop an economic development fund. He encouraged his audience to adopt black children and to become life long pen pals with prisoners. He encouraged his audience to give ten dollars a month to this fund and asked the "the ten million supporters back home" to do the same. Farrakhan estimated having a billion dollars in this fund within a year if everyone (blacks) would cooperate. One must note that this fund has existed for quite a few years. What Farrakhan called his Three Year Economic Program began on October 7, 1991. It is not part of a new agenda for Farrakhan. Many blacks have already been contributing to this fund and three years have long surpassed. Despite this, there doesn't seem to be any concrete evidence as to how this money is being spent.

No black organization would be accountable to anybody outside of us but accountable to us and we would free the NAACP, the Urban League, and all black organizations to work in the best interest of our people. How many of you would like to see all of our black organizations free?

When Farrakhan says that no black organization would be accountable to anybody outside of "us," there is no question that the "us" he is speaking about is black people. No matter how you slice it, these kinds of statements lend itself toward racial separatism. Often times, because of our struggles, those of us who are black, accept this kind of thinking. But suppose it were a white man standing on the steps of the capital saying things like "no white organization would be accountable to anybody outside of us [whites]"? Black people would find those statements to be racist. And if that is the case, then they are no less racist when Farrakhan says them.

With all of this in mind, there just might be another "us" that Farrakhan is referring to. It is possible that he is referring to the Nation of Islam as the "us". If indeed, somewhere in the future, black people would be accountable to the Nation of Islam for their every move, then the spirituality of American blacks would be in great jeopardy because The Nation of Islam teaches that Jesus Christ is nothing more than a prophet.

Farrakhan talks of freeing black organizations to work in the best interest of black people. He doesn't really say what these organizations need to be freed from. However, it is easy to conclude that he means black organizations should be freed from non-black organizations. Once again he lends himself towards the ideology of racial separatism. In order for a potential leader to become more influential among those whom he wishes to influence, he must attempt to put his audience in a vacuum away from the influence of others; hence, Farrakhan's emphasis on racial separatism.

Soon the leadership [he points to the people around him] is going to meet and work out the details of an exodus economic fund, and we're going to get back to you. This is not a one day thing. A task force will be formed right out of this leadership to make sure

that the things that we say today will be implemented so that next year on the day of atonement..... this will take place each and every year from now on until God says well done.

At this point of his speech, Farrakhan feels safe enough to identify himself and those around him as "the Leadership." Unfortunately, his audience may have agreed with his sentiments. This time, when speaking of his economic fund, he describes it as an "exodus" economic fund, again alluding to racial separatism. To make an exodus from something means to embark on a mass departure from it. Farrakhan wants black people to embark on a mass departure from white people, if at least not physically, spiritually. Farrakhan speaks of a task force being formed from within "the Leadership." Farrakhan says this task force will be developed to make sure that the details of this exodus economic fund are implemented. However, it is very difficult for an organization to police itself. Farrakhan goes on to say that his day of atonement will take place every year until God tells him to stop. Again, in saying this, he attempts to lend credibility to himself by implying that God has instructed him to do what he's doing.

We want an outside accounting firm and [will] scrutinize every dollar that was raised from your pockets to make the Million Man March a success. And if there is any overage it will not be spent. We will come back to this board of leadership [points to those around him] and we will account for every dime, every nickel, every dollar.

This excerpt of Farrakhan's speech contradicts what he said in the excerpt immediately preceding it. Farrakhan said that a task force would be formed from *within* "The Leadership" to police things. Then he says that an *outside* accounting firm will be policing some things (specifically the money). It's almost as if he realized that the second option would be more appealing to his audience. Farrakhan goes on to say that "The Leadership" (a phrase which he's using quite frequently at this point of his speech) will account for all of the money so that no-one will think there is a hidden agenda. Again, which is it? Will "The Leadership" account for the money, the task force within the Leadership, or an outside accounting firm?

When Farrakhan speaks of a hidden agenda he alludes to the possibility that some blacks may question his request for funds and begin wondering where the money is going. Farrakhan's hidden agenda has more to do with a spiritual quest as opposed to a financial one. However, it takes money to obtain enough visibility to influence people spiritually. Farrakhan needs the money to continue his campaign. He is campaigning to be seen as the undisputed leader of black America. If he can gain the title he seeks, then his influence in the black community will be overwhelming and his opportunity to propagate Black Muslim theology will soar even higher.

Now brothers, in closing I want to take this pledge.......

Farrakhan instructed his audience to repeat after him in making pledges. The pledges included: loving one's brother as one loves himself; improving one's spiritual, mental, social, and economic status; building businesses and the like as well as entering into international trade for the good of self, family, and black people, promising never to raise a gun or knife to any human being except in self defense; promising never to abuse one's wife by striking her or disrespecting her, promising never to engage in the abuse of children, sexual or otherwise; promising never to use the "B word" to describe any woman but especially any black woman, promising never to use drugs; and promising to support black newspapers, black radio, black television, and black artists who "clean up their acts."

Of course, for the most part, these are positive pledges. However, hidden within them are insidious suggestions. First, Farrakhan insidiously suggests that blacks should enter into international trade. Of course, there is nothing wrong with entering into international trade. However, no-one knew at the time that Farrakhan would decide to do business with Khadafy who is one of America's adversaries. By suggesting that blacks enter into international trade, Farrakhan was actually subliminally preparing his audience to accept the international "trading" he was about to embark upon with Khadafy: more on that later.

Secondly, Farrakhan suggests that his audience is to never use the "B word" to describe any woman. This is a good thing to suggest. However, Farrakhan takes it one step further by saying to his audience that they "especially" should not use the "B word" when it comes to addressing black women. The word "especially" insidiously implies that it is excusable to use the word when addressing women of other races.

The power of a pledge is great. When people pledge to do things they are giving their word. Consequently, their integrity is put on the line and they form a stronger bond to the person or organization with whom they are making the pledge. A pledge is a promise. Promises are not meant to be broken. Pledges bond people. Farrakhan's audience became more bonded with him when they made pledges with him. As human beings, we are greatly influenced by those we are bonded to. Many men at the March became greatly influenced by

Farrakhan because of the emotional bonding that the pledge produced.

This was a beautiful and peaceful meeting, probably one of the best that ever was held in Washington, formed by black people who want to atone to God and clear our slate.

Unquestionably, the best meeting, ever held in Washington was the March on Washington organized and headed by Reverend Doctor Martin Luther King, in the sixties. All races and both genders were invited to this March. Racial harmony was the primary issue that King addressed. Farrakhan's March is a far stretch from King's. However, Farrakhan knows that people will invariably compare his March to King's. Therefore, Farrakhan tries to give credibility to his March by indirectly attempting to put it in the same league as King's.

In the name of Allah, the beneficent, the merciful, praise be to Allah the Lord of the worlds, the beneficent, the merciful, master of the day of requital. Thee whom we worship, the needs seek. Guide us on the right path, the path of those upon whom you have bestowed favors not the path of those upon whom wrath is brought down nor those who go astray. Oh Allah, we thank you for this holy day of atonement and reconciliation......and as we leave this place let us be resolved to go home to work out this atonement and make our communities a decent, whole, and safe place to live. And Allah, we beg your blessings on all who participated, all who came that presented their bodies as a living sacrifice, holy and acceptable as their reasonable service. Now let us not be conformed to this world but let us go home transformed by the renewing of our minds and let the idea of atonement ring throughout America.

The preceding excerpt was part of Farrakhan's closing prayer. Farrakhan is a Black Muslim. He does everything in the name of Allah. In his prayer, he speaks of worshipping Allah. Because of this alone, Christians (black or white) have no business following this man. As Christians, we can not afford to separate the man from the message.

Again Farrakhan defines his March as a day of atonement but this time goes so far as to label it a *holy* day of atonement. The March promoted Nation of Islam theology and therefore can not be considered holy. Furthermore, Farrakhan describes all who came as those who have presented their bodies as a living sacrifice, holy and acceptable as their reasonable service. Sound familiar? It should. He has taken this from biblical scripture. Let's take a look:

> [36]For of him, and through him, and to him, are all things: to whom be glory for ever. Amen. (Romans 11:36)
>
> [1]I beseech you therefore, brethren, by the mercies of God, that ye present your bodies a living sacrifice, holy, acceptable unto God, which is your reasonable service.
> [2]And be not conformed to this world: but be ye transformed by the renewing of your mind, that ye may prove what is that good, and acceptable, and perfect will of God. (Romans 12:1-2)

As usual, Farrakhan has tried to blend biblical scripture with Muslim theology. He speaks of worshipping Allah while in the same breath uses biblical scripture to describe the black man as those who he says presented their bodies as a living sacrifice. However, when referring to those who have presented their bodies as a living sacrifice, holy and acceptable to God for reasonable service, the Bible is speaking of Christians. Part of following Christ is living holy, and in order to live holy one must give up certain things and make sacrifices. This is the duty of a Christian. When Farrakhan tells his audience not to be conformed to this world but instead to be transformed by the renewing of their minds, he uses scripture to allude to the Nation of Islam theology of the resurrection of the black man's mind and is, therefore, not using the scriptures in the biblical sense. Paul (the author of Romans) was instructing all Christians not to be conformed to this world. He was not, as Farrakhan would have us think, instructing only black people. Farrakhan ends his prayer with the following words:

And perhaps she [America] may do some act of atonement that you may forgive and those ill-effected may forgive, that reconciliation and restoration may lead us to perfect union with thee and with each other. We ask all of this in your holy and righteous name. Amen.

Finally, at the end of his speech, it looks as if Farrakhan speaks of all Americans reconciling with one another. However, Farrakhan says that in order for this to happen, America must "do some act of atonement." He never specifies what "act of atonement" would be acceptable to him for racial harmony and restoration. This is because Farrakhan's true agenda includes racial separatism, not racial harmony. This is evident in the majority of his speech. It appears as if the above statement has more to do with hindsight than with sincerity. Farrakhan can point to this statement when people, like me, accuse him of having racist ideologies.

Allah Akbar!

Farrakhan instructed his audience to repeat these two words several times before his departure from the steps of the Nation's Capital. These two words give praise to Allah which makes it again obvious that Farrakhan's main mission is to promote Black Muslim theology.

SUMMING UP THE MATTER

Farrakhan was very much aware that he was addressing an audience composed of blacks, most of which had a history of Christian experience. Observers pointed out that 98% of his audience that day were composed of men who were Christians or came from Christian backgrounds. Farrakhan was also aware that this March would be nationally televised. Consequently, Farrakhan was very careful with what he said. Instead of directly encouraging blacks to consider joining the Nation of Islam, he prayed to Allah and made indirect references to Black Muslim theology, while all the time quoting from the Bible and misrepresenting the scriptures. However, Farrakhan has not been as careful with his words when speaking in front of audiences composed predominantly of Black Muslims and Farrakhan supporters, as attested to in the discussion of the following speech presented in the next chapter: Farrakhan's 1996 Saviour's Day Speech.

CHAPTER FOUR

A BRIEF LOOK AT THE PRELUDE TO FARRAKHAN'S 1996 SAVIOUR'S DAY SPEECH

On February 25, 1996, Farrakhan spoke at the Nation of Islam's annual "Saviour's Day" event which took place at the U.I.C. Pavilion in Chicago. This was his first major speech after the Million Man March. The entire event was set on stage in front of a backdrop of two towering photographs. Those photographs were of Elijah Muhammad and Wallace Fard (whom Black Muslims refer to as Master Fard Muhammad). Black Muslims define their Saviour's Day as the annual observance of the anniversary of the birth of Wallace Fard. They consider Fard to be their Saviour. This train of thought goes completely against biblical doctrine. The Bible teaches us that Jesus Christ is our only Saviour. The Nation of Islam considers their Saviour's Day to be the holiest day of the Muslim calendar.

Before Farrakhan spoke at this event, a commentator and two speakers spoke ahead of him. The commentator was Jamil Muhammad. One of the speakers, Tynetta Muhammad, was introduced as "a wife of the honorable Elijah Muhammad." The other speaker was Reverend Ben Chavis, head of the National African Leadership Summit, who was, at the time a Christian minister, but has since become a Black Muslim and now calls himself: Benjamin Muhammad. Mr. Chavis had been ousted from his position as President of the country's National Association for the Advancement of Colored People (NAACP). The NAACP did not support the Million Man March.

Tynetta Muhammad and Chavis addressed the crowd briefly. A few excerpts from their remarks will be presented before we discuss Farrakhan's speech. Brief comments from Jamil Muhammad and Ishmael Muhammad (assistant minister to Farrakhan) will be presented as well. The things that they said are but examples of thought that point to the powerful influence that Farrakhan has over the minds of many black people.

Tynetta Muhammad

Tynetta Muhammad began her delivery by saying, "there is no God but Allah." She went on to say that Allah came to the United States in the person of Wallace Fard and she described Elijah Muhammad as "a divine leader, teacher, guide, and the most exalted Christ." She thanked Allah for giving his last call in "the person of Minister Louis Farrakhan."

By saying that there is a "most exalted Christ" implies that there is more than one Christ and that one Christ is more exalted than another. However, there is no *most* exalted Christ. There is only *one* exalted Christ and that is Jesus Christ.

Tynetta Muhammad continued by saying the following: "the 104th Sura is entitled the slanderer. Who is that talking about? Alright, the slanderer is now trying to slander the righteous man of God who is the only hope and friend of America and the world today."

When Tynetta asks who the slanderer is, she is alluding to her belief that the United States Government has slandered Farrakhan by accusing him of consorting with terrorists, namely, Muammar Khadafy. Her question is intentionally facetious. She implies that the slanderer is the United States Government. Tynetta goes on to describe Farrakhan as a righteous man of God. Lets look at what the Bible defines as a righteous man of God.

> 8 But what saith it? The word is nigh thee, even in thy mouth, and in thy heart: that is, the word of faith, which we preach;
>
> 9 That if thou shalt confess with thy mouth the Lord Jesus, and shalt believe in thine heart that God hath raised him from the dead, thou shalt be saved.
>
> 10 For with the heart man believeth unto righteousness; and with the mouth confession is made unto salvation.
>
> 11 For the scripture saith, Whosoever believeth on him shall not be ashamed.
>
> 12 For there is no difference between the Jew and the Greek: for the same Lord over all is rich unto all that call upon him.
>
> 13 For whosoever shall call upon the name of the Lord shall be saved. (Romans 10:8-13)

According to the above scripture references, in order to be saved (saved from eternal damnation, from hell) one must confess and believe in the Lordship and resurrection of Jesus Christ. Belief in Jesus Christ (salvation) leads to righteousness (verse 10). The Nation of Islam does not teach this. They teach that Fard is Lord and Saviour and that Jesus was never resurrected from the grave. Therefore they are not saved, and if they are not saved, they are not righteous. So, if the Nation of Islam is not righteous, and Farrakhan is the leader of the Nation of Islam, then Farrakhan can not be righteous either.

Tynetta depicts Farrakhan as being the only hope and friend of America and the world today. This is not true. Jesus is the only hope and friend of America and the world today as confirmed by the following scriptures:

> 24The Lord is my portion, saith my soul; therefore will I hope in him.
> 25The Lord is good unto them that wait for him, to the soul that seeketh him.
> 26It is good that a man should both hope; and quietly wait for the salvation of the Lord.
> (Lamentations 3:24-26)

> 1Paul, an apostle of Jesus Christ by the commandment of God our Saviour, and Lord Jesus Christ, which is our hope.
> (1 Timothy 1:1)

Jesus is described, not only as our hope, but as our God and Saviour. The scriptures in Lamentations instructs us to hope in the Lord. Jesus is our hope, not Farrakhan.

Tynetta Muhammad refers to Farrakhan as being the great and holy man that God has appointed for this day and time. She threatens the United States by stating that America would be in flames if it were to take a move against Farrakhan. However, Farrakhan challenged the government several times during this speech.

Tynetta Muhammad is mistaken when she says Farrakhan is holy because Farrakhan's calling is not in Christ. Farrakhan is not holy. He does not believe in the atonement of Jesus Christ but instead believes in what he calls the atonement of the Million Man March.

Reverend Ben Chavis/Benjamin Chavis Muhammad

Ben Chavis was introduced to the audience as a "brother and friend." Unfortunately he was one of the many Christians who put the quest for black unity above the gospel of Christ. He did this by supporting Farrakhan and the "Nation." Farrakhan made it clear, especially during this speech, that his mission is to promote Islam and encourage black Americans to become Black Muslims. At the time Chavis was a Christian. However, Chavis is no longer a Christian but is now a Black Muslim. Chavis became a Black Muslim in February of

1997. He is a victim of Farrakhan's craftiness; a casualty of spiritual warfare.

Chavis begins his speech by giving honor and all praise to God and greets the audience with the Muslim greeting, 'As-salaam-alaikum." Chavis could not bring himself to give honor and praise to Allah and therefore compromised by using the word "God."

Chavis thanked God for this "Saviour's Day," for the Million Man March, and for Louis Farrakhan. However, God does not condone this "Saviour's Day" because those in charge of the day are celebrating someone other than Jesus Christ as their Lord and Saviour. God does not condone the Million Man March because Farrakhan used it and continues to use the memory of its event as a tool to draw black people into the Nation of Islam. God does not support Louis Farrakhan because Farrakhan teaches false doctrine. Consequently, God does not sanction "Saviour's Day," the Million Man March, nor the teachings of Louis Farrakhan. Despite this, Chavis thanked God as though God sanctions these things.

Chavis moved on to articulate the following: "As a Christian minister, I am pleased, I am proud to stand here today, and I appeal to my other Christian ministers: don't let the devil divide you from truth. The truth is that the honorable Minister Louis Farrakhan, [his] vision for the Million Man March, his call was a call from God..... overwhelmingly, the majority of black people stand with Minister Louis Farrakhan."

This book documents various reasons as to why the Million Man March was *not* a call of God. However, Chavis was duped into thinking so, along with many other Christian blacks. Farrakhan teaches false doctrine (misinterpretation and perversion of biblical scripture) indirectly or directly during most of his speeches, including the speech he made at the Million Man March. Many Christians don't realize that he is doing this. However, there are some that do and follow him anyway. But, Farrakhan's call for better unification amongst blacks, does not give Christian blacks the luxury of following him. Chavis also said that most black people stand with Farrakhan. If this is true then an overwhelming amount of blacks are being swayed by Farrakhan's false doctrines. Chavis is a stunning example of Farrakhan's impact on the Christian black community in America. Because of Farrakhan's influence, Chavis has denied Christ when at one time he accepted him, or at least he said that he did.

Chavis also declared, "We want white America to stop interfering into the affairs of black America!" However, by conducting the Million Man March at the Nation's Capital, Farrakhan is not staying out of the affairs of "white America." It doesn't seem fair for the Nation of Islam and their supporters to employ a double standard. Furthermore, Farrakhan stated in his Million Man March speech that there are two

America's: one white and one black. He said this as if there should not be (and it shouldn't). But if the Nation of Islam complain about the racial divide in America, then it is hypocritical for them or any of their supporters to later say anything that would incite more division. Chavis' remark about keeping white America out of black America's affairs would certainly rate as rhetoric that incites racial division.

In their national paper, "The Final Call," the Nation of Islam have often times made statements that indicate their desire for blacks to live in separate territories or states from whites. They want the government to exempt all black people from paying taxes. They want equal but separate schools and they want interracial marriages to be prohibited. These are just some of the things that Chavis is supporting by becoming a Black Muslim.

Jamil Muhammad

Jamil Muhammad asked the Muslims in the audience from the Muhammad Mosque in London England to stand. When they did, Jamil Muhammad exclaimed, We're [black Muslims] all over the planet! It's too late devils! It's too late! You tried to stop us [blacks] but it's too late!"

Any time anyone from the Nation of Islam uses the word "devil" they are referring to white people. We know this because Elijah Muhammad labels white people as such in his book: MESSAGE TO THE BLACK MAN IN AMERICA. Black Muslims consider Elijah Muhammad to be a divine messenger of Wallace Fard. Therefore, Black Muslims see Elijah Muhammad's teachings as divine. In order to be considered a Black Muslim one must agree with Elijah Muhammad's teachings. Elijah Muhammad's description of white people as being devils is undeniably racist. Therefore, the Nation of Islam can accurately be described as a racist religion.

Ishmael Muhammad

Ishmael Muhammad introduced Farrakhan to the audience by uttering these words: "In the name of Allah the beneficent, the merciful, I bear witness that there is no God but Allah who came in the person of Master Fard Muhammad to whom praise is due forever and I bear witness that the honorable Elijah Muhammad is his messenger. I further bear witness beyond a shadow of a doubt that the man in our midst [Farrakhan] is a divine leader, a divine teacher and a divine guide. I speak of none other than our big brother and friend, our world president, our leader, the honorable Minister Louis Farrakhan."

Ishmael Muhammad goes on to describe Farrakhan as a representative of Elijah Muhammad.

The Black Muslims believe that God came in the person of Fard Muhammad while Christians believe that God came in the person of Jesus Christ. There are distinct historical differences between Fard and Jesus that give more weight to the argument that Jesus was indeed God incarnate, not Fard. Jesus, not Fard, resurrected from the grave. No-one knows whatever happened to Fard. Jesus, not Fard, was crucified on the cross because he declared he was God. Fard never said he was God. Jesus, not Fard, healed the blind and made the lame to walk. Jesus, not Fard, is the only person who ever lived who fits *all* of the characteristics of the messianic prophecies given by the Old Testament prophets. Consequently, Ishmael Muhammad is quite mistaken when bearing witness that God came in the person of Wallace Fard.

Ishmael Muhammad goes on to describe Farrakhan as "our world president." There is no person, at least not yet, who holds the title as world president. Farrakhan is not the president of any, city, country, or nation.

A DISCUSSION OF FARRAKHAN'S 1996 SAVIOUR'S DAY SPEECH

This "Saviour's Day" event came at a time when Farrakhan had recently returned from a meeting with Khadafy in Libya. It was reported that Khadafy wanted to give Farrakhan one billion dollars. Farrakhan and Khadafy agree with this report. Because Khadafy is considered one of America's adversaries, Farrakhan was accused by the American government of consorting with a terrorist. Many people, even black people criticized Farrakhan when it came to his dealings with Khadafy. Farrakhan was angered by the criticism and was not as careful about what he said at the "Saviour's Day" rally when compared to what he said at the Million Man March.

During the speech which he delivered on February 25, 1996 at the Saviour's Day Rally held at the U.I.C. Pavilion in Chicago Illinois, Farrakhan said........

I am a student of the Honorable Elijah Muhammad and I am eternally indebted for Allah's intervention in our affairs in the person of Master Fard Muhammad, the great Mahdi.

Saviour's Day

Farrakhan begins his speech by praising the name of Allah, the same as he did at the Million Man March. The above excerpt lets us know, without a doubt, that Farrakhan believes Wallace Fard to be God incarnate. He says it from his own mouth. The word "Mahdi" is an Islamic term for Messiah. Farrakhan and the Nation of Islam believe Fard to be the Messiah as well as to be God. For them, the Messiah and God are one in the same, just as it is for Christians.

I shall teach my children and through them my children's children to praise his name forever for raising up in our midst one that the world needs to become aquainted with, one that really [hesitates].....my mission is...to make his great commission known, and that is the honorable Elijah Muhammad."

Farrakhan has finally revealed, with some hesitation, his true agenda. This is what he is really all about. His main purpose in life is to make known the thoughts and teachings of Elijah Muhammad. However, he needs an arena in which to do it. The Million Man March was that arena.

As it is written in the holy Koran as well as in the Bible, Pharaoh and his magicians cast first, and these damnable liars [the United States government] have cast first. But it said when Moses and Aaron cast their rod it swallowed up their lies and today we will swallow up the lies and tomorrow Allah will swallow up the liars!

During the Reagan administration, Khadafy made terrorist threats against the United States. Therefore, the government has every right to question Farrakhan's seemingly "in your face" attitude in regards to his dealings with Khadafy. However, Farrakhan calls the U.S. government "damnable liars" for questioning his motives when it comes to his association with Khadafy. Farrakhan not only accuses the United States government of lying but compares the government to "Pharoah and his magicians" who he says cast first. Let's take a look at the scripture from whence his comparison is derived.

> 8And the Lord spake unto Moses and unto Aaron, saying,
> 9When Pharaoh shall speak unto you, saying, Shew a miracle for you: then thou shalt say unto Aaron, Take thy rod, and cast it before Pharaoh, and it shall become a serpent.

> 10And Moses and Aaron went in unto Pharaoh, and they did so as the Lord had commanded: and Aaron cast down his rod before Pharaoh, and before his servants, and it became a serpent.
>
> 11Then Pharaoh also called the wise men and the sorcerers: now the magicians of Egypt, they also did in like manner with their enchantments.
>
> 12For they cast down every man his rod, and they became serpents; but Aaron's rod swallowed up their rods." (Exodus 7:8-12)

Pharaoh, a King of Egypt who ruled sometime between 1500 B.C. and 550 B.C. during the time of Moses, had enslaved the Jews (Hebrews) and would not free them. Moses was assigned by God to lead the Hebrews to freedom. Aaron was to be Moses' assistant. According to scripture, in regards to this particular incident whereby rods turned into snakes, Aaron cast first, not Pharaoh. However, Farrakhan said Pharaoh cast first. Once again, he misquotes scripture. Farrakhan portrays the government, who he says cast their rod first, as liars when in actuality Farrakhan cast his "rod" first by consorting with Khadafy. When looking at biblical doctrine as compared to the doctrine of the Nation of Islam, Farrakhan and the Nation of Islam are the ones who are lying.

Farrakhan's misrepresentation of the above scriptural account is taken from the misrepresentation of the same account located in Sura number 20 of the Koran. Let's see what the Koran says:

They said, "Oh Moses, wilt thou first cast down thy rod, or shall we be the first who cast?"

He Said, "Yes, cast ye down first." And lo! by their enchantment their cords and rods seemed to him as if they ran.

70 And Moses conceived a secret fear within him.

We said, "Fear not, for thou shalt be the uppermost:

Cast forth then what is in thy right hand: it shall swallow up what they have produced: they have only produced the deceit of an enchanter: and come where he may, ill shall an enchanter fare."

And the magicians fell down and worshipped. They said, "We believe in the Lord of Aaron and of Moses." (Sura XX)

In the biblical account, God tells Moses to instruct Aaron to cast his rod when Pharaoh asks for a miraculous sign. According to the account in the Koran, the magicians give Moses the option whether to cast first or second and Moses instructs the magicians to cast first. In the biblical account Aaron casts his rod and it becomes a serpent. The magicians cast their rods which become serpents also. However, Aaron's rod swallows up the rods of the magicians. In the Koran's account, Moses is instructed to cast his rod and is told that his rod will devour the rods of the magicians, but the actual account of the devouring is never really told. The bottom line to all of this is that the Bible and the Koran give two different accounts of the same event. However, the words of the Bible are not to be altered or changed. The Koran frequently alters the words of the Bible.

By using the Koran's historical account of this particular interaction between Moses and Pharaoh as an analogy to compare the United States government with Pharaoh, Farrakhan presumptuously compares himself to Moses and Aaron, the good and righteous ones. He indirectly gives himself credibility on the level of Moses thereby subliminally suggesting that he is the Moses for the black race in America. Not only this, but he calls the U.S. government "damnable liars" and says that "Allah will swallow up the liars." Again, he is threatening the U.S. government.

A word of instruction to black people and to leaders in particular: whatever you read in the papers from our enemies you should not rush to comment because they put a microphone in your face. You should just be quiet and tell them that I have not heard from my brother yet but I'm sure that when he returns he will answer those questions.

Farrakhan considers the government and the press his enemies. He wants all black people to think as he thinks and to see the press and the government as adversaries. Farrakhan directs black people not to voice their opinions about him but instead to let him answer all of the questions and make all of the statements. He tells us that we should "just be quiet" when it comes to responding to questions about his affairs. His request is similar to the demands of a totalitarian regime.

Don't be so quick to jump out there because the enemy has said something in his press! That's his paper! That's his television! That's his radio! This is his world....for the time being!

The words "for the time being" heralded great applause from the audience. The inference being that eventually either Farrakhan, the Nation of Islam, blacks or all three would one day rule the world. When Farrakhan says "this is his world" the "his" he is referring to could only be either white people as a whole or the United States government. Since the United States government does not rule the world, Farrakhan must be referring to whites. Whites don't rule the world either, but in Farrakhan's eyes (as well as the eyes of many American blacks), they do. It is possible that Farrakhan's followers do see him as a world leader. Remember, Ishmael Muhammad introduced him as the world president. And as we saw in the previous chapter, Farrakhan himself implied that he was a President of sorts. However, the antichrist will be the only person that will become a world leader, and his leadership will be established before the great war of Armageddon (discussed in more detail later in the chapter).

February 26, 1877 in the holy city of Mecca in Arabia, this man [points to photograph of Fard], Master Fard Muhammad, was born. His father was an original black man and his mother was a woman from the caucasus [caucasoid] region.

From all indication, no one has ever known where Fard came from. All of a sudden, one fine morning in the summer of 1930, he appeared, selling linens, as a way of getting into the homes of blacks. He just as mysteriously disappeared. For years, the Nation of Islam accepted this account of Fard. Now, Farrakhan has given him a birth date and a history. Interestingly enough, Fard has a very American sounding name for someone who is said to have been born in Mecca.

Not only has Fard been given a birth place and date, but he has also been given a racial identity. Black Muslims believe he was Arab. There was a huge photograph of Fard used as a backdrop for this "Saviour's Day" event. The man in the photo (Fard) appeared to be white. This was explained away by Farrakhan who stated that Fard's father was an "original black man." It is unclear if the adjective "original" is used to connote the ancestry of Fard's father's genealogical line or the fact that scientists have proven that the first man "originated" from Africa. Farrakhan did not explain what he meant by the term "original." However, it is clear that, by posting Fard's photograph, Farrakhan put himself in a position of having to explain Fard's racial identity.

Farrakhan goes on to say that Fard's mother was from the "caucasus [caucasoid] mountain region." In other words, she was white. It is not clear what area of the world he is referring to when speaking of this mountain region. Interestingly enough, Farrakhan does not come right out and say that Fard's mother was white.

Despite Farrakhan's attempt to give Fard more of an identity and to assure his audience that Fard was a black man, when looking into the history of the Nation of Islam, we see that there is no certainty as to where Fard came from nor as to his racial identity. Of course, if the Nation of Islam considers Fard to be God, then Fard's racial identity shouldn't matter. But of course, it would matter if the Nation of Islam teaches that whites are devils, which it does. Therefore, Farrakhan must take great strides to convince his audience that Fard is black. Otherwise, according to their own racist theology, the "Nation" would be worshipping and giving all praises to a demon.

His [Fard's] father was a great wise scientist who would go and get bits of wisdom from here and there to give to his son.

In chapter One we learned that Elijah Muhammad believed and taught that twenty-four black god-scientists (including Allah) were born dating as far back as sixty-six trillion years ago. Elijah Muhammad names Yakub as one of the god-scientists who he says was born six thousand years ago for the purpose of creating the white race. Therefore, when Farrakhan speaks of Fard's father as being a "great wise scientist" he is actually making a racist statement incognito. Furthermore, as mentioned before, Wallace Fard dissappeared in 1934 as mysteriously as he appeared in 1930. Consequently, the existence of any historical information regarding Fard's Father becomes questionable, making Farrakhan's rendition of Fard's life history just as questionable.

His [Fard's] mission was to come among us at the proper time and under the right circumstances to bring about the resurrection of a mentally dead people, and to lay the foundation of a whole new world. This man [points to photograph of Fard], Fard Muhammad.

By referring to the resurrection of a mentally dead people, Farrakhan is once again referring to what Black Muslims call the resurrection of the black man's mind. Black Muslims believe that once this resurrection occurs, a whole new world will be upon us. They believe that black people will rule this whole new world. Once again, this goes completely against the doctrines of the Bible. The only resurrection that should be celebrated is the resurrection of Jesus Christ. Furthermore, the Bible indicates that Jesus will be the ruler of the new world (the new Jerusalem), after the Armageddon war. Let's take a look at some scriptures.

> 1 And I saw a new heaven and a new earth: for the first heaven and the first earth were passed away; and there was no more sea.

> [2]And I John saw the holy city, new Jerusalem, coming down from God out of heaven, prepared as a bride adorned for her husband.
> [3]And I heard a great voice out of heaven saying, Behold, the tabernacle of God is with men, and he will dwell with them, and they shall be his people, and God himself shall be with them, and be their God.
> [4]And God shall wipe away all tears from their eyes; and there shall be no more death, neither sorrow, nor crying, neither shall there be any more pain: for the former things are passed away.
> [5]And he that sat upon the throne said, Behold, I make all things new. And he said unto me, Write: for these words are true and faithful.
> [6]And he said unto me, It is done. I am Alpha and Omega, the beginning and the end. I will give unto him that is athirst of the fountain of the water of life freely.
> [7]He that overcometh shall inherit all things; and I will be his God, and he shall be my son.
> [8]But the fearful, and unbelieving, and the abominable, and murderers, and whoremongers, and sorcerers, and idolaters, and all liars, shall have their part in the lake which burneth with fire and brimstone: which is the second death. (Revelation 21:1-8)

Verse 6 defines God as Alpha and Omega. Alpha and Omega means: the beginning and the end or the first and the last. In John's prophetic vision depicted in the book of Revelation, Jesus, the son of man, defines himself as "the first and the last." Let's take a look:

> [10]I was in the Spirit on the Lord's day, and heard behind me a great voice, as of a trumpet,
> [11]Saying, I am Alpha and Omega, the first and the last: and, What thou seest, write in a book, and send it unto the seven churches which are in Asia; unto Ephesus, and unto Smyrna, and unto Pergamos, and unto

> Thyatira, and unto Sardis, and unto Philadelphia, and unto Laodicea.
> 12And I turned to see the voice that spake with me. And being turned, I saw seven golden candlesticks;
> 13And in the midst of the seven candlesticks one like unto the Son of man, clothed with a garment down to the foot, and girt about the paps with a golden girdle.
> 14His head and his hairs were white like wool, as white as snow; and his eyes were as a flame of fire;
> 15And his feet like unto fine brass, as if they burned in a furnace; and his voice as the sound of many waters.
> 16And he had in his right hand seven stars: and out of his mouth went a sharp two-edged sword: and his countenance was as the sun shineth in his strength.
> 17And when I saw him, I fell at his feet as dead. And he laid his right hand upon me, saying unto me, Fear not; I am the first and the last:
> 18I am he that liveth, and was dead; and, behold, I am alive for evermore, Amen; and have the keys of hell and of death. (Revelation 1:10-18)

Verse 17 identifies the Son of man (v. 13) as the first and the last (Alpha and Omega). We know that the Son of man is Jesus Christ and that the first and last is Alpha and Omega. Therefore, Jesus Christ is Alpha and Omega. It is Alpha and Omega that is to rule the New Jerusalem. God has laid the foundation of a whole new world through Jesus Christ, not through Fard. The new Jerusalem represents the new world. Only those saints who have confessed a belief in the Lordship and deity of Christ will be present with him in the New World. Jesus will rule the New World and those who worshipped him in spirit and in truth will be ruled by him. In the New World there will be no death, pain, suffering crying, or the like. What a wonderful revelation. But it is not the Revelation of Farrakhan, it is the Revelation of St. John given to us by God. It is not Farrakhan, blacks, or the Nation of Islam that will rule, but instead Jesus.

This man [points to photograph of Fard], Fard Muhammad, studied forty-two years to deliver us.

The word "us" is used to denote black people. It is clear at this point that Farrakhan is not talking about deliverance of black people from any type of oppression or discrimination. But instead, Farrakhan gives indication that he believes that black people need to be spiritually delivered, especially from the "black slave making white man's religion" of Christianity. Farrakhan's mission, as was Wallace Fard's, is to infiltrate Black Muslim Theology into the African-American community.

He studied [points to photograph of Fard] what he needed to know to accomplish his assignment, to raise you--black man, from a state of mental death and ignorance. His mission is to bring us into the light of divine wisdom and to connect us to the source of power with power!

This is classic Farrakhan rhetoric. Farrakhan never says where Fard studied. He doesn't inform us of what he means by "the light of divine wisdom" and he doesn't clarify what he means by connecting black people with the source of "power with power." However, by saying that Fard's mission was to bring blacks into a light of divine wisdom, Farrakhan is essentially saying that Black Muslim Theology, since Fard was the founder of it, is the way to divine revelation. But those who are impressed with Farrakhan's quest to bring more unity to black people will view this kind of talk as being profound instead of profuse, and will unfortunately become motivated by Farrakhan's apparent intellect.

You that study the Bible; the Bible teaches you that one would come in the last days and he would come without observation as a thief in the night. He would come in disguise. The prophet Habakkuk saw him coming. God, the book says, came from Teman and the holy one from mount Peran, said he had horns coming out of his hands and there was the hiding of his power and the curtains of Midian did shake and tremble. It's talking about a man..."

The book of Matthew 24:34-44 tells us, as does the following scripture reference, that Jesus will come in the last days as a thief in the night to establish his new kingdom on earth. The scriptures also tells us that no one will know when that day will be.

It must be emphasized that the Bible is not saying that Jesus is a thief but is instead giving an analogy as to how surprised everyone will be when he comes. We will be just as surprised when he comes as we would be if we encountered a thief in the night. However, this marks the first phase of his return: what Christians refer to as the rapture. The second phase of Christ's return is marked by the battle of Armageddon. This is an end-time battle that the Bible speaks of in which the Lord, his angels, and his heavenly hosts will defeat Satan and his demons. This day is called the day of the Lord. All Christians raptured (caught up in the air to be with Christ) during the first phase will fight in God's army during the second phase of his coming.

> 16For the Lord himself shall descend from heaven with a shout, with the voice of the archangel, and with the trump of God: and the dead in Christ shall rise first:
> 17Then we which are alive and remain shall be caught up together with them in the clouds, to meet the Lord in the air: and so shall we ever be with the Lord.
> (1 Thessalonians 4:16-17)

> 10But the day of the Lord will come as a thief in the night; in the which the heavens shall pass away with a great noise, and the elements shall melt with fervent heat, the earth also and the works that are therein shall be burned up.
> 11Seeing then that all these things shall be dissolved, what manner of persons ought ye to be in all holy conversation and godliness,
> 12Looking for and hasting unto the coming of the day of God, wherein the heavens being on fire shall be dissolved, and the elements shall melt with fervent heat?
> 13Nevertheless we, according to his promise, look for new heavens and a new earth, wherein dwelleth righteousness.
> 14Wherefore, beloved, seeing that ye look for such things, be diligent that ye may be found of him in peace, without spot, and blameless. (2 Peter 3:10-14)

Farrakhan does not give the identity of the one who comes as a thief in the night. We can safely assume that Farrakhan is not referring to Jesus Christ, as the Bible does. Farrakhan says that the one who will come as a thief will come in disguise. There is no indication in the Bible that Jesus will come in disguise. The Bible clearly identifies Jesus as the one who will come back as a thief in the night. He, and no one else, is identified as the one who will be ruler of a new world.

After the church is raptured, the inhabitants of the earth who are left will undergo a great and terrible seven year tribulation. The battle of Armageddon will occur at the end of the tribulation period. Let's take a look:

> 24 But in those days, after that tribulation, the sun shall be darkened, and the moon shall not give her light,
>
> 25 And the stars of heaven shall fall, and the powers that are in heaven shall be shaken.
>
> 26 And then shall they see the Son of man coming in the clouds with great power and glory.
>
> 27 And then shall he send his angels, and shall gather together his elect from the four winds, from the uttermost part of the earth to the uttermost part of heaven. (Mark 13:24-27)

The Son of man is Jesus Christ. He is the one that verse 26 says will be seen coming in the clouds with great power and glory; not Fard, not Elijah Muhammad, not Farrakhan. Farrakhan says, "he will come in disguise." However, Jesus will come without disguise and everyone will know who he is at the time of his return.

Farrakhan goes on to say that the prophet Habakkuk saw "him" coming and that this "him" came from Teman and the Holy One from Mount Paran. Farrakhan does not identify "him" as God. However, the Bible does. Let's see what the book of Habakkuk says.

> 1 A prayer of Habakkuk the prophet upon Shigionoth.
>
> 2 O Lord, I have heard thy speech, and was afraid: O Lord, revive thy work in the midst of the years, in the midst of the years make known; in wrath remember mercy.
>
> 3 God came from Teman, and the Holy One from mount Paran. Selah. His glory covered the heavens, and the earth was full of his praise.

[4]And his brightness was as the light; he
had horns coming out of his hand: and there
was the hiding of his power.
[5]Before him went the pestilence, and
burning coals went forth at his feet.
[6]He stood, and measured the earth: he
beheld, and drove asunder the nations; and
the everlasting mountains were scattered, the
perpetual hills did bow: his ways are
everlasting.
[7]I saw the tents of Cushan in affliction: and
the curtains of the land of Midian did tremble.
(Habakkuk 3:1-7)

During Habakkuk's prayer to the Lord he recalled how God brought the children of Israel out of Egypt. Israel's exodus from Egypt led them through the land of Teman (near Edom at the time) and Mount Paran which were both countries south of Judea. Some biblical commentaries describe Teman and Paran as cities and place Teman south of Canaan and Paran in Arabia.

Verse 4 speaks of God's brightness and figuratively speaks of God's power by describing horns coming out of his hands hiding his power. These "horns" are actually rays beaming from the hands of God emitting (or covering, hiding) the power he has within his hands. The Hebrew verb that gives the action of emitting rays is taken from the root meaning of the Hebrew word for "horns." Remember, as he prayed, this is how Habakkuk described God.

The book of Exodus gives the historical account of Moses leading the children of Israel out of Egypt. Egypt had enslaved the Israelites. Pharaoh, a king of Egypt at the time did not allow the Israelites to worship God. Because of this, God instructed Moses to lead the Israelites to freedom. Moses demanded that Pharaoh free the children of Israel. Pharaoh did not listen to Moses at first. Because of this, God sent pestilence and plague upon Egypt. It is this pestilence that Habakkuk recalls and refers to in verse 5. Habakkuk describes God as having burning coals going forth from his feet. One of Egypt's plagues (there were ten in all) was to suffer from hail. The hail was mingled with fire. When it fell, it burned. When Habakkuk speaks of pestilence and burning coals coming from the feet of God, he is speaking of one of the Egyptian plagues (hail) that God cursed Egypt with when Pharaoh refused to free the Jews. Habakkuk goes on to recall how God spread asunder the nations. Many theologians agree that these were the nations of Canaan that God disbanded.

The Midianites seduced Israel into worshipping false Gods. Therefore Moses made war against them as God commanded, hence: Habukkuk's account of the curtains of Midian trembling.

The focus here is that Habakkuk attributed all of the historical recollections in his prayer to the work of God. As we will see, Farrakhan attributes these works to someone else. Farrakhan says that in all these things "it's [the Bible or maybe Habakkuk] talking about a man." Farrakhan goes on to say the following:

Isaiah again said for unto us a child is born and unto us a son is given and a government shall be upon his shoulders and he shall be called wonderful, counselor, the mighty God, the prince of peace, the everlasting Father. And of the increase of his government of peace there would be no end. Yet he's a child born of a woman. John the Revelator, I think its the twelfth chapter of Revelation, he said there was a wonder in heaven, a woman clothed in the sun standing on the moon with twelve stars in her crown. The honorable Elijah Muhammad taught us that a woman clothed in the sun means the woman was pregnant. So this woman--pregnant--was going to bring forth a child that all the prophets heralded his coming. He would be a strange child, a man destined to rule the nations with a rod of iron, but born of a woman. Twelve stars--the major scientists backing up the prophecies. He was born February 26, 1877.

Earlier we noted that Farrakhan said that Fard was born on February 26, 1877. From the time in this speech that Farrakhan talks of the last days to the time Farrakhan talks of a child being born of a woman, he is referring to Fard, not Jesus. Farrakhan quotes from Isaiah 9:6 which reads:

> 6 For unto us a child is born, unto us a son is given: and the government shall be upon his shoulder: and his name shall be called Wonderful, Counselor, The Mighty God, The everlasting Father, The Prince of Peace.

The prophet Isaiah is not talking about Fard, he is talking about Jesus. Jesus was the child to be born in Bethlehem of a woman, the virgin Mary. Jesus is the one whom the government would persecute. He is the one whose name would be called Wonderful, Counselor, The Mighty God, The everlasting Father and the Prince of Peace. What Farrakhan is saying when he couples Fard's supposed birth date with the description of the Messiah (the child who is born) that the above scripture gives, is that Fard, not Jesus, is the Messiah. This is blasphemy.

Farrakhan also made reference to the vision of a woman "clothed in the sun, standing on the moon with twelve stars in her head. He was referring to the twelfth chapter of Revelation. Let's look at this chapter:

> 1And there appeared a great wonder in heaven; a woman clothed with the sun, and the moon under her feet, and upon her head a crown of twelve stars:
>
> 2And she being with child cried, travailing in birth, and pained to be delivered.
>
> 3And there appeared another wonder in heaven; and behold a great red dragon, having seven heads and ten horns, and seven crowns upon his heads.
>
> 4And his tail drew the third part of the stars of heaven, and did cast them to the earth: and the dragon stood before the woman which was ready to be delivered, for to devour her child as soon as it was born.
>
> 5And she brought forth a man child, who was to rule all nations with a rod of iron: and her child was caught up unto God, and to his throne.
>
> 6And the woman fled into the wilderness, where she hath a place prepared of God, that they should feed her there a thousand two hundred and threescore days.
>
> 7And there was war in heaven: Michael and his angels fought against the dragon; and the dragon fought and his angels,
>
> 8And prevailed not; neither was their place found any more in heaven.
>
> 9And the great dragon was cast out, that old serpent, called the Devil, and Satan, which deceiveth the whole world: he was cast out into the earth, and his angels were cast out with him.
>
> 10And I heard a loud voice saying in heaven, Now is come salvation, and strength, and the kingdom of our God, and the power of his Christ: for the accuser of our brethren is

> cast down, which accused them before our God day and night.
>
> 11And they overcame him by the blood of the Lamb, and by the word of their testimony; and they loved not their lives unto the death.
>
> 12Therefore rejoice, ye heavens, and ye that dwell in them. Woe to the inhabiters of the earth and of the sea! for the devil is come down unto you, having great wrath, because he knoweth that he hath but a short time.
>
> 13And when the dragon saw that he was cast unto the earth, he persecuted the woman which brought forth the man child.
>
> 14And to the woman were given two wings of a great eagle, that she might fly into the wilderness, into her place, where she is nourished for a time, and times, and half a time, from the face of the serpent.
>
> 15And the serpent cast out of his mouth water as a flood after the woman, that he might cause her to be carried away of the flood.
>
> 16And the earth helped the woman, and the earth opened her mouth, and swallowed up the flood which the dragon cast out of his mouth.
>
> 17And the dragon was wroth with the woman, and went to make war with the remnant of her seed, which keep the commandments of God, and have the testimony of Jesus Christ. (Revelation Chapter 12)

This was part of the prophetic Revelation given to Saint John the apostle in a vision from God while he was banished in exile on the island of Patmos. The woman in this vision is symbolic of Israel. Israel is referred to as a woman in Isaiah 54:5-6 as well as in other scriptures.

The sun, moon, and twelve stars are also symbolic of Israel as attested to in the thirty-seventh chapter of Genesis. This chapter gives account of a dream that Joseph had which he told to his brothers. Joseph's dream was that the sun, moon, and eleven stars bowed to him. Joseph had eleven brothers. Joseph's brothers hated him for his dreams. They questioned Joseph about this particular dream, asking him if the dream meant whether or not one day they and their parents would bow to Joseph. It so happens that Joseph became king of Egypt and Joseph's brothers did eventually end up bowing to him as King. Joseph was the son of Jacob. Jacob was blessed of God. Genesis 35:10 tells us that God renamed Jacob as Israel. All of Israel (the nation) are descendants of Israel (the man). The sun, moon, and twelve stars is symbolic of Joseph's family with the sun depicting Jacob (Israel), the moon depicting Rachel (Joseph's mother), and the twelve stars depicting Joseph and his siblings. The twelve stars do not represent twelve scientists, as Farrakhan would have you to think, but instead represents the nation of Israel.

The man-child that verse five speaks of is Jesus Christ, not Fard. Jesus has a genealogy and is a descendant of Israel. When looking at the Greek, "to rule" has the connotation of ruling as a shepherd rules. Hebrews 13:20 describes Jesus as "that great shepherd of the sheep." Furthermore, Psalms 2:9 tells us that Jesus will break the heathens (non-believers) with a rod of iron. The symbolisms of a man child ruling with a rod of iron unquestionably point toward Jesus, who was born, died, was resurrected, and is now ascended to the Father, not toward Wallace Fard who Farrakhan says was born in 1877.

Verse 11 tells us that the devil and his angels were overcome by the blood of the lamb, not by Wallace Fard. Jesus Christ is the lamb of God who shed his blood as a sacrifice for our sins. This is pointed out in St. John 1:29 which says: "The next day John seeth Jesus coming unto him and saith, Behold the Lamb of God, which taketh away the sin of the word."

The Bible doesn't say that Fard takes away the sins of the world. It is Jesus that takes away the sins of the world. There is no salvation in Wallace Fard, but Farrakhan and the Nation of Islam wants you to believe there is.

You see, the Lord is my shepherd I shall not want.....though we've [black people] been walking in a valley of the shadow of death we have feared no evil because the Lord, the Lord of the worlds, the Lord of creation is with us.

Farrakhan is quoting from the 23rd chapter of Psalms. It is quite evident by now that Farrakhan is not speaking of Jesus Christ when he uses the word "Lord." However, unsuspecting Christians and people unlearned in biblical doctrine will hear Farrakhan say something like what is quoted above, and conclude that Farrakhan believes Jesus Christ to be his shepherd. This is exactly what Farrakhan wants us to believe, especially those of us who are Christians. He realizes that he can not succeed in his mission without the support of Christian blacks.

Farrakhan implies that black people have been walking in the shadow of death and that those of us who are black should fear no evil because the Lord is with us. However, when he says this, the implication is that the Lord is with blacks because of all of the mistreatment and racial discrimination that blacks have experienced in America, and in some instances still continue to experience today.

However, the Bible tells us that God is with those who are with him. God is the shepherd of his sheep. God's sheep are those who believe him to be who he says he is. The color of one's skin or the injustices that one may have endured is not the deciding factor in one's salvation. In the preceding excerpt, Farrakhan gives the impression that the Lord is automatically the shepherd of all black people. However, the Lord is only the shepherd of those who believe in him. Of course, we know by now that the "Lord" that Farrakhan is speaking of is not the Lord the Bible speaks of and according to the Bible, a person's salvation solely rests on his or her belief in the Lord Jesus Christ. Salvation has nothing to do with race, as Farrakhan would have us believe.

He anointed our head with oil 'til our cup runneth over. He who? I'm talking about he [points], Master Fard Muhammad. That is he.

Farrakhan continues to quote the 23rd Psalm. The "he" whom the Bible is is referring to is not Wallace Fard as Farrakhan has said, but Yahweh, instead. Nowhere in the Bible is Wallace Fard recognized as God. As a matter of fact, Fard (according to Farrakhan) was born hundreds of years after the Bible was written. Despite this, Farrakhan continues to use biblical scripture in an attempt to give divine credibility to Fard.

You say but he's a man born of a woman. Well who was Jesus? Was he not a man born of a woman? Who was Muhammad? Who was Moses? Who was Abraham? Were they not men born of a woman?

The Nation of Islam believes that Jesus was no more than a prophet. Farrakhan lumps Jesus with Muhammad, Moses, and Abraham, who were all born of a woman. By doing this, Farrakhan again attempts to discredit the deity of Christ. Yes, Jesus, Muhammad, Moses, and Abraham were all born of a woman. But only one was born miraculously of a virgin woman, and that one is Jesus Christ.

Allah created the heaven and the earth. We don't know when. We just say, in the beginning.

Genesis 1:1 teaches us that "in the beginning God created the heaven and the earth. " Allah is the Arabic name for God. However, when Farrakhan uses the name, he is not talking about the God of the Bible. He is talking about Wallace Fard. When the Orthodox Muslims use the name, they are not talking about the God of the Bible either. They are talking about a god who is spirit only and does not represent himself in three persons as the Father, Son and Holy Ghost. Therefore, although it sounds biblically agreeable to say that Allah created the heaven and the earth, it is not. Of course, Farrakhan knows that when he uses the word "Allah" he is not speaking of the God of the Bible. However, many Christian blacks are not aware of this and unknowingly assume that Farrakhan is just as much of a Christian as he is a Black Muslim. A person can't be both. Furthermore, many blacks unknowingly assume that Farrakhan ascribes to biblical theology, but he doesn't. Instead, Farrakhan gives the impression that he does by using biblical scripture as bait to entice blacks into ascribing to Black Muslim theology. He is clever, well learned and can quote more scriptures than most Christians.

The real person don't have color. Color is what the real person comes in. So if you get color conscious, you lose reality. When you begin to think white or black you get all messed up because God is neither. He can come in any flesh. He can manifest in any flesh.

Biblical doctrine agrees with this. However, Black Muslim theology does not agree with this. How can it, when their doctrine considers whites to be devils? How can it when their mission statement includes the prohibition of interracial marriages or "mixing." The irony of it all, when it comes to the issue of race and the Nation of Islam, is that Wallace Fard looks like a white man. Many black people think he may have been a white man. Farrakhan leaves himself in a position where he has no option but to address this issue. Therefore, he emphasizes that God can manifest himself in any flesh. The problem here is that on one hand the Nation of Islam calls white people devils and on the other hand they tell us not to be color conscious. They are contradicting themselves in their own teachings.

There's a lot of wisdom in this world but you [blacks] are not the master of it. You are the subject and the object of it. And there is a few that are ruling that are masters and those are the few that the master [points to photograph of Fard] has come to set down!

Saviour's Day

Farrakhan is telling his audience that blacks should master and rule the world. He doesn't say it directly, but it is heavily implied. What Farrakhan is saying is that blacks have not mastered the world and now it's their turn to do so. This is indeed, racist ideology.

When he [Fard] said, 'accept your own,' he's telling you that your own is Islam.

This statement goes along with the Black Muslims' idea that Islam is the natural religion of the black man. There is no natural religion of the black man. No one is born a Muslim just as no one is born a Christian. In order to be a Muslim one must make a choice to become one. A black person is not automatically a Muslim simply because his or her skin is black. However, if Farrakhan can convince black people otherwise, then his mission to convert black people into the Nation of Islam will be made all the more easier.

You say you're a Christian. Who made you that? Lets talk. Did God make you that? No. Don't be angry with me. I love Jesus too. But Jesus never used these words 'I am a Christian.' Find it in the Bible! He never said that! Did He?!

The Muhammad of the sixth century never used the words "I am a Black Muslim" either. You won't find it in Koran. But yet, Farrakhan and the Nation of Islam choose to identify themselves in this manner. So what? It's simply a means of religious identification. It is the same with Christians.

Those who follow Christ have labeled themselves Christians for religious identification purposes. Leaders don't follow themselves, they lead other people to follow them. Those who follow Farrakhan might eventually label themselves as "Farrakhanians" but Farrakhan would not label himself that. So it was with Jesus. By saying what he said in the above excerpt, Farrakhan is indulging himself in a cheap semantic argument. He's grabbing at straws.

Farrakhan continues to attempt to discredit Christianity. His entire speech, up to this point, focuses on the promotion of Black Muslim theology. Remember, this is what Farrakhan and the Nation of Islam is really all about.

Find it in the Bible where Abraham and any of the prophets said 'I am a Jew.' They didn't say it! Don't be angry with me. As a Christian, that's not a bad name. But the truth of it is, the people believed Jesus to be the Christ, and so at Antioch, the disbelievers called the believers in Jesus as the Christ,

Christians. But no-where in the four gospels do you find Jesus saying 'I am a Christian."

Acts 11:26 indeed tells us that the word "Christian" was first used by the people of the city of Antioch when describing the disciples. However, the scripture does not say whether it was believers or non-believers who coined the term. It doesn't matter who coined the term or created the word. The word is fitting for anyone who believes in Christ. The question becomes, why has Farrakhan made such an issue of its origin? With this in mind, it is safe to say that his attempts to discredit Christianity border on the fanatical. Once again, Farrakhan says that Jesus never defined himself as a Christian. One does not have to define oneself as something to be that something. For example: I am a writer, but if I never identify myself as such, it would not take away from the fact that I am one. It is the same with Jesus. He did not define himself as a Christian but that does not mean he is not a Christian or that he did not uphold Christianity. Jesus, is the ultimate Christian and has defined himself as God. Not only has Jesus defined himself as God, but he has proven that he *is* God. This is what Farrakhan is really wrestling with. Farrakhan does not want to accept the fact that Jesus is God incarnate. The devil has had a hard time accepting it too.

Well, what is this Islam business. You don't find them saying I'm a Muslim [either]. Well, here's what they all said. Every prophet of God said 'I submit to obey God'.... Well, we say Muslim, that's what that means: one who submits to God.

Farrakhan's discussion of the etymology of the word "Christian" was introduced by him so he could make the above comment. His reasoning is as follows: every one who submits to God should call themselves Muslim because the word "Muslim" means "to submit." Therefore, he feels that if Christians say they submit to God then they should call themselves Muslims, not Christians. However, we should not confuse semantics with spirituality as Farrakhan would have us to do. Christians do not err to call themselves Christians because the word "Christian" defines someone who follows Christ and a true follower of Christ *submits* to the will of Christ. And when one submits to the will of Christ, one is submitting to God.

You say, I didn't expect this Farrakhan. I wanted you to talk about your trip. Well, don't trip on me. I'll get there.

Saviour's Day

Again, Farrakhan had just come back from Libya when he delivered this speech. Many black people were critical of his dealings with Khadafy. Despite this, Farrakhan's primary focus was Black Muslim theology, not the defense of his trip to Libya.

But he [Fard] came on July 4th to declare our [blacks] independence, to declare the black man free that we no longer have to bow down to the enemy [whites]. When he [the white man] calls, you don't have to answer. You're not bound to him anymore. Your time of servitude to the white man is up. It's over! It's done! It's through!

Great applause was received from the audience after this statement. Farrakhan is good at adding salt to a wound. Many blacks are still emotionally wounded from discriminatory experiences they, their relatives, or their ancestors have had to endure. Farrakhan is aware of this and often reminds blacks of certain injustices that have been imposed against them. These strategic reminders cause many blacks to emotionally bond with Farrakhan. From this bonding method, Farrakhan is able to influence many blacks to his way of thinking. However, he must keep implementing this bonding method on a consistent basis in order to continue to give rise to the probability of comradeship between he and his audience. Increased comradeship between Farrakhan and his audience automatically increases Farrakhan's ability to influence that same audience. Farrakhan wants to influence black people to join the Nation of Islam.

Farrakhan says that Fard came on July 4th. There is no historical data anywhere that reveals the date in which Fard first appeared in Detroit selling his wares. This is just another attempt on Farrakhan's part to give more credibility to his icon. Farrakhan chose the date of July 4th because it is Independence Day in America. By saying Fard first appeared on this date, Farrakhan indirectly correlates Independence Day with Fard. Farrakhan says that Fard came on that day to declare independence for blacks. His aim in saying these things is to encourage black people to look at Fard as a symbol of freedom.

Elijah was different because Elijah, when he heard the man [Fard], he had read the Bible. He studied it from a little boy. His father was a Baptist preacher. He knew that this man [Fard] was a Baptist preacher. He knew that this man [Fard] was the one that was to come. Somehow it was communicated to him.

Elijah Muhammad was raised in a Christian home. Farrakhan tells his audience this in another effort to give credibility to the Nation of

Islam. If Farrakhan can convince his audience that Elijah was the religious icon he believes him to be, then the fact that he (Elijah) professed to be a Christian and later became a Black Muslim may encourage other Christians to follow the same path as well as discourage non-Christians from following Christ.

Farrakhan also says that Fard was a Baptist preacher, however, there is no historical evidence to support this.

"Fard" means one we are obligated to obey.

In what language does the word "Fard" mean this? Farrakhan never says.

We are not obligated to obey Fard. Christ is the one we should obey as clarified by the following scripture reference.

> 8Though he were a Son, yet learned he obedience by the things which he suffered;
> 9And being made perfect, he became the author of eternal salvation unto all them that obey him; (Hebrews 5:8-9)

The "Son" that the scripture is referring to is Jesus Christ. Jesus, and no one else, is the author of eternal salvation, but only to those who obey him, not to those who obey Fard. Let's look further:

> 7And to you who are troubled rest with us, when the Lord Jesus shall be revealed from heaven with his mighty angels,
> 8Inflaming fire taking vengeance on them that know not God, and that obey not the gospel of our Lord Jesus Christ:
> 9Who shall be punished with everlasting destruction from the presence of the Lord, and from the glory of his power;
> 10When he shall come to be glorified in his saints, and to be admired in all them that believe (because our testimony among you was believed) in that day. (2 Thessalonians 1:7-10)

This is a message that is far more important to the black man (and any other man for that matter) than what Elijah Muhammad has said or what Farrakhan is is saying. Those who do not obey the gospel of Christ will not only forfeit eternal salvation (to live in God's heavenly kingdom forever) but they will be punished with everlasting destruction. To put it in plain English, they will go to hell, literally. We are obligated to obey God, not Fard.

Sooner or later every knee will bow and every tongue will confess that Master [Fard] came to North America.

Once again, Farrakhan takes biblical scripture and perverts it. Let's see how the actual scripture reads:

> 5Let this mind be in you, which was also in Christ Jesus:
> 6Who, being in the form of God, thought it not robbery to be equal with God:
> 7But made himself of no reputation, and took upon him the form of a servant, and was made in the likeness of men:
> 8And being found in fashion as a man, he humbled himself, and became obedient unto death, even the death of the cross.
> 9Wherefore God also hath highly exalted him, and given him a name which is above every name:
> 10That at the name of Jesus every knee should bow, of things in heaven, and things in earth, and things under the earth;
> 11And that every tongue should confess that Jesus Christ is Lord, to the glory of God the Father. (Philippians 2: 5-11)

In the last days every knee shall bow and every tongue shall confess that Jesus Christ is Lord, not that Fard came to North America. Farrakhan keeps twisting scripture in an attempt to give credibility to Fard.

This man [points to photograph of Fard], Fard Muhammad, I want you to hear his name. Burn it into your brains because in the next few days his power is going to be manifest! Burn it into your brains! He's your friend! He's your best friend! He is master of today! He's the Jesus you've been looking for! He's the Christ you've been talking about!

Farrakhan finally comes out and says what he really means. He has revealed his true thoughts about Jesus. He does not consider Jesus to be the Messiah. He considers Fard to be the Messiah. He does not consider Jesus to be the Christ. He considers Fard to be the Christ. This absolutely goes against biblical doctrine. Jesus is the only Christ. He is the only Messiah. He is our only Saviour. Fard is not the Jesus we've (Christians) been looking for and he is not the Jesus we've been talking about, but Farrakhan wants to convince blacks, especially Christian blacks, that Fard is the real Jesus. Jesus warned us about men like Farrakhan. We will take a look at these warnings in Chapter Seven.

Messiah is a human being in whom God is present. Look, look, look, look, look: the Messiah is not to be worshipped. But in him God is full and present. We should worship none but Allah. Christians, you make a mistake to worship Jesus! This is why you are powerless! Jesus never asked you to worship him!

Any Christian reading this should be appalled at these statements. The blasphemous statements that Farrakhan makes combined with his mission to promote Black Muslim theology is the very reason why Christians should not follow Farrakhan to Washington or anywhere else, because, to do so would be giving him support in what he says and does.

Farrakhan says that Jesus never asked us to worship him. He also says that it is a mistake to worship Jesus. These are blatant lies. Let's look at the scriptures:

> 1Then was Jesus led up of the spirit into the wilderness to be tempted of the devil. (Matthew 4:1)
>
> 8Again, the devil taketh him up into an exceeding high mountain, and sheweth him all the kingdoms of the world, and the glory of them;
> 9And saith unto him, All these things; will I give thee, if thou wilt fall down and worship me.
> 10Then saith Jesus unto him, Get thee hence, Satan: for it is written, Thou shalt worship the Lord thy God, and him only shalt thou serve. (Matthew 4:8-10)

Satan has always wanted to be in Jesus' position. Satan wants to be worshipped. He does not want Jesus to be worshipped. If Jesus was not to be worshipped then Jesus would not have told Satan that the Lord thy God should be worshipped. The Lord thy God, as we have seen in Chapter Two, is The Father, The Son, and the Holy Ghost. Jesus is part of the Godhead. He is the Son. He is the Lord thy God in the flesh. Therefore, he is to be worshipped.

Farrakhan also stated that Christians are powerless because they worship Jesus. Let's see what the Bible has to say about this.

> 17And the seventy returned again with joy, saying, Lord, even the devils are subject unto us through thy name.
> 18And he said unto them, I beheld Satan as lightning fall from heaven.
> 19Behold, I give unto you power to tread on serpents and scorpions, and over all the power of the enemy: and nothing shall by any means hurt you.
> 20Notwithstanding in this rejoice not, that the spirits are subject unto you; but rather rejoice, because your names are written in heaven. (Luke 10:17-20)

Jesus gave power to those who believe in him. He gave them power not only to tread on serpents but also to subject demons. However, it is made clear in verse 17 that this power comes through the name of Jesus Christ. Verse 19 tells us that Jesus gives his believers all power over the enemy. Satan and his demons are the enemy of the Christian. Those who believe in Christ are not powerless, as Farrakhan has stated, but are instead, quite powerful where spiritual matters are concerned. However, there is no godly power in the name of Fard.

Jesus, two thousand years ago was not the Messiah. Jesus, two thousand years ago, was a prophet, but the Messiah comes in the last days. There's the Mahdi [points to photograph of Fard]. Elijah Muhammad is the Messiah!

The crowd roared when Farrakhan said these things. Farrakhan seems a bit confused himself. A couple of excerpts back, he says that Fard is the Christ (Messiah). Now, he says Elijah Muhammad is the Messiah. Which is it? Neither. We saw, when looking at the book of Revelation that Jesus is the Messiah and will come again in the last days with the sound of a trumpet. Elijah Muhummad is not the Messiah. He is not the one whom the Bible says will come through the clouds in the last days. Elijah Muhammad is dead. Jesus has been resurrected from the grave, is alive, and sits on the right hand of the throne of God as attested to in Hebrews 12:2 which says, "Looking unto Jesus the author and finisher of our faith; who for the joy that was set before him endured the cross, despising the shame, and is set down at the right hand of the throne of God."

That man [points to photograph of Elijah] you say is dead, I told you in 1981, he's alive!

There is no evidence anywhere that Elijah Muhammad is alive. However, Farrakhan knows that Elijah Muhammad's life and death can not compare to the life, death, and resurrection of Jesus Christ. Therefore, Farrakhan attempts once again to give credibility to Elijah by indirectly insinuating that he too has risen from the grave.

Now I'm telling you, that's the Messiah [points to Elijah] and that's the guide [points to Fard], the master, and both of them are backing me up!

As we will see later, Farrakhan and his followers consider him to be a divine leader. However, Farrakhan must convince others of his proclaimed divinity. For Farrakhan to say that Elijah (whom he considers to be the Messiah) and Fard (whom he considers to be God as well as the Messiah) are backing him up, convinces many of his followers, Christian and non-Christian alike, that what he is doing is of divine order. However, we have seen that from a Christian standpoint, what Farrakhan is saying and doing is not of a divine order. God has not instructed Farrakhan to do and say any of the things he is doing and saying.

Bring me before Congress! Its time for the showdown anyway!

In January and February of 1996, Farrakhan toured the Middle East and Africa. He called this his "World Friendship Tour." He visited twenty nations during his tour, one of which was Libya. The Libyan leader is Muammar Khadafy, dictator and all-around terrorist who is suspected in the alledged bombing of the Pan Am aircraft 103 which disintegrated over Scotland in 1988. Not only this, but during the Reagan Administration, Khadafy blatantly threatened the United States with terrorists acts. He was silenced with an American bomb attack. Clearly, Khadafy is no friend of the United States.

Khadafy wanted to give Farrakhan a billion dollars. The money was to be used for the infiltration of an Islamic legislative lobby inside

America. Even Khadafy has been quoted as saying that Farrakhan is the tool he is using to fight America from the inside. If indeed Farrakhan has joined forces with Khadafy to fight America from the inside, then that puts Farrakhan on the same level as an international spy, a traitor, or a double agent.

Khadafy describes Farrakhan as America's "loophole." Khadafy's main goal in life is to promote Orthodox Islam. This is what he lives for. In his country, there is no freedom of religion. Those who are not Muslims are persecuted. Khadafy, along with others in Islamic countries, believes that all those who are not Muslims should be killed or enslaved. This is the basis of the Jihad ("Holy War"). Farrakhan has aligned himself with a terrorist who believes in the killing and enslaving of those who are not Muslims. Therefore, to align one's self with Farrakhan is to align oneself with Khadafy. Part of Khadafy's objective is to convert as many American black men to Islam as possible. This way he can train terrorists within America itself. The easiest targets are blacks who are bitter about racial injustices in America. They convert easily since Islam has a strong anti-establishment message.

During the tour, Farrakhan visited Iran (along with his entourage of 35 people) where he was a speaker at an annual political celebration given to commemorate the overthrow of a government once lead by Shah Mohammad Reza Pahlavi. At this celebration, the audience would often times chant "Death to America." During his address at this celebration, Farrakhan supported the audience's sentiments of America and referred to America himself as "the Great Satan."

Many Islamic Middle East leaders saw the Million Man March as their inroad to eventually bringing the United States under Islamic rule. Farrakhan also sees things this way. His agenda goes beyond American black unity.

With all this said, it is amazing that Farrakhan wasn't arrested as soon as he returned to American soil. He is quoted himself as having had expected to be jailed. However, when he returned, the U.S. government did not jail him. They did, however, consider prosecuting him for breaking laws regarding international associations. The F.B.I also began a complete investigation of him and the Nation of Islam. Representative Peter King felt that Farrakhan should be brought in front of the International Relations Human Rights Committee. Farrakhan, was of course, aware of all the hoopla and challenged the government, insisting to be brought before congress. He seemed to revel in the drama of it all.

Farrakhan wants to be considered a martyr. He erroneously puts himself in the position of what some think a martyr is. If one is martyred for a cause then their credibility concerning that cause is greatly increased. Farrakhan literally invites the American government to a "showdown." The government has verbally criticized Farrakhan for his dealings with Khadafy. If the government did decide to bring Farrakhan before the congress, then, in the eyes of many blacks, he'd be considered a hero and a martyr of sorts which would give him a greater ability to psychologically impact those who would think of him as such.

I asked the Reverend Doctor Benjamin Chavis to be the National Director of this March [Million Man March] because I didn't want it to seem like a Muslim thing.

Farrakhan is basically admitting to using Chavis as a smoke screen and unfortunately Chavis fell for it. Farrakhan says he didn't want the March to seem like a "Muslim thing" as if it wasn't a Muslim thing. It was a Muslim thing. However, during his speech at the March, Farrakhan did not reveal what he has revealed in this speech. Therefore people were unaware that the primary purpose of the March was to encourage blacks to become part of the Nation of Islam. Farrakhan does not want it to "seem like a Muslim thing" because he is fully aware that many Christians would not follow him if they knew that it really is a Muslim thing. So, he uses Christians who become infatuated with him, like Mr. Chavis (who claimed to be a Christian at the time), to blind the eyes of vulnerable Christian blacks who are still bitter against whites.

What you did black people, you allowed me and the Nation of Islam and black people to enter the hearts of the people of the earth.

Farrakhan is addressing himself to those who attended and supported the Million Man March. Farrakhan's primary goal is not only to propagate Black Muslim theology throughout America but all over the world. What he is saying here is that the support that black people gave him during the March was the catalyst he needed to allow him to begin to push the Nation of Islam internationally. Christians can not righteously and spiritually afford to be a part of this.

I am not saying that there are not good Americans, white and brown and black and yellow and red.

Maybe Farrakhan is not saying it in the above excerpt, but Black Muslim theology teaches that white people, all of them, are devils. Devils (demons is the more accurate word, Satan is the devil, the fallen angels are demons) are bad. They are not good in any way.

Therefore, for Farrakhan to imply (he never really said it) that some whites are good, goes against the teachings of the religion that he has deemed as his primary goal to promote. White Americans can not be good if they are all demons. Therefore, when Farrakhan says some whites are good, he can't really mean it because he is the leader of a religion that teaches otherwise.

My job was to get up quickly and get out of America and connect the Nation of Islam and black America to Africa, to the middle East, and to the Muslim world.

Farrakhan says it again and again: Spreading Black Muslim theology is his number one quest in life. He even wants to connect the Nation of Islam to the Muslim world. Orthodox Muslims see the Nation of Islam as a cult of their religion. Farrakhan knows this. However, it doesn't matter to him, especially since he believes he has the support of Khadafy. Farrakhan will not rest until he can convince as many people as possible worldwide to join the Nation of Islam.

You [government] want me dead but you're going to pay a price to get that result. Whatever you do to me over here, they're going to do to you over there. God has blessed me to make that connection.

Here we see Farrakhan actually threatening the United States government. However, there is no indication that the government has threatened him. What Farrakhan must realize is that the only reason he can publicly speak is because the government allows him to speak. The government is upholding the constitution of free speech. If the government wanted Farrakhan dead he'd be dead, simple as that. There is no indication, as of yet, that the government wants him dead. The government wants Farrakhan to stop consorting with the enemy (Khadafy). This is an understandable request. If Farrakhan does not stop consorting with Khadafy then the government might begin to consider Farrakhan to be an enemy agent. It makes sense that the government would feel this way.

Farrakhan says he has a "connection." He means a connection with the Middle East. Essentially, Farrakhan is saying that if the United States government hurts him, then his friends in the east will hurt the Americans that are over there. Farrakhan may have also meant that his friends would hurt the United States government. These are large words which draw large responses. When a person speaks against his own government, he risks being reprimanded by that same government.

They [the United States government] never want to see us [blacks] in unity with those [African Ancestors] from [whom] they disconnected us. Kunte Kinte was a Muslim.

With this statement, Farrakhan has again mixed his message of black unity with his message of Muslim theology and implies that the United States government does not want blacks to research their genealogy. He implies that the government does not want black people to unite with Africa at all. Then he says Kunte Kinte was a Muslim. Kunte Kinte was the center of Alex Haley's genealogical book. Mr. Haley, a well renowned black author who is now deceased, researched his family tree. Kunte Kinte was at the core of that family tree. Mr. Haley's book entitled "Roots" was made into a mini series in the late seventies. Mr. Haley as well as the mini series gained great acclaim. This was the first time America really took a strong look at the devastating effects slavery had on the African American community. Therefore, to bring up the name Kunte Kinte strikes a chord in the hearts of many black Americans. So, what does Farrakhan do? He couples Kunte Kinte with Islam by saying that Kunte Kinte was a Muslim, with the purpose of driving blacks toward Islam.

[They want to] take you out of the name of your own people, take you from the culture of your own people, rob you of the history of your own people, take you from the God of your own people, the religion of your own people.

Once again Farrakhan throws salt in the emotional wounds of black people as a tool to lead them to "the religion of [their] own people." He considers this religion to be the Nation of Islam (as initially taught by Fard). Let's see what the Bible has to say:

> 9 Lie not one to another, seeing that ye have put off the old man with his deeds;
> 10 And have put on the new man, which is renewed in knowledge after the image of him that created him:
> 11 Where there is neither Greek nor Jew, circumcision nor uncircumcision, Barbarian, Scythian, bond nor free: but Christ is all, and in all. (Colossians 3:9-11)

The Bible tells us that when one comes to Christ he is a new creature. Verse 10 above concurs with that by saying that those in Christ have put on the new man. Verse 11 teaches us that anyone can be a new man in Christ, and when in Christ, all men are the same. If all men are the same in Christ, then Christianity is a religion for everyone. Let's look further:

> [13]For by one Spirit are we all baptized into one body, whether we be Jews or Gentiles, whether we be bond or free; and have been all made to drink into one Spirit.
> (1 Corinthians 12:13)

Christianity is not a religion for the Jews only. It is a religion also for the Gentiles. A Gentile is anyone who is not a Jew. Jews are the descendants of Abraham who came through the line of Jacob (Israel). They are more so a nation of people rather than a race of people. Because of Abraham's faithfulness, God promised a certain land (Jerusalem) to his descendants. Therefore they are called the children of the promise (the chosen ones). However, in order to receive the promise, they must confess Christ just like anybody else. The Gentiles can be baptized into the body of Christ as quickly as any Jew can. A bound man (a slave) can be baptized into the body of Christ as quickly as any free man can be. All that is needed is a heartfelt confession of Christ as Saviour. Man makes religion into a "racial thing." God does not. With God its a "spiritual thing." The Nation of Islam errs when they insist that Islam is the "natural religion of the black man," because by saying this, they are making their religion into a "racial thing." God is not a God of races. The true and living God is a God for **all** people. Let's look at another scripture that emphasizes this further:

> [26]For ye are all the children of God by faith in Christ Jesus.
> [27]For as many of you as have been baptized into Christ have put on Christ.
> [28]There is neither Jew nor Greek, there is neither bond nor free, there is neither male nor female: for ye are all one in Christ Jesus.
> [29]And if ye be Christ's, then are ye Abraham's seed, and heirs according to the promise. (Galatians 3:26-29)

This scripture reference is similar to the one quoted from Colossians. However, verse 29 of the third chapter of Galatians takes matters further by informing us that those of us who are not natural Jews are spiritual Jews once we accept Jesus as our Saviour. We are considered by God as descendants (seed) of Abraham once we accept Christ. Therefore, the promise is just as available to the Gentiles as it is to the Jews. And **all** who believe in Jesus Christ are God's chosen people. Knowing this, we see that God is no respecter of persons (Acts 10:34). Unlike, the Nation of Islam, Christianity is for everybody.

Marcus Garvey, that beloved elder statesman....Marcus Mosiah Garvey will rise with us. He was trying to tie us to Africa. They didn't like that so they trumped up charges against him.

This excerpt was included in order to reveal Farrakhan's admiration for Garvey. Remember, Garvey hated whites to the point where he felt biracial blacks could not be trusted because they had too much white in them. Garvey also agreed with racial separatism to the point where he convinced many blacks that they should be living in Africa. Consequently Garvey established a Back to Africa movement that was unsuccessful.

Some of you scared Negroes [have] pictures that got Martin King on your walls today and got Malcolm on your walls today. Ah, but I'm the living inheritor of that legacy! Where's my picture on your wall?!!

Farrakhan has thrown aside any humility he may have portrayed at the Million Man March. He clearly wants to be idolized. He wants black people to put up pictures of him in their homes. He wants a legendary status and feels that he is the living inheritor of Martin Luther King's and Malcolm's legacy. Farrakhan wants to have the same influence in the American black community that these men did. He wants to be glorified and honored and puts any black person who does not do so into the category of a "scared Negro."

I'm going to deal with Brother Khadafy and this billion dollars. When the Million Man March was over, the first call I got internationally was from Muammar Khadafy.

Khadafy and Farrakhan are using each other to promote their own agenda. However, they have different agendas. Khadafy is an Orthodox Muslim and his goal is to convert people to Islam. Farrakhan's goal, on the other hand, is to convert black people to the Nation of Islam. Farrakhan knows that Khadafy does not really believe in the teachings of the Nation of Islam and Khadafy knows that Farrakhan does not really believe wholeheartedly in the teachings of Orthodox Islam, because Orthodox Islam is not a color-conscious religion, whereas, the Nation of Islam is. As a result, we have two shrewd men using one another for their own personal gain. The question therefore becomes: who's fooling who?

I'm like David. My brother Saul got a sword. I'm ready to fight Goliath but I don't need my brother's sword. I picked up five smooth stones in a brook. The giant looks at the little boy and says 'who does he think he is coming out after me? I'm just a servant of the Lord.' But I've got a smooth stone, only one. I don't need more than one to do the job.

Farrakhan is comparing himself to David who is spoken of in the Bible. David defeated Goliath with just a slingshot and a stone. The historical account of his victory is located in the seventeenth chapter of the book of Samuel. The account tells us that David carried five smooth stones as ammunition against Goliath. However, it only took the first try with the first stone to defeat the giant. Again Farrakhan attempts to give himself credibility by comparing himself with a popular, well-loved biblical historical figure: David. When Farrakhan speaks of Saul (the king of Israel at the time David defeated Goliath) he is actually referring to Khadafy. Khadafy has weapons just as Saul did. However, Farrakhan has indirectly stated, as the following excerpt points out, that he doesn't need Khadafy's weapons to accomplish his goal, just as David told Saul.

I told brother Khadafy I don't need that [weapons]. I will produce a revolution with the help of God and this book [holds up the Koran].

Farrakhan has just told us that he and Khadafy were speaking of weapons and revolution. It is no wonder the United States government is not pleased at their association with one another. Farrakhan intends to produce his revolution with the help of the Koran. The word "revolution" means to overthrow the government.

What revolution are you going to produce Farrakhan? See, it's a quiet revolution. See, Farrakhan will overthrow the government of your mind. See, that's what Jesus was all about. Jesus was all about changing the way you think.

Farrakhan cleared this up because plotting to overthrow the government is a Federal offense. However, Farrakhan definitely wants to "overthrow the government of the black man's mind." This "overthrow" idea goes hand in hand with the Nation of Islam's "resurrection of the black man's mind" theology. Farrakhan says that Jesus was "all about changing the way you think." By saying this, Farrakhan indirectly implies that a change or "resurrection" of the black man's mind is something that Jesus wants. Although Farrakhan sees Jesus as no more than a prophet, he realizes that a great majority of black people see him on a much higher plane. Therefore, Farrakhan erroneously implies that Jesus is going to resurrect the black man's mind.

Farrakhan says that his revolution is a quiet one. However, it is not. Conducting a Million Man March on the steps of the Capital is far from quiet. Associating with Muammar Khadafy, a known terrorist, and rubbing it into the face of the American government is far from quiet. Giving speech after speech in an effort to convert black people to the Nation of Islam is far from quiet.

And when he [Khadafy] saw the Million Man March he saw my words come to reality and he called me on the phone. He said, 'Brother, the wealth of Libya I will put behind the Nation of Islam.' That's what he said! That's more than a billion! And I'm going to accept it! It ain't a business transaction! It's a grant to help me with the work of the resurrection of the black men and women of America!

The audience gave Farrakhan a standing ovation during this part of his speech. If Farrakhan was able to reap "the wealth of Libya" he would use it to promote the Nation of Islam. The Nation of Islam goes against the principles of Christianity which makes it (the Nation of Islam) a false religion. No Christian worth his or her salt (remember, Matthew 5:13 tells us that Christians are the salt of the earth) should be following a man who has the religious intentions that Farrakhan does.

If you're [the government] going to deny black people the help of their own brother [Khadafy] then we're going to rise up against you.

Once more, Farrakhan threatens to rise up against the United States government if it continues to block him from his financial dealings with Khadafy. However, this time he has stated that black people as a whole will rise up with him. This is simply not true. I certainly don't plan to rise up against the American government for the sake of the Nation of Islam.

Some of you silly Negroes, you offer condolences to the damn crackers [white people] that hung your people and you make excuses for them. But if I do a statesman-like thing to go and say to the president [of Nigeria whose son had recently died in a plane crash] 'we're sorry for the loss of your son....

Farrakhan calls blacks who have a forgiving attitude towards discriminatory whites, "silly Negroes" and goes on to refer to white people as "damn crackers": this from a man who claims not to be a racist; from a man who claims not to be color-conscious!

Farrakhan visited Nigeria as well as many other African countries during his trip overseas. Black people who have criticized Farrakhan concerning his journey specifically criticized his dealings with Khadafy. Those same black people did not criticize Farrakhan for giving condolences to the Nigerian president. However, Farrakhan has lumped everything together. He feels that anyone who criticizes his dealings with Khadafy is also criticizing his entire tour of Africa and the Middle East.

I know they say I'm not supposed to travel to Libya by executive order of the President [of the United States]. I obey him as long as it don't conflict with my religion. I respect the President. I know he has the power of this country and I'm under his presidency. I know that. I'm not a disrespectful person, but I've got to respect God. You [the government] got an embargo on my brother and I don't believe your embargo is justified where you say a hundred and some odd Americans were killed as though your hands are clean. Bring me before congress! I'd like to show you the blood on the hands of the government of the United States of America!

There is no question that the American government has blood on its hands. It has the blood of African slaves on its hands who were beaten, burned, raped, murdered, and separated from their families. It has the blood of many black Americans who were accused, tried, and executed [hung] by white angry mobs throughout American history. During these awful times the American government sat back and did nothing. It took the civil rights movement of the sixties to stop many of the atrocities committed against blacks. However, the fact that those atrocities occurred does not give Farrakhan a license to threaten the government and consort with a known international terrorist.

Farrakhan has more than hinted at a desire to overthrow the government. To attempt to do so would be treason. It is one matter to attempt to turn the government's way of thinking around to a more civil or moral one, but it's another matter to incite a revolution against it.

Treason is not only a federal crime, it is wrong (1 Peter 2:13-14). The Bible tells us that we are not to repay evil for evil (Romans 12:17). Therefore, Farrakhan errs in his attempt to justify his dealings with Khadafy.

They [Indian Muslims of South America] treated me like a king. Just remember when they crucified Jesus, that's what they put on the cross: Jesus, King of the Jews. Don't you forget it because you're about to see your scripture fulfilled.

Farrakhan continues to compare himself with Jesus. His logic is as follows: since the Indian Muslims of South America treated him like a king and Jesus was called a king then he is just as much of a king as Jesus. Farrakhan even goes further to say that we [Christians] are about to see our scripture fulfilled. What he means is that we are about to see our scripture fulfilled through him. As we will see later, Farrakhan believes that the government wants to "crucify" him. The scriptures were fulfilled with the crucifixion of Jesus. However, Farrakhan is implying that the scriptures will be fulfilled with his [Farrakhan's] "crucifixion." Lets take a look at the scripture that Farrakhan is referring to:

> 43And immediately, while he yet spake, cometh Judas, one of the twelve, and with him a great multitude with swords and staves, from the chief priests and the scribes and the elders.
>
> 44And he that betrayed him had given them a token, saying, Whomsoever I shall kiss, that same is he; take him, and lead him away safely.
>
> 45And as soon as he was come, he goeth straightway to him, and saith, Master, master; and kissed him.
>
> 46And they laid their hands on him, and took him.
>
> 47And one of them that stood by drew a sword, and smote a servant of the high priest, and cut off his ear.
>
> 48And Jesus answered and said unto them, Are ye come out, as against a thief, with swords and with staves to take me?

> 49I was daily with you in the temple teaching, and ye took me not: but the scriptures must be fulfilled. (Mark 14:43-49)

According to the biblical historical account, Judas, one of Jesus' twelve disciples, betrayed Jesus for thirty pieces of silver. He led the Roman guards to where Jesus was in order that they may take him away to be crucified. Before being taken away, Jesus told his captors that the scriptures must be fulfilled. In other words, Jesus had to be crucified in order for the Messianic prophecies of the Old Testament concerning him to come to fruition. It was prophesied, in part, that the Messiah would be crucified. Farrakhan has used the words "to see your scripture fulfilled" to imply or subliminally suggest that he, instead of Jesus, is the Messiah who is to be crucified.

I want you to see your Bible being fulfilled. That man [points to photograph of Fard] and these two men [points to photographs of Fard and Elijah], you don't know too much about them. This one [Elijah] you know more [about] than Master Fard. But I'm more visible than both of them. But I'm less, so far less than both of them.....But God has made me in America to walk in the footsteps of Jesus. Listen, this [America] is a modern Rome. The Jews don't like me. They didn't like Jesus.

Farrakhan claims to be more visible than Elijah, whom he considers to be the Messiah, and Fard, whom he considers to be God incarnate. Although he says that he is less than both of them, in the next breath he says that God has made him to walk in the footsteps of Jesus. Jesus is truly God incarnate and is greater than Elijah or Fard. Therefore, Farrakhan is likening himself to God when he says that God has made him to walk in the footsteps of Jesus. Although Farrakhan doesn't believe Jesus is who he said he is, of course, many Christian blacks do. This being the case, Farrakhan makes certain to compare himself as favorably as he can with Jesus Christ. But God has not made Farrakhan to walk in the footsteps of Jesus. How could he, when Farrakhan doesn't believe in the biblical identity of Jesus? Once again, Farrakhan is simply trying to credit himself in the eyes of blacks but specifically in the eyes of Christian blacks. The black church is his trump card.

The Million Man March was akin to Jesus going to the tomb of Lazarus and calling Lazarus out of the tomb.

Saviour's Day

The scriptures tell us of the historical account in which Lazarus died and Jesus called him from the tomb. Jesus brought Lazarus back to life. Farrakhan compares the Million Man March to Jesus' miraculous raising of Lazarus. What Farrakhan is really saying is that the Million Man March has resurrected the minds of black people just as Jesus resurrected Lazarus from the grave. By saying this, Farrakhan is saying that he has just as much power as Jesus and is also describing the Million Man March as miraculous. The Million Man March was far from miraculous. It was a March, not a miracle. Farrakhan does not have the power that Jesus has no matter how many times he compares himself to Jesus. Farrakhan is not Jesus. He is not anybody's Saviour. He is not the Messiah.

All Jesus said was 'Lazarus come forth' and he came forth, His hands bound, his feet bound and a napkin over his eyes. And Jesus said 'Satan loose him and let him go.' I created no black man. I have no control over none. I just made a call and they started coming from every corner of America and from different parts of the world, and [they] came to Washington D.C. Washington today is like Jesus going to Jerusalem or like Paul going to Rome.

Again, Farrakhan is comparing his audience at the Million Man March to a dead Lazarus that was risen from the grave. Jesus and Paul, as well as all of Jesus' disciples, traveled to different cities and countries to spread the Word of God. Farrakhan is trying to spread the word of the Nation of Islam and compares himself to Jesus and the apostles when he says that going to Washington D.C. in today's time is like Paul going to Rome in New Testament times. Wherever Paul went, he went there to preach the gospel and wherever Farrakhan goes he goes there to preach another gospel: the gospel of the Nation of Islam.

Farrakhan says that Jesus told Satan to loose Lazarus and let him go. However, the Bible's account of the event gives no indication that Jesus ever said this to Satan. Again, Farrakhan has misquoted the scriptures. Let's see what the scriptures say.

> [17]Then when Jesus came, he found that he had lain in the grave four days already. (St. John 11:17)
>
> [23]Jesus saith unto her, Thy brother shall rise again.

> 24 Martha saith unto him, I know that he
> shall rise again in the resurrection at the last
> day.
> 25 Jesus said unto her, I am the
> resurrection, and the life: he that believeth in
> me, though he were dead, yet shall he live:
> 26 And whosoever liveth and believeth in
> me shall never die. Believest thou this?
> 27 She saith unto him, Yea, Lord: I believe
> that thou art the Christ, the Son of God, which
> should come into the world. (St. John 11:23-27)
>
> 41 Then they took away the stone from the
> place where the dead was laid. And Jesus
> lifted up his eyes, and said, Father, I thank
> thee that thou hast heard me.
> 42 And I knew that thou hearest me always:
> but because of the people which stand by I
> said it, that they may believe that thou hast
> sent me.
> 43 And when he thus had spoken, he cried
> with a loud voice, Lazarus, come forth.
> 44 And he that was dead came forth, bound
> hand and foot with graveclothes: and his face
> was bound about with a napkin. Jesus saith
> unto them, loose him, and let him go. (St. John 11:41-44)

This is the only biblical account of Jesus calling Lazarus from the grave. Jesus did not tell Satan to loose Lazarus. He told the people who were around him to loose Lazarus from his grave clothes. However, since Farrakhan has compared himself to Jesus and has compared black Americans to Lazarus, it is not surprising that he misquotes the scripture in order to say that Satan bound Lazarus. This way he can compare Satan, who he says bound Lazarus, to the white man, who he says continues to bind the black man. Here we have, once again, another piece of "blue-eyed devil" rhetoric.

I knew that the Million Man March was going to lead to my crucifixion. I knew it.

Farrakhan wants black people to look at him as Christians look at Jesus. No one has crucified Farrakhan. However, he strategically refers to any criticism he suffers as a result of the March as a crucifixion. Just using the word "crucifixion" is evidence that Farrakhan wants to be thought of in the same light as Jesus. If he can get black people to look at him in a divine way, half the battle is won. It will then be easier for him to promote his poisonous false doctrine.

But I'm here and I'm not running from you [government]. I'll be in Washington if you subpoena me. And you do with me as is written but remember that I have warned you that Allah will punish you.

When Farrakhan tells the government to do with him as it is written, he is again talking about the crucifixion. Farrakhan acts as if he believes that he is the Messiah that the Bible is talking about. It was written that Jesus would be crucified, not Farrakhan. Farrakhan speaks as if he wants to be crucified in some way. In his mind, any harm that would come to him would give him more credibility in the minds of black people.

You are wicked deceivers of the American people. You have sucked their blood. You are not real Jews, those of you that are not real Jews. You are the synagogue of Satan and you have wrapped your tentacles around the U.S. government and you are deceiving and sending this nation to hell. But I warn you in the name of Allah, you would be wise to leave me alone. But if you choose to crucify me, know that Allah will crucify you.

It appears as if Farrakhan is speaking to the Jews. He blames the Jews, or better yet, those who say they are Jews and are not real Jews, for the flaws within the government. He calls these "Jews" the synagogue of Satan and accuses them of sending the American nation to hell. It is no wonder that the Jews accuse Farrakhan of being anti-semitic. One can only guess at the underlying meaning behind what he says here.

On a spiritual level and according to the Bible, as we have seen, the only "real Jews" are people who have accepted the Lord Jesus Christ. At any rate, Farrakhan again speaks of people crucifying him. This time it seems as if he is directing his message to the Jews. The Jewish community has criticized Farrakhan on occasion, with just cause, because of the derogatory things he has said about them. However, Farrakhan sees this criticism as a type of crucifixion. Again, he is putting himself in the same light as Jesus. It appears that Farrakhan is telling the Jews that if they continue to criticize ("crucify") him then Allah will crucify or punish them. Farrakhan's verbal attacks against the Jews are perplexing indeed.

At this point of the speech, someone in the audience cried out, "I love you Farrakhan!" Farrakhan responded with the following:

I love you too and I will prove it by giving my life to prove my love for you, and greater love hath no man that he lay down his life for his friends. And I say this, I was born into the world for this.....But I don't believe that Allah wants me dead.

Again, Farrakhan has taken something Jesus said and attributed it to himself. Lets take a look:

> 12This is my commandment, That ye love one another, as I have loved you.
> 13Greater love hath no man than this, that a man lay down his life for his friends.
> 14Ye are my friends, if ye do whatsoever I command you. (St. John 15:12-14)

Jesus laid down his life for his friends. Jesus described his friends as those who do whatsoever he commands. Therefore, those of us who are truly Christians are friends of Jesus and do what he asks.

Farrakhan wants to be on the same plane with Jesus. So he speaks of laying down his life for his friends. However, Farrakhan has not laid down his life for anyone. He is still alive. Furthermore, since Farrakhan has used verse 13 for his gain it would seem that verse 14 would follow. Therefore, friends of Farrakhan are those who will do whatsoever he commands of them. Bearing this in mind, Christians can not afford to be Farrakhan's "friend" because Farrakhan's command is that every black person join the Nation of Islam. Farrakhan closed his speech in prayer to Allah.

SUMMING UP THE MATTER

Farrakhan was more bold in this speech than he was at the Million Man March. He had to be careful what he said at the March as to make sure not to alienate many of the Christians in the audience. However, his Saviour's Day speech was conducted in front of an audience composed of mostly Black Muslims. Therefore, he felt at liberty to expose himself in a more direct way. Farrakhan made it clear during this speech that the Saviour he worships is not Jesus Christ but instead Wallace Fard. Farrakhan also revealed that his main mission in life is to promote the Nation of Islam and its teachings worldwide.

Saviour's Day

Farrakhan barely touched upon the issue of black unity during this speech. Instead he focused on Black Muslim theology and made it a point to try to discredit Jesus and the Bible while at the same time comparing himself to Jesus whenever he felt it might add to his own credibility.

In the next chapter, we will discuss the speech Farrakhan gave at the New Bethel Church in Detroit. In this speech, Farrakhan goes even further than paralleling himself to Jesus. He actually says, among other things, that he is "a Jesus" which means that he considers himself to be a type of Jesus: **a type of god.**

CHAPTER FIVE

A DISCUSSION OF FARRAKHAN'S 1996 NEW BETHEL CHURCH SPEECH

On April 16, 1996 Farrakhan spoke at the New Bethel Church in Detroit Michigan. He entitled this speech: "Reports on the World Friendship Tour." When speaking of the World Friendship Tour Farrakhan is referring to his Middle East travels to Libya and surrounding lands. New Bethel Church is a Christian Church. Therefore, there were many Christians in the audience when Farrakhan spoke there. Because of this, as we will see, Farrakhan was not as blatant in his teaching of Black Muslim theology with this audience as he had been when addressing his Saviour's Day audience. However, throughout his address at New Bethel, Farrakhan still attempts to encourage his audience to embrace Islam, and in his effort to do so, Farrakhan once again perverts the meaning of many biblical scriptures, even going so far to say that he, himself, is a Saviour; a Jesus.

During the speech which he delivered on April 16, 1996 when reporting on his "World Friendship Tour" at the New Bethel Church in Detroit Michigan, Farrakhan said.........

In the name of Allah the beneficent, the merciful....we thank God for Moses and the Torah, for Jesus and the Gospel, for Muhammad and the Koran.

Farrakhan begins as he usually does. The irony here, however, is that Farrakhan thanks Allah for Muhammad and the Koran in a place where no such thanks should be uttered from one's lips: the church.

I am eternally grateful to Allah for his intervention in our affairs in the person of Master Fard Muhammad, the great Mahdi who came among us here in Detroit in 1930 and began the Nation of Islam....he found a man here in Detroit who was named Elijah Poole and he taught that man for three years and four months.

New Bethel Church

Again, the first thing Farrakhan does is promote the Nation of Islam. Unfortunately, he is aloud to do this inside of a church. Since Farrakhan's primary target is the church, it behooves him to find ministers who welcome him into their pulpits. Interestingly enough, the Nation of Islam would never allow a Christian to come into their mosque and preach the gospel of Christ. They wouldn't hear of it. Furthermore, Christians are heavily persecuted in Islamic countries and are often times, jailed, tortured, enslaved, or even killed simply for being a Christian. The doctrine of their religion allows this. Despite this, there are many Christian ministers who allow Farrakhan to preach in their pulpits.

And though he is physically absent, he is very [much] spiritually present.

The person whom Farrakhan deems physically present is Elijah Muhammad. However, there is no indication that Elijah Muhammad is spiritually present. Jesus Christ rose from the grave and is sitting on the right hand side of the Father, not Elijah Poole. Therefore, Jesus Christ is spiritually present, not Elijah Muhammad. It was Jesus who said the following:

> [19]Go ye therefore, and teach all nations, baptizing them in the name of the Father, and of the Son, and of the Holy Ghost:
> [20]Teaching them to observe all things whatsoever I have commanded you: and lo, I am with you alway, even unto the end of the world. Amen. (Matthew 28:19-20)

It was Jesus who told us that he would be with us always, not Elijah Muhammad. Elijah Muhammad died and did not rise from the grave. However, Jesus was resurrected in a body and then ascended to the Father. Under threat of death, many witnesses attested to his resurrection. No one has ever claimed to see Elijah Muhammad in a body after his death. Elijah Muhammad can not copycat the miracle of the resurrection of Jesus Christ, no matter how hard Farrakhan tries to convince us that he has.

So tonight we will commune. Tonight we will eat the bread. Tonight we will drink the blood. But what are you talking about Farrakhan? The scripture says man can not live by bread alone.

Jesus instructed his believers to participate in a holy ritual which Christians call communion. Jesus first introduced communion to his apostles. The following scripture references clarify the communion procedure.

> 23 For I have received of the Lord that which also I delivered unto you, That the Lord Jesus the same night in which he was betrayed took bread:
>
> 24 And when he had given thanks, he brake it, and said, Take, eat: this is my body, which is broken for you: this do in remembrance of me.
>
> 25 After the same manner also he took the cup, when he had supped, saying, This cup is the new testament in my blood: this do ye, as oft as ye drink it, in remembrance of me.
>
> 26 For as often as ye eat this bread, and drink this cup, ye do shew the Lord's death till he come.
>
> 27 Wherefore whosoever shall eat this bread, and drink this cup of the Lord, unworthily, shall be guilty of the body and blood of the Lord.
>
> 28 But let a man examine himself, and so let him eat of that bread, and drink of that cup.
>
> 29 For he that eateth and drinketh unworthily, eateth and drinketh damnation to himself, not discerning the Lord's body.
>
> 30 For this cause many are weak and sickly among you, and many sleep.
>
> 31 For if we would judge ourselves, we should not be judged.
>
> 32 But when we are judged, we are chastened of the Lord, that we should not be condemned with the world. (1 Corinthians 11:23-32)

Christians call the above ritual "communion" because by engaging in the breaking of bread and drinking of the cup, Christians are communing with God and one another. When Christians engage in communion, they are engaging in an act that gives reverence and remembrance to the Lord. The bread and drink become symbols of the body of Christ. Christians are commanded not to partake of such a holy observance unless they are worthy to do so. In order to be worthy one must, of course, believe in the Lordship and deity of Jesus and be living a holy life. If Christians are not living holy and partake of communion anyway, they will be condemned and may even become ill. Therefore, they must examine and judge themselves so as not to be condemned with the world. Farrakhan also speaks of eating the bread and drinking the blood. But his idea of all this is different from what Jesus had to say about it. The following excerpt gives us better insight into Farrakhan's thinking on the subject of communion.

So after supper he brake the bread and he gave a little piece to this one and that one [be]cause he didn't want any of the disciples to think they had the whole loaf. He wanted the disciples to understand that in him, in unity we got the whole loaf. So don't you take your piece and run off. But let's take our pieces and come to the common table and share the word of God. Muslims and Christians and Jews and Buddhists and Hindus and people who have scripture and people who receive no scripture but built their life on the natural principles that are in the very creation of God. We all can come to the table with our piece of bread.

The partaking of the bread and the cup is not for Muslims, Buddhists, Orthodox Jews, and Hindus but for Christians. One can not be worthy to partake of the body of Christ unless they believe in what that body stands for. St. John 14:6 tells us that Jesus told his disciples that he is the way, the truth, and the life and that no-one can come to God except they come through him. Therefore being worthy to partake in the symbolic eating and drinking of Jesus' body includes not only following the Lord's commandments but believing in the Lord as well.

As Farrakhan spoke more about the breaking of bread he stated that those who broke bread and drank of the cup had to examine their lives and that their lives had to be lived in accordance to how Jesus lived his life. However, Farrakhan stops there. Farrakhan does not go on to say that one must believe in the Lordship of Christ in order to have communion with God. He does not say it, because he does not believe it. Furthermore, Farrakhan has no problem instructing others to live as Jesus lived because he believes that Jesus was a righteous man. But, a righteous man is all Farrakhan believes Jesus was. He does not believe that Jesus is the everlasting Saviour for all mankind.

You came tonight to see your brother. You line the streets in the cold and the snow and some sleet and rain. But what came you out to see? A reed shaking in the wind? A man dressed in fine rainment? A prophet? More than a prophet.

The last sentence was not a question but a statement. Farrakhan considers himself more than a prophet. He considers himself to be a Messiah. This is something that he says verbatim later on in this speech.

And so tonight we're going to break some bread.

Remember, Farrakhan is in a church addressing mostly Christians. He has to get the Christians on his side and attempts to do so by speaking of breaking bread together. Farrakhan is very familiar with the scriptures and uses them to his advantage when trying to sway Christians to his way of thinking.

See, we always get caught up in [the] physical person that carries the spirit or the essence of God.

Farrakhan is speaking about himself and indirectly instructs his audience (the majority of whom were Christians) not to get "caught up" in the fact that he is the leader of the Nation of Islam whose theological doctrines go against everything Christianity stands for. He is speaking of himself when he refers to the "physical person that carries the spirit or the essence of God."

Farrakhan does not carry the spirit or the essence of God because he is not of God. He is not of God because he does not believe in the deity and resurrection of the Lord Jesus Christ. Chapter Seven will deal more with this.

I am honored to be in this holy place and I thank the Reverend Smith, Doctor Smith, for allowing us to meet here tonight.

Reverend Smith errs in allowing Farrakhan to speak at his church because by doing so he has allowed a man to stand in his pulpit who gives praises, glory, and honor to Fard Muhammad and not to Jesus Christ.

But those that saw it [the Million Man March] through the lens of the television; those who saw disciplined men, saw an army and just like the Bible teaches in the book of Ezekiel that when the dry bones stood up, they stood up an exceedingly great army. Now you may rejoice in what you saw but others said, 'if we smite the shepherd we may scatter the sheep.'

New Bethel Church

God gave a prophetic vision to Ezekiel concerning Israel. In the thirty-seventh chapter of Ezekiel, Israel is compared to a valley of dry bones that are brought back to life. Once breath was breathed into them they appeared as a great army. Theologians have pointed to this prophecy as one of many that predict the reunification of the Israeli Nation. This reunification actually came to past in 1948 under the support of the United Nations. Israel (the land) became a state in the Middle East having as its neighbor Arab Muslims. It is there that the nation of Israel was reunited.

Farrakhan compares his audience at the Million Man March to the nation of Israel. He calls his audience an army. Ezekiel refers to the renewed Israel as an army. A group of unified people does not necessarily make an army. However, an army must be unified. Furthermore, armies are formed and prepped for battle. Therefore, it stands to reason that since Farrakhan is referring to his audience as an army then he must be planning to go into battle. But his audience must first be unified and then prepped for whatever battle Farrakhan has in store for them. In the discussion of the next speech we will see that Farrakhan's subtleties are brought to life and that he is indeed planning to go into battle and to take his army with him. His battle is against the white man and his army is the black man.

Martin Luther King did his speech in nineteen minutes. Well let's applaud Dr. King, but Dr. King don't have my job. Dr. King could explain a dream in nineteen minutes but I was doing a delicate brain operation.

Farrakhan constantly compares himself to Martin Luther King. He wants to be thought of in a greater light than the celebrated leader. Consequently, Farrakhan often times attempts to discredit King. Farrakhan demeans King's "I have a Dream" speech by implying that his two hour and fifteen minute Million Man March speech was on the level of a "delicate brain operation" whereas King's speech at Washington was no more than a nineteen minute speech about a dream. Farrakhan's Million Man March speech was not on the level of a delicate brain operation, but instead was on the level of a delicate brain*wash* operation. Farrakhan also implies that he has a greater job to do than King did and Farrakhan believes that his attempt at racial separatism is a higher calling than King's attempt at civil rights and integration.

I stood in the east and spoke with my face shining west, as lightning shineth from the east even unto the west so shall the coming of the son of man be!

Again, Farrakhan has likened himself to Jesus Christ. Let's take a look at the scripture reference that he is referring to:

> 27For as the lightning cometh out of the east, and shineth even unto the west; so shall also the coming of the Son of man be.
> 28For wheresoever the carcase is, there will the eagles be gathered together.
> 29Immediately after the tribulation of those days shall the sun be darkened, and the moon shall not give her light, and the stars shall fall from heaven, and the powers of the heavens shall be shaken:
> 30And then shall appear the sign of the Son of man in heaven: and then shall all the tribes of the earth mourn, and they shall see the Son of man coming in the clouds of heaven with power and great glory.
> 31And he shall send his angels with a great sound of a trumpet, and they shall gather together his elect from the four winds, from one end of heaven to the other. (Matthew 24:27-31)

Biblical scholars have assessed that the Son of man spoken of in verse 30 refers to Jesus Christ. Verses 29 through 31 describe the battle of Armageddon. These scriptures are similar to previous scriptures quoted from the book of Mark. Jesus will come back in the clouds after the seven year tribulation (discussed in Chapters Four and Six). This event will represent his second coming. When Jesus comes back, he will gather his believers from the four corners of the earth (the four winds) to fight this battle with him. Verse 27 tells us that Jesus will come as the lightning comes out of the east and shines to the west. When referring to the Million Man March, Farrakhan says he stood in the east and spoke with his face shining to the west, then he immediately quotes Matthew 24:27. By aligning himself with this particular scripture, Farrakhan is saying that he is the Son of man and that the battle of Armageddon is already upon us. However, the above scripture reference is speaking of the second coming of Jesus Christ, not the coming of Louis Farrakhan.

But back at the ranch: the enemy said it was a good message but the wrong messenger. They got black people to condemn me.

Farrakhan considers the enemy to be the white man. The message he is talking about is the message he delivered at the Million Man March. Many people, black and white, felt that Farrakhan's message at the March was a good one despite their distaste for him personally. However, the message was not a good one because it underhandedly promoted racial separatism and Black Muslim theology. Anything good in the message was overshadowed by those two things.

In the meantime, I became depressed because I saw my crucifixion coming.

Again, as in his Saviour's Day speech, Farrakhan intentionally uses words and phrases that compare him to Jesus Christ. In this instance he has used the word "crucifixion." He wants to paint a picture of himself as a suffering Messiah in the minds of unsuspecting people.

You see, the scriptures of the Bible and the Koran are really a roadmap and a plan for the salvation of an entire people. And all I was doing was following the script.

As we have seen in Chapter One, there is historical and scientific evidence that the Bible is the Word of God and is the "roadmap" to salvation, not the Koran. The Bible is the roadmap to salvation for all people, not just a specific people. However, Farrakhan's use of the phrase "an entire people" indirectly suggests a particular group of people. The particular people he indirectly refers to are black people.

And if the prophets wrote of enslaved people in the past that God gave a deliverer to and you are an enslaved people in the present, where is your deliverer? Where's your Moses? Where's your Jesus? Where's your Muhammad? Where's your David? Your Solomon? Your Daniel? Your Ezekiel?

Farrakhan considers black people an enslaved people and is attempting to convince his audience of that. However black people are no longer physically enslaved in America. Slavery was abolished years ago. Despite this, black Americans as well as other American minorities have had to overcome discriminatory practices and fight for civil rights. In many instances, blacks and minorities find themselves still struggling for certain justices and equalities. However, to describe black people as enslaved is to rip off the scab from that ever festering sore. Many blacks who identify with being "enslaved" will be more likely to identify with Farrakhan. Farrakhan knows this. Farrakhan further nurses his notion of the enslaved black by telling his audience that they need a deliverer. Farrakhan fancies himself as the black man's deliverer and his aim is to convince as many blacks as possible of this.

God ran out of juice huh?....He made deliverers for them folk back there that weren't in the condition that we're in but he's too damn weak to make one for us?! Is that what you faithless people think?! You like to talk about Moses! You like to sing about the children of Israel! You like to talk about Jesus and the woman at the well! Well, damn it! There's a woman here whose got an issue of blood! Whatcha gonna do for her?!

Farrakhan is good at abusing his audience. Any one who does not agree with what Farrakhan is saying is "faithless" along with a whole list of other negative adjectives. Farrakhan indirectly compares blacks to the woman with the issue of blood. Let's take a look at what the Bible says about this woman:

> [43]And a woman having an issue of blood twelve years, which had spent all her living upon physicians, neither could be healed of any,
> [44]Came behind him, and touched the border of his garment: and immediately her issue of blood stanched.
> [45]And Jesus said, Who touched me? When all denied, Peter and they that were with him said, Master, the multitude throng thee and press thee, and sayest thou, Who touched me?
> [46]And Jesus said, Somebody hath touched me: for I perceive that virtue is gone out of me.
> [47]And when the woman saw that she was not hid, she came trembling, and falling down before him, she declared unto him before all the people for what cause she had touched him, and she was healed immediately.
> [48]And he said unto her, Daughter, be of good comfort; thy faith hath made thee whole: go in peace. (Luke 8:43-48)

Theologians have deciphered that this woman had been bleeding vaginally for twelve years. She suffered for these twelve years until she was able to touch the hymn of the garment of her deliverer: Jesus Christ. The woman had faith that the Lord would heal her. Her faith, along with God's will, did indeed heal her. Farrakhan believes that this woman is symbolic of black America. He believes that black America has been suffering at the hands of white America. Consequently, Farrakhan believes that black America needs a deliverer. He believes that he is that deliverer. However, in order to get cooperation from the American black community, Farrakhan has to convince black people to have faith in him. He wants black people to have the kind of faith in him that the woman with the issue of blood had in Jesus Christ.

You deny God in the present and glorify him in the past.

God is the same God today as he was yesterday. However, Farrakhan doesn't see it that way. Farrakhan looks at Fard Muhammad as the God of the present. Farrakhan views Jesus as a great man who is dead and gone. He believes that Jesus Christ was the Messiah of the time in which he lived. Farrakhan does not consider Jesus to be a present day Messiah. This kind of thinking is contrary to biblical doctrine. Jesus Christ said that he would always be with us. Furthermore, Jesus is described as "Alpha and Omega, the first and last" in Revelation 1:11. If Jesus will always be with us and is the first and the last, then he is the God of the past and the present. Therefore, to glorify him is to glorify the God of the past and the present. Farrakhan would like Christians to believe that by glorifying Jesus Christ they are glorifying a God of the past only.

I went to the East because the Nation of Islam is bigger than me. One day I won't be with you, but the Nation must survive.

Here is additional proof that Farrakhan's main mission is to promote the Nation of Islam. The land in the East that he is referring to is Libya. Remember, Farrakhan made a pact with Khadafy to further advance the Nation of Islam.

And I've got to say this white folks, I've got to say it. Not [to] all but to those I'm talking to. You're such wicked liars.

This is a racist statement. A racist statement is one that negatively describes an entire race of people or promotes hate against a particular race.

Farrakhan does not specify which "white folks" he is referring to because he is referring to white people in general. Farrakhan attempts to cloak his racism by saying that he is not making this statement to all white folks. However, racism is hard to cloak. It's easy to decipher whether or not a statement is racist. Simply rephrase the statement so that the racial comment refers to whatever race you are. If you find the statement to be racist in content after rephrasing it, then it is just as racist if you apply it to another race besides your own. This is how the statement looks when I rephrase it to apply to my race: "And I've got to say this black folks, I've got to say it. Not to all but to those I'm talking to. You're such wicked liars." If I heard a white person say that, I'd say he was a racist, wouldn't you? If so, then those of us who are black can not support any ethnic slurs and racist comments from Farrakhan. We can not uphold any double standards when it comes to this.

I'm going to quote you some Bible now. So if I'm anti-semitic then all of you better burn the Bible. And I want to see you Christians lead the ritual of burning since you ain't got the courage to read the scriptures.......Jesus had a problem with those who called themselves Jews. I didn't write the Bible. You look at it tonight.

Jesus only had a problem with the Jews when the Jews refused to acknowledge him as God. Despite a wealth of proof to the contrary, there are many Jews who do not believe that Jesus is the Messiah that is prophesied of in the Old Testament. They are still waiting for their Messiah to come. Many Jews who lived during Old Testament times also believed the same way. For this reason, Jesus told us that only a remnant (a small portion) of the Jews would actually be saved. The Jews are referred to as God's chosen people because God made a promise to Abraham that his (Abraham's) descendants (the Jews) would inherit a land flowing with milk and honey (Jerusalem). However, the promise does not automatically save a Jew. A Jew must still believe in the Lordship of Jesus Christ to inherit the promise.

During Old Testament times the Jews often turned away from God and began worshipping false gods. This is evident when we look at their exodus from Egypt. Although Moses led the Jews to freedom with God's assistance, they constructed a golden calf and worshipped it. There are many instances besides the worshipping of the golden calf in the Old Testament where the Jews turned from God. These are the times God had "a problem" with them. However, Farrakhan tries to make it appear as if God has a "problem" with all Jews today. He goes on to imply that Jesus was anti-semitic and says that those Christians who speak against anti-semitism should burn the Bible; his reasoning being that the Bible, in his estimation, is anti-semitic. Hogwash! The

Bible does not contain anti-semitic doctrine within its pages, neither was Jesus anti-semitic during his ministry on earth. God only turned from the Jews when the Jews turned from him. Moreover, the Jews are the seed of Abraham to whom the promise was given. Furthermore, the Bible informs us that Jesus was a Jew. How could Jesus be anti-Jewish when he was a Jew himself? How could the Bible be labeled as anti-Jewish when it gives account of the covenant God made between himself and the Jews regarding the promised land? How could the Bible be labeled as anti-Jewish when it gives an account of how God freed the Jews from their slavery in Egypt? Clearly, Farrakhan is unjustified in his statements.

Look, don't say Jesus paid it all and then say he's coming back to judge us and some he's going to send into everlasting damnation. If he paid it all, there ain't no such thing as damnation for us in our craziness. So there shouldn't be a judgement.

Jesus did pay the price for all of us. He paid the price of salvation with his blood. Therefore, salvation is free and available to everyone. However, in order to reap the benefits of this free and available gift, one must accept and worship he who shed the blood. Although the blood was freely given, one must still choose whether or not to accept the free gift.

Farrakhan says that there is no such thing as damnation and that there shouldn't be a judgment, but the Bible tells us that there is a hell (damnation) and there is a day of judgment. Once again, Farrakhan blatantly contradicts the Word of God. The following scriptures tell us about God's judgment:

> 12 And I saw the dead, small and great, stand before God; and the books were opened: and another book was opened, which is the book of life: and the dead were judged out of those things which were written in the books, according to their works.
>
> 13 And the sea gave up the dead which were in it; and death and hell delivered up the dead which were in them: and they were judged every man according to their works.
>
> 14 And death and hell were cast into the lake of fire. This is the second death.
>
> 15 And whosoever was not found written in the book of life was cast into the lake of fire. (Revelation 20:12-15)

There will be a judgment. At the time of that judgment, those whose names are not found in the book of life will be cast into the lake of fire. The lake of fire is a type of hell. Those whose names are in the book, will be those who accepted Jesus as Lord and Saviour when they were living. They will be spared everlasting damnation and instead will enjoy everlasting life with God in his kingdom which has no end.

Jesus had a problem with the Jews. It got so bad till Jesus said one day when they said to him, 'God is our father' and Jesus answered saying, 'If God were your father you would love me, for I proceeded forth from God but now you seek to kill me, a man that has told you the truth.' He said, 'I know you, you are of your father, the devil.'

Let's take a look at the scripture reference that Farrakhan is referring to:

> 37 I know that ye are Abraham's seed; but
> ye seek to kill me, because my word hath no
> place in you.
> 38 I speak that which I have seen with my
> Father: and ye do that which ye have seen
> with your father,
> 39 They answered and said unto him,
> Abraham is our father. Jesus saith unto them,
> If ye were Abraham's children, ye would do
> the works of Abraham.
> 40 But now ye seek to kill me, a man that
> hath told you the truth, which I have heard of
> God: this did not Abraham.
> 41 Ye do the deeds of your father. Then
> said they to him, We be not born of
> fornication; we have one Father, even God.
> 42 Jesus said unto them, If God were your
> Father, ye would love me: for I proceeded
> forth and came from God; neither came I of
> myself, but he sent me.
> 43 Why do ye not understand my speech?
> even because ye cannot hear my word.
> 44 Ye are of your father the devil, and the
> lusts of your father ye will do. He was a
> murderer from the beginning, and abode not
> in the truth, because there is no truth in him.

> When he speaketh a lie, he speaketh of his own: for he is a liar, and the father of it. (John 8:37-44)

Jesus has a problem with **anyone** who does not accept him as Lord and Saviour, not just the Jews. Jews are no exception. In the above scripture, Jesus is addressing the Jews. However, he is addressing those Jews who don't believe in his Lordship. Farrakhan intentionally and strategically doesn't quote the scriptures that tell us what Jesus says to the Jews who do believe in him. But we will quote them here:

> 31Then said Jesus to those Jews which believed on him, If ye continue in my word, then are ye my disciples indeed;
> 32And ye shall know the truth and the truth shall make you free. (John 8:31-32)

Those who are disciples of Jesus are children of God. Those who are not disciples of Jesus are children of the devil. A disciple by definition is a follower. One can not follow Jesus if they don't believe in what he stands for.

The Jews are the descendants of Abraham. However, a Jew can be disinherited from the promise God made to Abraham simply by refusing to accept Jesus as Lord and Saviour. In that sense, he is no longer a child of the promise. Jesus made it plain: those who do not believe in the deity of Christ are children of the devil. As we can see from the scriptures quoted, Jesus was only talking to Jews who had not accepted him as Saviour, not to Jews in general.

Farrakhan attempts to discredit the Jews because they are Abraham's descendants and therefore the children of the promise. Since they are the children of the promise, they are God's chosen people. Farrakhan wants to convince us that black people, instead of the Jews, are God's chosen people. In order to do this, he tries to put Jews in a negative light and downplays their relationship with God as well as misrepresents what the Bible has to say about them.

There's none righteous. There's none good. No, not one. That's Paul talking. Who was Paul talking to? Jews.

Yes, Paul was talking *to* the Jews *about* everybody. Romans 3:10 tells us that none are righteous. Romans 3:23 is more specific concerning righteousness when it says, "For all have sinned, and come short of the glory of God." By saying these things, the Bible is telling us that no one is born righteous. Belief in the Lordship of Jesus

Christ is what makes one righteous. However, it is the blood of Chris and a belief in the redemptive power of that blood that saves us, not righteousness. Although we should strive to be as righteous as possible, none of us would ever be righteous enough to deserve a place in heaven. It is better that we are promised a place in spite of ourselves. We are promised a place in heaven as long as we believe in the deity of Christ. Notice, the scriptures say that none are righteous and that all have sinned. The words "none" and "all" include everybody.

I'm not trying to show myself as any anti-semitic person because I'm not that at all. I don't hate Jewish people.

Agreed. It doesn't appear as if Farrakhan hates the Jews. Instead, it appears as if he hates white people. Farrakhan's criticism of the Jews stems from jealousy, not hate.

And somebody tells you Farrakhan is out there calling himself Jesus and all of a sudden you don't love me.

Notice, Farrakhan didn't say that this "somebody" wasn't telling the truth. Christians can not afford to support a man who claims, directly or indirectly, to be Jesus. Farrakhan has made unmistakably strong indirect claims to being the Messiah. Because of this, he has been the target of some strong criticism from a few Christians. Those who have criticized him have not said they do not love him. Christians are commanded to love everyone, friends and enemies alike. However, to love someone does not mean that you can not rebuke, correct, or criticize him or her.

If you love everybody then your love should include me, Christian. You don't love me? What have I done? Did I rape your mother? Did I rob you? Did I take away your name? Your language? Your culture? Your God? Your religion? Your country? Did I kidnap you? But you can make excuses for the white man, but you won't even come next door to see about your brother. Maybe he's an Arab. Maybe you could help him. Maybe you could redeem him, if only you loved him. But you hate me without a cause.

I haven't heard any Christians say that they hate Farrakhan. This is something Farrakhan has drudged up in order to evoke sympathy for his plight. Again, by indirectly bringing up the perils of slavery, Farrakhan throws salt into the emotional wounds of American blacks.

hurch

ınderstands that he must get Christians to see him in a ıt in order for his plan of racial separatism and theological ιo work. His plan can not work without the Christian. becomes uncomfortable when Christians question him becaus he knows that he stands for everything they do not. The trouble is, many Christians either don't know what Farrakhan really stands for, won't accept that what he stands for is contrary to Christianity, or will water down what he stands for in the name of Afrocentricity.

I tied the Nation of Islam to the Muslim world.

There is no question that Orthodox Islam is one of the fasted growing religions worldwide. Farrakhan knows this and therefore understands how important it is for him to attempt to "tie" the Nation of Islam and Orthodox Islam together. Remember, Orthodox Muslims do not agree with the doctrines of the Nation of Islam. They see the Nation of Islam as a cult and a hindrance. Farrakhan feels that he had a successful trip to the Middle East. Considering his quest to promote Black Muslim theology worldwide, he just may have. Farrakhan wants Orthodox Muslims to embrace the Nation of Islam. He feels that this connection was made as a result of his journey to Libya and his talks with Khadafy. However, it is questionable whether or not Farrakhan has influenced the Middle East on the level that he thinks he has. Both he and Khadafy are very shrewd men and it is my estimation that they are using each other for their own separate gain.

We['re] little silly children. [Some say] my Jesus [is] bigger than your Muhammad. My Muhammad [is] bigger than your Jesus. Well my Moses [is] bigger than both of them. And if Moses, Muhammad and Jesus came in the room they would be hugging and kissing each other.

No they would not. If Moses, Muhammad and Jesus came into the room, Jesus would hug Moses and rebuke Muhammad. Muhammad was a false prophet. The Bible tells us to beware of false prophets; but more on this in Chapter Seven.

So we came back home and the scriptures fulfilled: a prophet is not without honor except in his own house.

Once again, Farrakhan uses the scriptures to indirectly compare himself to Jesus. Let's take a look:

> [1]And he went out from thence, and came into his own country; and his disciples follow him.
> [2]And when the sabbath day was come, he began to teach in the synagogue: and many hearing him were astonished, saying, From whence hath this man these things? and what wisdom is this which is given unto him, that even such mighty works are wrought by his hands?
> [3]Is not this the carpenter, the son of Mary, the brother of James, and Joses, and of Judah, and Simon? and are not his sisters here with us? And they were offended at him.
> [4]But Jesus said unto them, A prophet is not without honour, but in his own country, and among his own kin, and in his own house. (Mark 6:1-4)

Jesus was better received outside of his homeland than inside. Farrakhan left the states and was well received during his visit to Africa and the Middle East. Since he received much criticism for his dealings with Khadafy, he has made himself akin to a prophet and is saying that the scriptures are being fulfilled through him. The scriptures were fulfilled through Christ, not through Farrakhan. However, Farrakhan sees himself as the prophet who is without honor in his hometown and compares himself to Jesus who was often times dishonored in his own land.

What [are] you investigating? Whose gonna play Pontius Pilate? We already see the Jews. We already see the scribes and we already see the Pharisees and the Sadducees. What [did] you charge Jesus with? Blasphemies! Sedition! Seven Hundred Club [says] he's blasphemous. He said he's the Messiah! He said he's Jesus!

Others have quoted Farrakhan as saying he's Jesus. Even though Farrakhan appears to be upset by the accusation, he never really comes out and says that he never said it. Again, as indicated in the preceding excerpt, Farrakhan likens himself to Jesus by trying to convince his audience that he is going through the same things Jesus went through. Pontius Pilate was the Roman governor of Judea at the time of Jesus' crucifixion. Pilate had the power to stop the crucifixion. Instead, he let the crowd of people (Jews and Gentiles alike) decide on who should be crucified: Jesus or Barabbas. Barabbas was a murderer that was being held in custody at the time. The angry crowd of people prompted Pilate to crucify Jesus instead of Barabbas. They hated Jesus because he claimed to be God and accused him of blasphemy because they didn't believe that he was God. Pilate begrudgingly went along with the request of the people even though he knew that Jesus had done nothing wrong. So when Farrakhan asks, "Whose going to play Pontius Pilate?.." he is planting a seed in the minds of those in his audience. That seed says that Farrakhan will also be accused of blasphemy and have to stand before a Pontius Pilate.

Farrakhan goes on to identify the staff of the 700 Club (A Christian syndicated talk show) as modern day Pharisees and Sadducees who accused him of claiming to be God. The Pharisees were a religious group of people who opposed Jesus because Jesus did away with Old Testament law. The Pharisees still wanted to continue to abide by the rituals and laws of the Old Testament despite the lack of necessity to do so. Jesus fulfilled the law by shedding his blood on the cross. After the death and resurrection of Jesus Christ it was no longer necessary to follow the laws of Moses and of the Old Testament. The law was a shadow of things to come. However, the Pharisees along with the Sadducees didn't see it that way.

Farrakhan targets the 700 Club because in 1996, it aired a taping in which Glenn R. Plummer (President of the Christian Television Network), exposed Farrakhan's claims to be Jesus. During the program, Farrakhan was criticized for these claims. Curiously, in defending himself, Farrakhan does not say that there must have been some misunderstanding, but instead likens himself to Jesus who was also accused of blasphemy. However, the difference between Jesus and Farrakhan is that Jesus was accused of blasphemy and was innocent of the charges, because he indeed, is God. On the other hand, Farrakhan has been accused of blasphemy and is guilty of the charges, because he indeed, is not and never will be God. The very fact that Farrakhan compares his experience of being accused of blasphemy to Jesus' experience of being accused of blasphemy is but one more proof that Farrakhan sees himself as suffering in the same ways Jesus did because he sees himself, as we will soon see, as today's Jesus. What Mr. Plummer pointed out is the following: Farrakhan was noted to have said that: 1) the historical Jesus was not the Messiah, 2) seventy-five percent of what we read in the Bible that refers to Jesus is referring to a man of the future other than Jesus, 3) Jesus was not born in Bethlehem but instead in Sandersville Georgia [Elijah Muhammad's birthplace] 4) the Old Testament Elijah and the New Testament Jesus are one in the same and 5) that he (Farrakhan) is Elijah.

Elijah was a prophet of the Old Testament. Since Farrakhan thinks that he is Elijah and that Elijah and Jesus were the same person (which they were not), then it is reasonable to conclude that Farrakhan thinks he is Jesus.

Since Farrakhan thinks that seventy-five percent of what the Bible says about Jesus Christ is not referring to the Jesus of the New Testament but instead refers to a man of the future, then it is reasonable to conclude that Farrakhan believes that he is this man of the future, since Farrakhan thinks he is Jesus. Elijah Muhammad was born in Sandersville Georgia in the early 1900s. Farrakhan thinks that Jesus was not born in Bethlehem but instead in Sandersville Georgia. Therefore, it is reasonable to conclude that Farrakhan believes that Elijah Muhammad is Jesus. The question then becomes: How could Farrakhan believe that both he and Elijah Muhammad are Jesus? The answer to this question comes with the discussion of the next excerpt.

Farrakhan is misguided in his thinking. The Jesus Christ that the Bible refers to is the literal Jesus that walked the earth approximately 2000 years ago. It is talking about the Jesus that was crucified and then resurrected from the grave. The Bible never refers to Jesus being born in Sandersville Georgia. The Bible indicates that Jesus was born in Bethlehem. The Bible never refers to any other Messiah aside from Jesus. The Bible never gives reference to Muhammad as being the Messiah nor does it give reference to Elijah Muhammad being Jesus nor does it give reference to Farrakhan being Jesus. The Bible never talks about two different Jesuses. The same Jesus that was resurrected and ascended to the Father is the same Jesus that will come back to gather his people from the four corners of the universe to establish a new Jerusalem on earth. Farrakhan is not Jesus, no matter how much he'd like to be.

Well, I want to make it clear: Jesus is too big. Jesus is too powerful. I'm not even worthy to unlace his shoes. It said, all power in heaven and earth has been turned over into his hands. I'm not that one. But I am *a* Jesus! Listen! Wait a minute! I am *a* Messiah! I am *a* Saviour! And I am *a* deliverer! And I am *a* restorer! And I am *a* finder and seeker of the lost under *the* Jesus: the Messiah, the Saviour, The redeemer, the restorer.

At one point Farrakhan alludes to a belief that he is Jesus and at another point he says he believes he is a *type* of Jesus. To say either is blasphemous. Apparently, Farrakhan believes that Jesus served his purpose for the time in which he lived and it's Farrakhan's turn now. Farrakhan believes in evolving Messiahs: when one dies another comes along to take his place. This is how Farrakhan can believe that

Elijah Muhammad was "a Jesus." However, there is but one Messiah and his name is Jesus. The Bible never taught that there was or would ever be more than one Jesus or that types of Jesus Christs would evolve through the years. As a matter of fact, the Bible says just the opposite. Jesus warned us about people like Farrakhan that would say, directly or indirectly that they are Jesus. Let's take a look:

> 4And Jesus answered and said unto them, Take heed that no man deceive you.
> 5 For many shall come in my name, saying I am Christ; and shall deceive many.
> (Matthew 24: 4-5)

Farrakhan stated that he is a "finder and seeker of the lost under *the* Jesus." By making this statement, Farrakhan has used Jesus' name to say he is a type of Christ. Therefore, Farrakhan has come in the name of Jesus claiming to be Christ (v. 5). The following is a scripture reference that identifies Jesus as the Messiah. Jesus is the only person that the Bible gives that distinction to. The Bible never says that there will be other Christs after Jesus.

Farrakhan says that he is a deliverer. To deliver someone means to rescue them from something. The word "deliver" is synonymous with the word "redeem." Both words indicate freedom from something. Christ came to redeem us from our sins. He did so by shedding his blood. Christ is our deliverer, not Farrakhan. Farrakhan has not shed any blood for redemption of sin. There is no redemptive power in the blood of Farrakhan. There is only redemptive power in the blood of Christ. By calling himself a deliverer, Farrakhan is also calling himself a redeemer. However, Christ is our redeemer and none other. Let's see what the Bible has to say about redemption.

> 11But Christ being come an high priest of good things to come, by a greater and more perfect tabernacle, not made with hands, that is to say, not of this building;
> 12Neither by the blood of goats and calves, but by his own blood he entered in once into the holy place, having obtained eternal redemption for us.
> 13For if the blood of bulls and of goats, and the ashes of an heifer sprinkling the unclean, sanctifieth to the purifying of the flesh:
> 14How much more shall the blood of Christ, who through the eternal Spirit offered himself

> without spot to God, purge your conscience from dead works to serve the living God?
>
> [15]And for this cause he is the mediator of the new testament, that by means of death, for the redemption of transgressions that were under the first testament, they which are called might receive the promise of eternal inheritance. (Hebrews 9:11-15)

Jesus Christ is our redeemer. Through his blood is the forgiveness of sins. The flesh is purified by believing upon the name of Jesus Christ. As the scriptures indicate above, during Old Testament times, the sacrificial blood of animals redeemed people from sin. However, when Jesus sacrificed himself for the sins of the world, then the blood of animals was no longer needed because the blood of Jesus took its place. Neither Fard, Farrakhan, or Elijah Muhammad has shed any sacrificial blood. None of them have been nailed to a cross and crucified for the soul-sake of man. Only Jesus fits this bill.

Jesus is the mediator of the New Testament and he is the way to God, not Farrakhan, not Fard, not Elijah Muhammad.

Farrakhan says that he is a Saviour. But the Bible tells us that there is no Saviour other than Jesus Christ.

SUMMING UP THE MATTER

When speaking at New Bethel, Farrakhan was quick to apply biblical principles to himself and the Nation of Islam thereby perverting the meaning of communion, the crucifixion, Ezekiel's vision of the dry bones, and the plan for salvation. Ultimately, Farrakhan refers to himself as a Saviour and a Messiah. To do so is blasphemous. The irony here is that Farrakhan is allowed to blaspheme God inside of the very place where blasphemy should be forbidden: the church. If this isn't enough, Farrakhan, in his speech that he delivers at Chicago's Mosque Maryam (discussed in the following chapter), takes his distorted interpretations of the scriptures even further when speaking on the doctrine of the mark of the beast found in the book of Revelation. He also, without apology, unveils his avid hatred of white people and reveals, without a doubt, that he is indeed a racist.

CHAPTER SIX

A DISCUSSION OF FARRAKHAN'S 1996 MOSQUE MARYAM SPEECH

On June 9, 1996 Farrakhan spoke at the Mosque Maryam in Chicago Illinois. He entitled this speech: "God's Divine Destruction on America; Can she avert it?" The majority of his audience were Muslims. Consequently, Farrakhan unveiled certain areas of his beliefs that he is more careful to mask when addressing a Christian audience.

In this speech, Farrakhan states that God will destroy America because of her historical mistreatment of blacks. He says that the destruction is targeted towards white people and that, because of this, black people should not integrate with whites in any way. Farrakhan is quoted as saying that the church has made black people "niggers." Farrakhan says that whites, all over the earth, are under a death sentence. He says that Islam will rule the world and that Jesus was a Muslim. Let's take a closer look.

During the speech which he delivered on June 9, 1996 when he spoke of "God's Divine Destruction" at Mosque Maryam in Chicago Illinois, Farrakhan said……..

In the name of Allah the beneficent, the merciful.....

Again, Farrakhan gives praise to Allah, not to God as Christians know him.

I believe him to be the Messiah that the world is waiting for.

Farrakhan is speaking of Elijah Muhammad. He believes Elijah Muhammad to be the Messiah that the world is looking for which implies that Jesus was not the Messiah that the world has been looking for. Again, this train of thought clearly goes against biblical doctrine.

America and her people which includes you, face divine destruction. In the book of Revelations the thirteenth chapter, the eighteenth verse, it reads: Here is wisdom. Let him that hath understanding count or calculate the number of the beast for it is

the number of a man, six hundred threescore and six. Some translations say it is the number of a man, six six six.

Farrakhan believes that God will destroy America because of her mistreatment of blacks over the years. He ties this destruction into the Bible's account of a man who will rise up, set himself in the temple at Jerusalem, and claim to be God. He is called the beast and his number is 666. Let's take a look at the scripture Farrakhan quotes from:

> [13] Here is wisdom. Let him that hath understanding count the number of the beast: for it is the number of a man; and his number is Six hundred threescore and six. (Revelation 13:18)

The beast that the scripture is referring to is the antichrist. The antichrist is the one who will claim to be God. The book of Revelation speaks of two beasts. One is the beast of the sea who is the antichrist and the other is the beast of the earth, who is the false prophet. The following scripture reference gives us more information about the first beast.

> [1]And I stood upon the sand of the sea, and saw a beast rise up out of the sea, having seven heads and ten horns, and upon his horns ten crowns, and upon his heads the name of blasphemy.
>
> [2]And the beast which I saw was like unto a leopard, and his feet were as the feet of a bear, and his mouth as the mouth of a lion: and the dragon gave him his power, and his seat, and great authority.
>
> [3]And I saw one of his heads as it were wounded to death; and his deadly wound was healed: and all the world wondered after the beast.
>
> [4]And they worshipped the dragon which gave power unto the beast: and they worshipped the beast, saying, Who is like unto the beast? who is able to make war with him?
>
> [5]And there was given unto him a mouth speaking great things and blasphemies; and

power was given unto him to continue forty
and two months.

[6]And he opened his mouth in blasphemy
against God, to blaspheme his name, and his
tabernacle, and them that dwell in heaven.

[7]And it was given unto him to make war
with the saints, and to overcome them: and
power was given him over all kindreds, and
tongues, and nations.

[8]And all that dwell upon the earth shall
worship him, whose names are not written in
the book of life of the lamb slain from the
foundation of the world. (Revelation 13:1-8)

As noted before, the book of Revelation was written by the apostle John who was banished to the Island of Patmos during the time of its writing. Revelation is the last book of the Bible and is comprised of the visions of John during his time at Patmos. While John was in the spirit, he saw the risen Lord, Jesus Christ, who instructed him to reveal the account of the visions that God would give to him while he was in exile on the Island. The visions of John that are documented in the book of Revelation correlate with the visions and prophecies recorded in the Old Testament book of Daniel.

In verse 1, the ten horns and crowns represent multiple nations that have combined together to create a new world order. The antichrist will be in charge of all nations. Verse 2 tells us that the dragon will give the antichrist great power. The dragon is symbolic of Satan. Verse 3 indicates that the antichrist will be able to work miracles and that people will marvel at him. Verse 4 tells us that people will worship Satan and the antichrist. Verse 5 tells us that the antichrist will be a great charismatic speaker although what he speaks will be blasphemous. The verse also tells us that the antichrist will reign for forty-two months. Forty-two months is three and a half years: the latter half of the seven-year tribulation. During this second three and a half years, the antichrist will claim to be God, and people will believe him, except for the very elect of God (discussed in more detail later on in this chapter).

The second beast that the book of Revelation speaks of is the beast that arises out of the earth. Let's take a look:

[11]And I beheld another beast coming up
out of the earth; and he had two horns like a
lamb, and he spake as a dragon.

> 12And he exerciseth all the power of the
> first beast before him, and causeth the earth
> and them which dwell therein to worship the
> first beast, whose deadly wound was healed.
> 13And he doeth great wonders, so that he
> maketh fire come down from heaven on the
> earth in the sight of men,
> 14And deceiveth them that dwell on the
> earth by the means of those miracles which
> he had power to do in the sight of the beast;
> saying to them that dwell on the earth, that
> they should make an image to the beast,
> which had the wound by a sword, and did live.
> 15And he had power to give life unto the
> image of the beast, that the image of the
> beast should both speak, and cause that as
> many as would not worship the image of the
> beast should be killed.
> 1 And he causeth all, both small and great,
> rich and poor, free and bond, to receive a
> mark in their right hand, or their foreheads:
> 17And that no man might buy or sell, save
> he that had the mark, or the name of the
> beast or the number of his name. (Revelation
> 13: 11-17)

As we have seen earlier, the scriptures go on to tell us that the mark of the beast is the number of a man whose number is 666.

Verse 11 tells us that there will be another beast coming out of the earth. He will have horns like a lamb but speak like a dragon. The lamb symbolizes Christ. However, we know that the beast is not the Christ. Instead, this beast will trick people into believing he is the Messiah. He will have an outer Christ-like appearance but will be like Satan on the inside. Therefore, despite his messianic outward appearance, this second beast will really be a devil in sheep's clothing, a fake.

Verse 13 tells us that the second beast will also have great miraculous power just like the antichrist will. Verse 14 reveals that man will be fooled by these miracles and will, as a result, succumb to the second beast who paves the way for the first beast and convinces men to make an image to the first beast, the antichrist. Satan attempts to copycat the Trinity. Instead of the Father, Son, and Holy Ghost, Satan will establish the rule of Satan, the antichrist, and the false prophet.

The second beast is considered to be the false prophet paving the way for the coming of the antichrist much like John the Baptist paved the way for the coming of Jesus.

Verse 15 teaches that anyone who does not worship the image of the antichrist during those times will be killed. Verse 16 tells us that the antichrist will mandate that the people of the earth wear his symbol (666) in their hands or foreheads in order to buy and sell. In other words, this mark will be as money is today. Without it, a person will become destitute. However, anyone who takes the mark will be pledging his allegiance to the antichrist. It will be a symbol of their worship unto him. Therefore, during those times, true Christians will not take the mark and be sorely persecuted.

We have to compute now what the number means. So we are dealing with a man that has characters like a beast. The book of Revelation closes or is the closing of the Bible. It talks about four beasts, one of those beasts more terrible than the others and that beast was taken and utterly destroyed and its body given to the burning flames. Now you have a beast being destroyed and you have fire and you have to calculate time. Now, the honorable Elijah Muhammad is a principle helper in that calculation.

The Bible does not say anything about Elijah Muhammad aiding in the calculation of the number 666. It is the number of a man. There is no calculation involved.

The honorable Elijah Muhammad has taught us that what we are entering into now is the judgment of the present world and its order. This world belongs to the Caucasian people.

Farrakhan believes that the world belongs to white people. He also says Elijah Muhammad taught that the world will be judged. Accordingly, Farrakhan believes that whites, not blacks, will be judged. The following scripture reference tells us what the Bible says about God judging the world:

> 4And I saw thrones, and they sat upon them, and judgment was given unto them: and I saw the souls of them that were beheaded for the witness of Jesus, and for the word of God, and which had not worshipped the beast, neither his image, neither had received his mark upon their

foreheads, or in their hands; and they lived
and reigned with Christ a thousand years.
5 But the rest of the dead lived not again
until the thousand years were finished. This is
the first resurrection.
6 Blessed and holy is he that hath part in
the first resurrection: on such the second
death hath no power, but they shall be priests
of God and of Christ, and shall reign with him
a thousand years.
7 And when the thousand years are
expired, Satan shall be loosed out of his
prison,
8 And shall go out to deceive the nations
which are in the four quarters of the earth,
Gog and Magog, to gather them together to
battle: the number of whom is as the sand of
the sea.
9 And they went up on the breadth of the
earth, and compassed the camp of the saints
about, and the beloved city: and fire came
down from God out of heaven, and devoured
them.
10 And the devil that deceived them was
cast into the lake of fire and brimstone, where
the beast and the false prophet are and shall
be tormented day and night for ever and ever.
11 And I saw a great white throne, and him
that sat on it, from whose face the earth and
the heaven fled away; and there was found
no place for them.
12 And I saw the dead, small and great,
stand before God: and the books were
opened: and another book was opened,
which is the book of life: and the dead were
judged out of those things which were written
in the books, according to their works.
13 And the sea gave up the dead which
were in it: and death and hell delivered up the
dead which were in them: and they were
judged every man according to their works.
14 And death and hell were cast into the
lake of fire. This is the second death.

> [15]And whosoever was not found written in the book of life was cast into the lake of fire. (Revelation 20:4-15)

As we can see, the judgment of God has nothing to do with race. Christians living during tribulation times will be beheaded for their belief in Christ. However, God will judge them as righteous for not taking the mark of the beast and they will reign with Christ in his earthly kingdom which will last a millenium (a thousand years). After Christ's thousand year reign on earth Satan will once again be loosed and he will again deceive many people. Afterwards, God will cast Satan into Hell along with the antichrist and the False Prophet. Verse 12 tells us of the book of life in which the dead will be judged. Man will be accountable for his deeds and anyone whose name is not found written in the book of life will be cast into Hell. God is not playing. Hell is very real. Only those who believe in the deity of Christ and confess him as Lord and Saviour, and believe in his resurrection, will find their names in the book of life.

The Holy Koran says that Allah created the Heavens and the Earth in six periods of time. So, six is the number of the originator and six is the number of the beast. The honorable Elijah Muhammad taught us that the white race is not a natural man but a man that came through a process of birth control through a system of grafting. You can take it our leave it. The white people are not an ancient people. They are a new people on our Earth. So, the first six which is six hundred could refer to the six hundred years that it took on the Island of Patmos or Pilan to graft this new people out of the original.

The Bible teaches that God, not Allah, created the heavens and the Earth (Genesis 1:1). The scriptures go on to tell us that God created the Earth in six days which Farrakhan says is six periods of time. Farrakhan therefore concludes that six is the number of "the originator." By this he means that six is the number of God. Farrakhan also states that six is the number of the beast. Neither statement is true. Nowhere does the Bible indicate that six is the number of God. Furthermore, 666, not 6, is the number of the beast.

The Bible doesn't teach that the white man was grafted. Moreover, the Bible does not attribute the first 6 in 666 to anything and certainly not to six hundred years in the grafting of the white man. Farrakhan says that the white man is not a natural man but that he came through a process of birth control through a system of grafting. What he means by this is unclear. However, many Black Muslims believe that the white race is a mutant race of people. Black people would, with just cause, label any white person a racist who would say these things about black people. They sound just as racist coming from Farrakhan when he says these things about white people.

Now either white people were here and they didn't come from us or they did come from us. And their scholars are saying today that the original people are the black people of the Earth. They are bearing witness to the honorable Elijah Muhammad. So then if you can not produce a white man naturally, then what was the process by which he was brought on the Earth and for what purpose was the white man brought here? This is not racist teachings. This is actual facts.

Scientists have indeed estimated that the first man on Earth originated in Africa. Consequently, it would seem that the first man would have been a person of color. If we were to nationalize this man, we would have to say that he was an African. However, this scientific information does not mean that those with African blood (i.e. black Americans) are superior to any race in any way.

Farrakhan believes that since the first man was black then all white people came from black people and therefore, anything not black is unnatural, a mutation. If we look around us there are many races aside from the black race (i.e. Chinese, Hispanics, Italians, e.t.c.). The question then becomes for anyone who accepts Farrakhan's race ideologies: What about the people from all the other races, are they mutants too?

Farrakhan speaks as if God has no say in genetics. With all the different colors of people on the planet one can only logically conclude that God intended to create different races. To bring the point home further and for the sake of analogy, let's take a look at Eve:

> 21And the Lord God caused a deep sleep to fall upon Adam, and he slept: and he took one of his ribs, and closed up the flesh instead thereof;
> 22And the rib, which the Lord God had taken from man, made he a woman, and brought her unto the man.
> 23And Adam said, This is now bone of my bones, and flesh of my flesh: she shall be called Woman, because she was taken out of Man.

> [24]Therefore shall a man leave his father and his mother, and shall cleave unto his wife; and they shall be one flesh. (Genesis 2:21-24)

Eve was made from Adam. However, Adam and Even were considered to be one flesh. Consequently, they were equals even though Eve came from Adam and even though they had distinct physical differences from one another. Furthermore, although Eve was produced from "the original man," she was not a mutant. Therefore, if we were to agree with Farrakhan when he says that white people "came from" black people, so what if they did? Both races are equal in status to one another. Neither is superior. If a man and a woman, who have bodies succinctly different from one another, were made equal, despite the fact that one came from the other, then certainly blacks and whites, who have no difference from one another besides skin color, would also be equal to one another. It doesn't matter which race was created first.

By saying that white people "came from" black people, and that white people are not "naturally" produced, Farrakhan is implying that blacks are superior to whites. Since Farrakhan deems whites to be unnatural, he figures that there must be some special purpose for their earthly existence; a purpose he believes, and has convinced others, is negative. However, white people are just as natural and normal as anyone else. It is Farrakhan and the Nation of Islam who tag them as mutants.

Even if there were a race of people produced "unnaturally", that race of people would be no less human than other races. Is a test tube baby less of a human being than a baby formed in the womb? Of course not. Although man interfered with the "natural" process of a test tube baby's conception, God created both the test tube baby and the naturally procreated baby equally.

Jesus said to the Jews, "I know you. You are of your Father, the devil. He was a liar and a murderer from the beginning. So, if the Father was a liar and a murderer from the beginning, the lying and murder was born into the very nature of the people. Listen, the island of Patmos or Pilan was a womb and whatever goes on outside the womb affects the nature of that which is being formed in the womb. If lying and murder, murder of the darker, saving the lighter, marrying the lighter onto the lighter, murdering, the darker saving the lighter, and this went on for 600 years until a pale people was produced. Human beings, but a different kind of human being.'

When speaking of Jesus addressing the Jews as devils, Farrakhan is referring to the eighth chapter of the book of John. However, Farrakhan leaves out some important things in regards to his reference. Farrakhan made reference to this scripture in his speech at New Bethel. Let's look at it again:

> 33They answered him, We be Abraham's
> seed, and were never in bondage to any man:
> how sayest thou, Ye shall be made free?
> 34Jesus answered them, Verily, verily, I say
> unto you, Whosoever committeth sin is the
> servant of sin.
> 35And the servant abideth not in the house
> for ever: but the Son abideth ever.
> 36If the Son therefore shall make you free,
> ye shall be free indeed.
> 37I know that ye are Abraham's seed; but
> ye seek to kill me, because my word hath no
> place in you.
> 38I speak that which I have seen with my
> Father: and ye do that which ye have seen
> with your Father.
> 39They answered and said unto him,
> Abraham is our father. Jesus saith unto them,
> If ye were Abraham's children, ye would do
> the works of Abraham.
> 40But now ye seek to kill me, a man that
> hath told you the truth, which I have heard of
> God: this did not Abraham.
> 41Ye do the deeds of your father. Then
> said they to him, We be not born of
> fornication; we have one Father, even God.
> 42Jesus said unto them, If God were your
> Father, ye would love me: for I proceeded
> forth and came from God; neither came I of
> myself, but he sent me.
> 43Why do ye not understand my speech?
> even because ye cannot hear my word.
> 44Ye are of your father the devil, and the
> lusts of your father ye will do. He was a
> murderer from the beginning, and abode not
> in the truth, because there is no thruth in him.
> When he speaketh a lie, he speaketh of his

> own: for he is a liar, and the father of it. (John 8:33-44)

Again, Jesus was specific in what he was saying regarding these matters. Many of the Jews felt that they were automatically saved since they were descendants of Abraham. However, Jesus made it clear that what saves them is not their genealogy, but instead whether or not they believed in the things that Jesus was saying.

When looking again at the preceding excerpt of his speech, Farrakhan mixes the above scripture reference with his own procreation theory. Farrakhan figures that the Jews are the children of the devil and are therefore liars and murderers (the devil is described in the Bible as a liar and a murderer). He then accuses the ancient Jews of murdering the darker skinned people and marrying or saving the lighter skinned people in order to mix with them and produce a "pale" people or white people. Now, in order for Farrakhan to believe this, he'd have to believe that the Jews were pale enough or white enough to pull this off. Think about it. What sense does this line of reasoning really make?

Let us make man in our image and after our likeness and let us give them power and dominion. That's how the white man got power. It was given to him divinely, but a certain limit and term was set on the white man's rule. Why was their term limited? It was limited because their rule would be contrary to the eternal principles of truth and justice upon which the universe is based, and since the universe is based on the eternal principals of truth and justice, no unjust world can have any permanence in a universe balanced by justice. Are you listening? Good. Good. So, then if white folk created or made a world that is unjust, lies and murder and stealing at the root of this world, then this world can have no permanence in God's universe of truth. So then would come a time when this world would be judged and destroyed.

Farrakhan begins the above excerpt by loosely quoting the following scripture:

> 26 And God said, Let us make man in our image, after our likeness: and let them have dominion over the fish of the sea, and over the fowl of the air, and over the cattle, and over all the earth, and over every creeping thing that creepeth upon the earth. (Genesis 1:26)

Farrakhan then says that this is how the white man "got power." His reasoning in coupling the above scripture with his notion of how the white man got power is not made clear. However, it appears as if Farrakhan believes that God gave the white man limited worldly power. Farrakhan goes on to blame the white man for all of the injustices in the world and expresses a belief that because of this, the white man will soon be destroyed.

Eve, not the white man, was the first human being to bring sin into the world by eating the fruit of the tree of Knowledge of good and evil (Genesis 2: 17) and tempting her husband to do so as well. Before this, there was no earthly sin.

The devil is described in the Bible as a liar and a thief. It was Satan who convinced Eve to eat the fruit by lying to her when he told her that she and Adam would be like gods if they did so. Technically, then, he was the first actual being (angelic being) to bring sin into the world. Furthermore, the Bible tells us that Cain, not the white man, was the first murderer. He killed his brother, Abel. There is no indication in the Bible as to the color of Cain's skin. Even if we knew what race of people Cain belonged to, it would not matter. Does the sin of one black man mark the whole race? Of course not. Does the sin of one white man mark the whole race? Of course not. Clearly, Farrakhan has racist views when it comes to the issues of skin color.

Farrakhan's theory about whites creating an unjust (sinful) world is contradicted by his belief that blacks were the first ("original") people on Earth. If this is so, then Adam and Eve were black. If Adam and Eve were black and they were the first human beings to commit sin, then one could just as well erroneously conclude that blacks brought sin into the world. See what kind of problems this line of thinking creates? Instead, it should be said that Adam and Eve brought sin into the world by disobeying God's command not to eat the forbidden fruit. God does not make this a black and white issue and neither should we.

So we have 600, meaning the years it took these people to produce out of the original. There were 60,000 human beings, black human beings involved in that process. And the last 6 represents two things. I'll get to the second thing that it represents later. But the first thing that the 6 represents is 6,000 years. After he had gone six thousand years his time is up, then God comes and the process of removal of his power and authority and himself begins.

Farrakhan is saying that it took 600 years for the white race to be produced, there were 60,000 human beings involved in this so-called production, and that the last 6 of the number 666 represents 6,000 years of white rule that is about to end. There is no biblical, historical, or scientific support anywhere for his assessment. Farrakhan's understanding of the number of the beast (666) is misguided.

Look, here's another angel flying in the midst of heaven having the everlasting gospel to preach. Here is the Bible [holds Bible up] and that which Jesus was given is called Bushra or Ingil which is gospel. Here's the book, Bible [holds Bible up]. Is this [Bible] the everlasting gospel?! Just think. Is this Koran [holds Koran up] the everlasting gospel?! Is it? How do you know? How do you know? There's got to be proof. Either it is or it isn't. If this is not the everlasting gospel [holds both books up] then there's a time set on these books! Well that's a fact. But we have to know. Look brothers and sisters. Neither of these books is the everlasting gospel.

Farrakhan made reference to Revelation 14:6-7. Let's take a look at it:

> 6And I saw another angel fly in the midst of heaven, having the everlasting gospel to preach unto them that dwell on the earth, and to every nation, and kindred, and tongue, and people.
> 7Saying with a loud voice, Fear God, and give glory to him; for the hour of his judgment is come: and worship him that made heaven, and earth, and the sea, and the fountains of waters.

Farrakhan says that neither the Bible nor the Koran is the everlasting gospel. He is right when he says this about the Koran but errs in saying this about the Bible. Verse 6 above tells us that the everlasting gospel will be preached to them that dwell on the earth. As pointed out by the scripture below, no other gospel should be preached other than that of the gospel of Jesus Christ. Let's look further:

> 1Paul, an apostle of Jesus Christ by the commandment of God our Saviour, and Lord Jesus Christ, which is our hope;
> 2Unto Timothy, my own son in the faith: Grace, mercy, and peace, from God our Father and Jesus Christ our Lord.

> [3]As I besought thee to abide still at Ephesus, when I went into Macedonia, that thou mightest charge some that they teach no other doctrine, (1Timothy 1:1-3)

When Paul wrote the letter to Timothy he realized that some Christians were lending an ear to a different doctrine other than that which was taught by Christ. Not only were some lending an ear, but many were teaching a different gospel. Paul clearly points out that there is no other gospel other than that of Jesus Christ. Let's look further:

> [7]Whereof I was made a minister, according to the gift of the grace of God given unto me by the effectual working of his power.
> [8]Unto me, who am less than the least of all saints, is this grace given, that I should preach among the gentiles the unsearchable riches of Christ;
> [9]And to make all men see what is the fellowship of the mystery, which from the beginning of the world hath been hid in God, who created all things by Jesus Christ:
> [10]To the intent that now unto the principalities and powers in heavenly places might be known by the church the manifold wisdom of God,
> [11]According to the eternal purpose which he purposed in Christ Jesus our Lord: (Ephesians 3:7-11)

Paul tells us that God commissioned him to be a minister of the gospel. Paul's duty was to preach the gospel according to God's eternal purpose which is manifested in Jesus Christ. If God's eternal purpose is manifested in Jesus Christ, then it stands to reason that the gospel of Christ is eternal. An eternal purpose coincides with an eternal gospel. Remember, John 1:1 tells us that "the Word was with God and the Word was God." John 1:14 goes on to say that "the Word became flesh." Therefore, we know that Jesus is God. He is the Word of God. God is eternal. Jesus is also eternal since he is God incarnate. He is part of the Godhead. He is Alpha and Omega and was with God in the beginning (John 1:2). So, if Jesus was the Word, and the Word was God, and God is eternal, then the Word (the everlasting gospel) is eternal.

Farrakhan goes on to use the following scripture in an effort to convince us that the Bible is not the eternal gospel:

> 9But as it is written, Eye hath not seen, nor ear heard, neither have entered into the heart of man, the things which God hath prepared for them that love him. (1 Corinthians 2:9)

If one looks at this scripture by itself, one might indeed conclude that the gospel of Christ is not eternal since the scripture does say that man has not heard or seen the things that God has prepared for him. We have certainly heard of Heaven, so what could this mean? Farrakhan neglects to continue quoting verses 10 through 16, which gives us a clearer understanding of what verse 9 means. Let's take a look:

> 10But God hath revealed them unto us by his Spirit: for the Spirit searcheth all things, yea, the deep things of God.
>
> 11For what man knoweth the things of a man, save the spirit of man which is in him? even so the things of God knoweth no man, but the spirit of God.
>
> 12Now we have received, not the spirit of the world, but the spirit which is of God; that we might know the things that are freely given to us of God.
>
> 13Which things also we speak, not in the words which man's wisdom teacheth, but which the Holy Ghost teacheth; comparing spiritual things with spiritual.
>
> 14But the natural man receiveth not the things of the Spirit of God: for they are foolishness unto him: neither can he know them, because they are spiritually discerned.
>
> 15But he that is spiritual judgeth all things, yet he himself is judged of no man.
>
> 16For who hath known the mind of the Lord, that he may instruct him? But we have the mind of Christ. (1 Corinthians 2:10-16)

God does not reveal his purpose to us by natural means but instead ultimately by spiritual means. The things that God has prepared for Christians are revealed to Christians by his spirit. This does not discredit the Bible because the second book of Timothy 3:16 tells us that scripture is given by inspiration of God. If it is inspired of God then it is spiritually inspired. As verse 16 implies: in order to understand God's purpose, we must have the mind of Christ. Verse 9 teaches us that God has prepared for those who love him, things that the eye has not seen, nor the ear heard, nor things that have entered into the heart of man. However, verse 10 clarifies that whatever these things are, they are revealed to us by the spirit of God, not by another gospel, as Farrakhan would have us to think.

There must be an everlasting gospel that will be preached on the other side of the destruction of this world. So a new book is coming!

Farrakhan says a new book (another gospel) is coming, thereby attempting to discredit the already existing one. However, the scriptures below speak against another gospel and tell us that those who purpose to preach another gospel other than the gospel of Christ, will be cursed.

> 6 I marvel that ye are so soon removed from him that called you into the grace of Christ unto another gospel:
> 7 Which is not another; but there be some that trouble you, and would pervert the gospel of Christ.
> 8 But though we, or an angel from heaven, preach any other gospel unto you than that which we have preached unto you, let him be accursed.
> 9 As we said before, so say I now again, If any man preach any other gospel unto you than that ye have received, let him be accursed. (Galatians 1:6-9)

Verse 7 tells us that those who preach another gospel, aside from the gospel of Christ, pervert the gospel of Christ by doing so. Farrakhan preaches another gospel and uses the Bible to do it, thereby perverting the gospel of Christ. Verse 8 and 9 informs us that anyone who perverts the gospel of Christ by teaching another gospel is cursed. This means that Farrakhan is cursed. The question then becomes: why would anyone want to follow someone who is cursed?

Now God has set down his decision. He intends to wipe out America.

There is nothing in the Bible to indicate this.

Now what is your position, black man, in the judgment? Whether you know it or not, you are the reason why God is judging America.

Farrakhan believes that God will judge America harshly for her historical mistreatment of black people. However, there is no biblical indication of this.

It is your [blacks] mistreatment at the hands of white people that has caused God to send down his judgment on America. Now you in your silliness are so forgiving, white folk ain't even asked for forgiveness. I want you to hear me. White folk haven't even acknowledged that they did you wrong. They have not repented for what they did to your fathers and what they're doing to you and what they plan against your future. But God knows their thoughts, their plans and because he knew them before they came into existence, he planned their destruction before they were born.

Farrakhan labels any black person as "silly" who has forgiven America for her discriminatory and racist practices over the years. Let's see what the Word of God says about forgiveness:

> 14For if ye forgive men their trespasses, your heavenly Father will also forgive you:
> 15But if ye forgive not men their trespasses, neither will your Father forgive your trespasses. (Matthew 6:14-15)

The Bible teaches us to forgive people regardless of whether or not they have repented of their sin against us. Granted, this is not an easy thing to do. However, it is not white people, per se, that black people should forgive but instead black people must learn to forgive the United States government. The fact that the government is run by white people and is responsible for allowing the mistreatment of blacks over the years, does not put white people at fault, but instead puts the government at fault for the injustices committed against blacks over the years. It was the American government that allowed slavery, that instilled Jim Crow laws, allowed lynchings to go unpunished, promoted segregation, and violated the human rights of blacks. There were many whites who fought against these atrocities. The Civil War is a clear example of this. Without the whites of the North who fought the whites of the south against slavery, American blacks may have well been enslaved far into the twentieth century. There are just as many white people who fought for civil rights as there are who fought against it.

Jesus taught that we must learn to forgive others of their transgressions against us if we expect God to forgive us of our transgressions against him. Granted, it is very difficult to forgive a group of people that have not asked for forgiveness. But often times, God forgives people who have not asked to be forgiven. He did so when he was on the cross and said "Father forgive them; for they know not what they do" (Luke 23:34). If we, who are Christians, strive to be more Christ-like, then that must include the ability to forgive, with or without an apology.

Farrakhan goes on to say that God planned the destruction of white people "before they were born." This is simply not biblical. The Bible shows us that God did indeed destroy nations of people that refused to acknowledge him as God (i.e. Hittites, Amalekites), but nowhere does it teach that God planned the destruction of white people before they were born. The book of Genesis gives account that God destroyed the entire world, except Noah and his family, because the world refused to live righteously and to acknowledge him as God. The Bible also tells us that God destroyed the cities of Sodom and Gomorrah because the people of those cities turned from him and lived unholy lives. However, God never destroyed a people because of the color of their skin. When Farrakhan says that God planned the destruction of white people before they were born, he is essentially saying that God planned their destruction because they are white. By saying these things, Farrakhan insults our intelligence when trying to convince us that his views of white people are not racist ones.

Black people in America, whether you want to believe it or not, are very special to the Lord of creation.

The Bible teaches us that the *Jews* are God's "special" people. Let's take a look:

> 6 For you are a holy people to the Lord your God. The Lord your God has chosen you out of all the peoples on the face of the earth to be his people, his treasured possession.

> 7 The Lord did not set his affection on you
> and choose you because you were more
> numerous than other peoples, for you were the
> fewest of all peoples. 8 But it was because the
> Lord loved you and kept the oath he swore to
> your forefathers that he brought you out with a
> mighty hand and redeemed you from the land
> of slavery, from the power of Pharaoh king of
> Egypt. 9 Know therefore that the Lord your God
> is God; he is the faithful God, keeping his
> covenant of love to a thousand generations of
> those who love him and keep his commands,
> 10 But
>
> Those who hate him he will repay to
> their face by destruction;
> He will not be slow to repay to their
> face those who hate him.
>
> 11 Therefore, take care to follow the commands,
> decrees and laws I give you today.
>
> 12 If you pay attention to these laws and are
> careful to follow them, then the Lord our God
> will keep his covenant of love with you, as he
> swore to your forefathers. (Deut 7:7-12)

Verse 6 says that the Jews (we know the scripture is talking about the Jews because verse 8 talks about them being delievered from Egypt) are God's people and that they are his treasured possession out of all the people on the face of the earth (verse 6). This makes them pretty special, don't you think? The Bible does not say this about blacks. However, as discussed in previous chapters, any person can become a Jew and be heir to the promise by confessing a belief in Jesus as Lord and Saviour and by believing in his resurrection. Blacks are no more special than any other "gentile" unless they confess Christ. Upon confessing Christ, they become just as special as any Jew. Again, the reason why the Jews are special is because they are the children of the promise (verse 8) that God made to Abraham. However, no Jew will enter the kingdom of heaven unless he believes in the deity of Christ.

Some might say that since God sees the Jews as special, then he is favoring one race over another. But we must remember that in God's eyes, the Jews are a *nation* of people, not a *race* of people and that their specialization has only to do with God's promise to them. There may be many black people who are of Jewish decent and not even know it.

Farrakhan is in competition with the Jews. It is disturbing to him that they are called God's chosen people. Because of this, Farrakhan tries desperately to discredit them and then sets out to convince everyone that black people are God's chosen.

For his purpose you have been chosen to be God's people to do a very special work for God. But you are all wrapped up in the people he came to destroy. You want to integrate with your enemy. You want to marry your enemy. You are in love with your enemy. So, if God sends down his judgment on the enemy that you are in love with, you say 'no God, I ain't going with you if I can't bring white folk with me.'

Farrakhan is clearly against interracial marriages. He is against integration of any kind among blacks and whites. This kind of thinking is unquestionably bigoted. God banned marriages between a believer and unbeliever when he instructed Christians as follows: "be ye not unequally yoked together with unbelievers" (2 Corinthians 6:14). However, there is no indication in the Bible that God had a problem with interracial marriages. Poor race relations between black and white America is a man made problem, not a God made problem.

Now, it's not an accident that in today's times your churches are being burned down. You want to call Farrakhan 'antichrist' but I'm not burning churches. I respect the church as a house of God.

During the time of this speech, black churches were being burned down in certain southern states. Although there is no indication that Farrakhan is burning down churches, he is definitely blaspheming God within them. Therefore, he is doing something even worse, since blasphemy against the Holy Ghost is the only sin that the Bible teaches is unforgivable (Matthew 12:31-32). Every time Farrakhan speaks against the deity of Christ and tries to discredit the Godhead of the trinity (Father, Son, Holy Ghost), he is blaspheming God.

And with the cross, they went into Europe, Africa, Asia, and they gave people religion [holds up the Bible] and took away the freedom, the justice, the equality, the raw materials of the darker people of the Earth.

Farrakhan is indirectly saying that the white man forced the religion of Christianity on the people of Europe, Africa, and Asia. However, Christianity really begins in the Old Testament with the occurrences of the Messianic prophecies. The law of Moses was a shadow of present-day Christianity. All of the teachings in the Bible come from the same God. So, to say that Christianity was brought to certain countries by white people, would be to deny that there were black "Christians" in the days of Moses and Jesus. With the current trend in the black community to prove that many of the historical biblical characters were people of color, Farrakhan puts himself in a strange dilemma by inferring that the white man brought in Christianity.

With the cross, they slaughtered the native people in the western hemisphere, murdered the Careb Indians, enslaved the blacks. In the name of Jesus you were heathens and unworthy to be looked upon as an equal to white people. So the church made you a nigger! Listen to me! not the church of Jesus Christ but a false church operating in Jesus' name. And every one of us that have believed in that false church are like people committing fornication with her. You're laying down with a whore and a whore is not teaching you good manners or good morals. You are a funky, filthy, lowdown people that have been made that way by your so-called Christian masters!

Farrakhan is crafty with his words. The false church that he believes is operating in Jesus' name is any church that does not state a belief in Fard Muhammad as God. However, he does not say this. Farrakhan is most influential at inciting blacks to feel harshly against whites when he says things similar to what he said in the above excerpt. It is true that white slave owners of America's antebellum southern history used the Bible to try to justify their mistreatment of blacks. However, this does not make the church of Jesus Christ a false church, but instead makes the doctrine of the cursed black, a false doctrine.

During the times Africans were enslaved in America, many whites misinterpreted what the scriptures teach concerning slavery thereby erroneously convincing other whites, and even some blacks, that the Bible teaches that blacks are cursed to be slaves. As discussed previously, the Bible doesn't teach this. However, the misinterpretation was the tool that was needed to decrease the probability of a slave revolt as well as ease the minds of the slave owners.

Contrary to what Farrakhan said, the church did not make black people "niggers." Instead, black people were considered to be such by many whites (church-goers included) who felt biblically justified in their bigotry and cruelty. Today, many bigoted whites try to justify their bigotry by misinterpreting and misrepresenting the scriptures. As a matter of fact, not only bigoted whites do this, but bigoted blacks do this as well: Farrakhan is a prime example. However, the Bible is not to blame for a person's misuse and interpretation of it. People who have racist views will always try to justify those views by implying that God condones them.

You're not out of this brothers. You're not out of this sisters. You're wrapped up in the white man and his aim is 'if I'm going down, you are the people of God alright, but I'm going to take you down with me!' That's his aim.

Any black person that does not share Farrakhan's racist views is categorized as a person who is "wrapped up in the white man." This is a great psychological ploy of his. Because of the mistreatment blacks have suffered in the hands of America over the years, very few black people would welcome a description of this kind. In the American black community, a black person "wrapped up in the white man" is considered as a black person who does not understand or care about the racial injustices imposed upon blacks over the years. Therefore, to say this to a black person is demeaning and insulting, and Farrakhan knows this. Consequently, many blacks are influenced by Farrakhan's public reprimand of blacks who do not agree with his way of thinking. Thus, they are emotionally and psychologically blackmailed or duped into lending an ear to his rhetoric.

Look at the warner [one who warns] that comes to the Babylon. What is the word? Come out of her my people that you be not partaker of her sins and of her plagues. For her sins have reached unto heaven. Don't integrate in her. Come out! Come out! Come out of her way of thinking. Come out of her name. Come out of her false worship!

The Koran describes Muhammad as a "warner." The "warner" that Farrakhan is speaking of in the above excerpt is himself. He fancies himself as one who is giving a warning to the black people of America. He is telling black people to leave America before it is destroyed. He likens America to the evil ancient city of Babylon. The people of that city denied God. Therefore, God instructed the Jews not to integrate with them. God gave these instructions because of the Babylonians unbelief, not because of their race.

America defines itself as a Christian nation. This does not mean it is perfect. Farrakhan sees Christianity as the white man's religion and the Nation of Islam as the black man's religion. It therefore makes sense that he would see American as a sort of Babylon. Since America defines itself as a Christian nation, and to be a Christian means to follow Christ; Farrakhan believes that Americans are worshiping a false God. He therefore compares America to ancient Babylon. However, the comparison is an incorrect one because the Babylonians *were* worshipping false gods. If America were an Islamic country instead of a Christian one, Farrakhan would not compare it to ancient Babylon.

Farrakhan believes that black people should live in a separate society from white people. This is what he means when he instructs black people to "come out of her." He also means that blacks should come out of or come away from a Christian way of thinking and begin to think as a Muslim thinks.

You see, the Caucasian was given six days, so when Moses came, he gave them a reminder of their doom. He said, 'now six days you do your work but in the seventh day you rest. That is a holy day that must be consecrated to God.'

Farrakhan is actually saying that God instituted the sabbath as a reminder to white people of what he says is their impending doom. Where does he get this stuff? There is no biblical indication that this is the case. Instead, the Israelites were commanded to rest on the sabbath day as a way to give honor to God. God worked six days to create the heavens and the earth. He rested on the seventh day. Therefore, he also established a seventh day of rest for his people.

A day with the Lord is as a thousand years. So, what God was giving them through Moses was this: You've got six thousand years, white folks, to raise hell on this earth. But in the seven thousandth year, and this is why you have a group of people called the Seventh Day Adventist who believe that God would come in the seventh day or the seven thousandth year from Adam. So, now what you call the day, the sabbath, is really a thousand year period where the whole earth would be cleansed from the work of Satan. And it starts on the coming of the Mahdi and the messiah or God's presence in the world then that millenium begins, that sabbath begins. So you're being called now to come out of the six day work of the enemy.

This is heresy. Farrakhan is fixated on six thousand years. He feels that the white man's time is up. Farrakhan says that during the seven thousandth year (which he says is upon us) the black man will reign. Farrakhan believes we are in the seven thousandth year which he says began in 1930 when Fard (the “Mahdi”) first appeared. Farrakhan believes that during this thousand year period (from 1930 to 2930, by his calculation) black people will rest from the work of “the enemy.”

<u>Mosque Maryam</u>

We already know, from previous discussion, that Farrakhan believes that white people are the enemy.

And then in Mark it says: the sabbath was made for man and not man for the sabbath. The seventh day was made for you, the original man, to clean up, to get up from the dust of the white man's world!

When speaking of the "original man," Farrakhan is referring to black people. By saying that the sabbath day was made for the original man, Farrakhan is again implying that God made the sabbath day for the black man. Let's take a look at what the scriptures have to say:

> 27And he said unto them, The sabbath was made for man, and not man for the sabbath: (Mark 2:27)

Once again, Farrakhan misinterprets the scripture. He is correct when he says that the sabbath was made for man, but wrong to imply that it was made for the black man in order that he may get away from the white man's world. The sabbath day was made for any man who confesses a belief in Jesus Christ, regardless of the color of his skin. The sabbath was a day of rest. Therefore, rest was made for mankind. God realizes how important it is for the human race to rest and, as the following scripture shows us, he has a certain rest that is available for us to enter into.

> 9There remaineth therefore a rest to the people of God.
> 10For he that is entered into his rest, he also hath ceased from his own works, as God did from his.
> 11Let us labour therefore to enter into that rest, lest any man fall after the same example of unbelief.
> 12For the word of God is quick, and powerful, and sharper than any two edged sword, piercing even to the dividing asunder of soul and spirit, and of the joints and marrow, and is a discerner of the thoughts and intents of the heart. (Hebrews 4:9-12)

The kind of rest that is spoken of above, goes beyond a sabbath day rest. Instead, the scriptures are speaking of a spiritual rest that is provided for the people of God. In other words, because of the rest God gives them, God's people are given a certain amount of peace despite their troubles in life. Verse 9 specifically states that rest was made for the people of God. However, Farrakhan says that God's rest was made for the black man to get away from the white man. As shown, the scriptures do not say this. God's rest is for any man who is a believer in Jesus Christ.

This is the day that was made to get you up. But the white man is not--he's not made for this day. This is the day that he rests! He is to die! And the only way he can escape it is if he's born again! And I don't mean going back into the womb of black people but his mind has to be destroyed and a new mind be put in him. Otherwise, otherwise all of them are sentenced to death, every white man on earth!

Farrakhan believes that the only way the white man can escape death is to be born again. It is true that we must be born again in order not to experience a spiritual death. However, Farrakhan's concept of what it means to be born again differs radically from the Bible's teaching on what it means. Remember, Farrakhan does not believe in the resurrection of Jesus Christ but instead talks about the resurrection of the black man's mind. Farrakhan believes that part of that resurrection includes separation from white people. Farrakhan does not make clear what kind of new mind the white man would have to have in order to be considered born again. According to the Word of God, when a person confesses a belief in Jesus Christ, he is then born again, because he has put away his old life and has begun a new one in Jesus, as the following scripture tells us:

> 17Therefore if any man be in Christ, he is a new creature: old things are passed away; behold, all things are become new.
> (2 Corinthians 5:17)

Jesus' explanation of what it means to be born again is found in the book of St. John, among others:

> 3Jesus answered and said unto him, Verily, verily I say unto thee, Except a man be born again, he cannot see the kingdom of God.
> 4Nicodemus saith unto him, How can a man be born when he is old? can he enter the

> second time into his mother's womb, and be born?
>
> [5]Jesus answered, Verily verily, I say unto thee, Except a man be born of water and of the Spirit, he cannot enter into the kingdom of God.
>
> [6]That which is born of the flesh is flesh; and that which is born of the Spirit is spirit.
>
> [7]Marvel not that I said unto thee, Ye must be born again. (John 3:3-7)

As we can see, Jesus' definition of being born again has nothing to do with the renewing of the white man's mind but instead deals with the renewing of one's spirit. Farrakhan has perverted the meaning of what it means to be born again. In speaking with Nicodemus, Jesus explained that one must be born of water and the spirit in order to be born again. In order to be born of the spirit a person must believe in the resurrection and Lordship of Jesus Christ. However, being born again is a two-fold process: being born of water as well as the spirit. The word "water" in the scripture is used symbolically when speaking of the baptism of the Holy Ghost, as the following scripture reference attests to:

> [37]In the last day, that great day of the feast, Jesus stood and cried, saying, If any man thirst, let him come unto me, and drink.
>
> [38]He that believeth on me, as the scripture hath said, out of his belly shall flow rivers of living water.
>
> [39](But this spake he of the Spirit, which they that believe on him should receive: for the Holy Ghost was not yet given; because that Jesus was not yet glorified.) John 7:37-39

Jesus was glorified on the day of his resurrection. Many of those who had been saved before the resurrection had not yet received the spirit of God even though their salvation was sure. However, after Jesus ascended into heaven following his resurrection from the grave, the Holy Ghost (the spirit of God) was then given to those who were saved, just as it is today. To distort the meaning of what it means to be born again, as Farrakhan has done, is grievous to God.

They're all under the death sentence and you are under that sentence too. Because you've become just like them. You're just

a black-white man. Did you hear what I said?! You ain't no black man! You're a white man in black skin because your mind has been so destroyed! The mark of the beast is in your forehead! You think like the white man!

Once again, Farrakhan, by coining the term "black-white man," demeans any black person who would dare to embrace a white person. Farrakhan tells his audience that blacks who integrate with whites in any way are sentenced to death. Farrakhan believes, just by virtue of them being white, that white people have the mark of the beast. He even goes so far as to say that blacks who "think like the white man" (integrate with whites) have the mark of the beast. This is clearly racist thinking and racist theology, but God is not a racist and therefore, Christians can not justifiably support a man like Farrakhan, who apparently is. White people don't have the mark of the beast. As a matter of fact, no-one has the mark of the beast, yet.

The Messenger said the Islamic world will be the ruler. We are the people to rule in the next world and that's why they are so afraid of Islam.

This is an absolute lie. As we have seen, the book of Revelation speaks of a new Jerusalem whose King will be Jesus Christ. This new Jerusalem represents this "next world" that Farrakhan is referring to. Christianity represents Jesus Christ. Jesus will rule the next world. He is not a Muslim. Therefore, the next world will not be ruled by the "Islamic world."

Jesus was a Muslim. Moses and the prophets were Muslims.

The trick here is that Muslims will say that the word "Muslim" means to submit to God. They will then say that everyone who submits to God is therefore a Muslim. They will then tell Christians that they (Christians) are really Muslims because Christians submit to God and that's what the word "Muslim" means: to submit. This is all a play on words; a clever game with semantics. First of all, there is more meaning to the word "Muslim" than just to submit to God. The word Muslim automatically identifies the person describing themselves as such, with Islam. Furthermore, Muslims don't believe in the same God that Christians believe in. The god that Muslims submit to is Allah; a false god. Christians don't submit to Allah. Christians submit to Yahweh; the one and only true God. Muslims don't submit to Yahweh. So when Muslims say that the word "Muslim" means to submit to God: what God are they talking about? Allah of course. Well then, Christians certainly can't be referred to as Muslims because Christians do no submit to Allah. Jesus certainly can't be referred to as a Muslim because he did not submit to Allah. Moses and the Prophets can not be referred to as Muslims because they did not submit to Allah. Don't be deceived.

Moreover, Muslims do not believe in the resurrection of Jesus Christ. To say that Jesus was a Muslim is to say that Jesus did not believe in his own resurrection. Furthermore, Muhammad did not establish the Islamic religion until six hundred years after the death and resurrection of Jesus Christ and not until approximately sixteen hundred years after the death of Moses. Therefore, logistically speaking, neither Jesus nor Moses could have been a Muslim. Farrakhan goes beyond the ridiculous in his attempt to convince black people of his belief that Islam is the religion of the black man.

There are white people who know that the end is in sight and all they want to know is can they be saved. Now I'ma tell you something sisters: that's why white men are hitting on you so tough.

Farrakhan is actually implying that the only way whites can be saved is to become sexual intimate with black women. This indicates that Farrakhan believes that blacks are superior to whites, much like the Mormons and the Ku Klux Klan believe that whites are superior to blacks.

You know what they want [white men from black women]? They want to get you pregnant so that their seed will see the hereafter. And you're walking around carrying white men's babies and you don't even know that they say 'Ah, I made it in the hereafter. I know my time is up but I mixed my blood with hers and I'll make it in the hereafter. Dumb woman.

There is nothing in the Bible that bases a white man's salvation on whether or not he impregnates a black woman. This kind of ungodly thinking comes from Farrakhan, the Nation of Islam, and the early teachings of Elijah Muhammad.

The honorable Elijah Muhammad told us of a great mother ship that is made like the universe: a sphere and spheres within spheres. The white folk call them unidentified flying objects. They're coming out with a movie to let you know that's about to come down. But he put it in film and I said I'm not going to let him [white people] give you a false version. I'm going to tell you what the real deal is so you won't be tricked.

It has been said that Farrakhan believes that Elijah Muhammad is on a space ship circling the earth.

They saw UFO lights. Now in the book of Ezekiel it talks about the different colors, the amber, the red. The different colors that the lights would be on the wheel.

The "they" that Farrakhan is referring to are pilots who he allegedly says saw an unidentified flying object fitting the above description. The scripture reference that Farrakhan is speaking of in the book of Ezekiel is cited below:

> 3The word of the Lord came expressly unto Ezekiel the priest, the son of Buzi, in the land of the Chaldeans by the river Chebar; and the hand of the Lord was there upon him.
> 4And I looked, and, behold, a whirlwind came out of the north, a great cloud, and a fire infolding itself, and a brightness was about it, and out of the midst thereof as the colour of amber, out of the midst of the fire.
> 5 Also out of the midst thereof came the likeness of four living creatures. And this was their appearance; they had the likeness of a man.
> 6 And every one had four faces, and every one had four wings. (Ezekiel 1:3-6)

The four living creatures represent angels in the order of Cheribims. There are different orders of angels. The Bible teaches us that the Cheribim angels are assigned to cover the throne and glory of God. Let's look further:

> 15Now as I beheld the living creatures, behold one wheel upon the earth by the living creatures, with his four faces.
> 16The appearance of the wheels and their work was like unto the colour of a beryl: and they four had one likeness: and their appearance and their work was as it were a wheel in the middle of a wheel.
> (Ezekiel 1:15-16)

> 25 And there was a voice from the firmament that was over their heads, when they stood, and had let down their wings.
>
> 26 And above the firmament that was over their heads was the likeness of a throne, as the appearance of a sapphire stone: and upon the likeness of the throne was the likeness as the appearance of a man above upon it.
>
> 27 And I saw as the colour of amber, as the appearance of fire round about within it, from the appearance of his loins even upward, and from the appearance of his loins even downward, I saw as it were the appearance of fire, and it had brightness round about.
>
> 28 As the appearance of the bow that is in the cloud in the day of rain, so was the appearance of the brightness round about. This was the appearance of the likeness of the glory of the Lord. And when I saw it, I fell upon my face, and I heard a voice of one that spake. (Ezekiel 1:25-28)

The appearance of a man in verse 26 refers to the appearance of the likeness of the glory of the Lord in verse 28. This is the lamb of God (Jesus Christ). Ezekiel's vision has nothing to do with Elijah Muhammad and the wheels do not describe a UFO. Instead, the wheels are a symbolic indication of God's throne. Ezekiel was given visions from God in order that he may prophecy to Israel who had, as a nation, turned against God at that time.

There will be three hard years, believers, that we will have to endure. But one year will be harder than all the rest. And the Bible says if those days were not shortened for God's elect sake, not one soul would be left alive on the earth.

According to the books of Daniel and Revelation, the antichrist will enter the temple in Jerusalem and reign for seven years. During his reign, no-one will be able to buy or sell without his mark (666) upon their hands or foreheads (probably some kind of computer chip devise). This has been tagged by Christians as the seven year tribulation. After the first three and a half years of his reign, the antichrist will claim to be God. Let's take a look:

> [36]The king will do as he pleases. He will exalt and magnify himself above every god and will say unheard-of things against the God of gods. He will be successful until the time of wrath is completed, for what has been determined must take place. [37]He will show no regard for the gods of his fathers or for the one desired by women, nor will he regard any god, but will exalt himself above them all.
> [38]Instead of them, he will honor a god of fortresses: a god unknown to his fathers he will honor with gold and silver, with precious stones and costly gifts. He will attack the mightiest fortresses with the help of a foreign god and will greatly honor those who acknowledge him. He will make them rulers over many people and will distribute the land at a price. (Daniel 11:36-39)

The "king" that the above scripture is referring to is the antichrist. Remember, the book of Revelation tells us of a man whose number is 666 and that without this number no one will be able to buy or sell. This "king" and the man whose number is 666 are the same person. The antichrist will exalt himself above the God of gods. The God of gods is Yahweh (Jehovah) spoken of in the Old Testament, which is the same God as the Father, Son, and Holy Ghost spoken of in the New. Remember, false gods are indicated in the Bible by using the lower case "g" for the spelling of God. Therefore any god that the antichrist honors will be a false god. The scripture reference is focusing on the fact that this "king" will think of himself as God and will convince most of the world of the same.

As we have seen before, the book of Revelation tells us that the antichrist will be able to deceive people with his ability to do the miraculous (Revelation 13:14) and that he will direct the people of the earth to make an image of him in order that they may worship his image (Revelation 13:15). Not only this, but the Bible tells us that the antichrist will have the ability to make this image come to life.

During the antichrist's reign, he will make a covenant with the people of the earth. The people will bring sacrifices and offerings unto him. In the beginning, everything will go smoothly until he claims to be God. Then, those who do not accept him as God will be beheaded. the Bible calls this: the abomination of desolation. Let's take a look:

> [9]He will confirm a covenant with many for one 'seven.' In the middle of the 'seven' he will put an end to sacrifice and offering. And on a wing of the temple, he will set up an abomination that causes desolation, until the end that is decreed is poured out on him. (Daniel 9:27)

The end that is decreed upon the antichrist is the one in which he is defeated by the Son of Man (Jesus) and the saints during the war of Armageddon which comes after the seven years. Bible scholars have assessed that the "one seven" the above scripture refers to is symbolic of seven years. Three and a half years is the middle of seven years. Remember, during these seven years of tribulation, believers in Jesus Christ will have to go underground since they will not be able to take the mark of the beast. Consequently if these days were not shortened for the sake of the saints (believers) no one would be left alive on the earth after it was all over.

In the last excerpt we looked at, Farrakhan spoke of this time of tribulation. However, the "believers" that he speaks of are not those who believe in the gospel of Christ but instead, those who believe in the false doctrine of Elijah Muhammad. The Bible does not recognize Fard Muhammad as God. When the Bible talks about believers, it is always referring to those who believe in Jesus Christ. There is no exception to this. The Bible is very clear: those who do not believe in the deity and Lordship of Jesus Christ live the eternity of their afterlives in hell. They will be there along with the antichrist, Satan, and his demons.

The enemy is so angry with God over his growing loss of prestige and power that he's determined to take every one of us down with him. He set the white male on you [points to the black women in the audience]. He set the white female on you [points to the black men in the audience]. He knew that God wanted you to separate and out of his rebelliousness he said 'let's force integration.'

Farrakhan is referring to white people as the enemy. There is no biblical indication that God wants white people to be separated from black people. The Word of God does not command any race to separate from another race.

Farrakhan blames white people for integration of the races by saying it was forced. However, blacks and whites alike had a hand in American integration between the races. Furthermore, integration is a good thing, not a bad thing. It is a good thing to be at peace with and get along with one's neighbors. Jesus instructed us to love our neighbors as we would love ourselves (Mark 12:30-31). Since white people and black people live in the same country (America) they are neighbors to one another. Segregation can not be a part of the formula that says love thy neighbor, because two neighbors who separate from one another are no longer neighbors. Therefore, if one is to love his neighbor he must integrate with him, not separate from him. Racial integration is not biblical.

Brothers, leave the white woman alone.

Farrakhan says things like this and then wants people to believe he is not a racist. There is nothing wrong with interracial marriages. Nowhere in the pages of the Bible is interracial marriage condemned.

Let's calculate some time on the last six. Since Master Fard Muhammad came in 1930, sixty years from 1930 is 1990. Right? If it's not to exceed ten years then the year 2000 would be the end. So if you calculate from the time of Master Fard's coming, you don't have but five more years of grace. But I think the time begins from the time he establishes his servant, the Honorable Elijah Muhammad. If that is true you got four more years....you got eight years to make up your mind.

Farrakhan delivered this speech in 1996. Despite the preposterousness of it all, he miscalculates his own formula. 1996 to the year 2000 is four years, not five. At first Farrakhan takes his calculations from the time Fard Muhammad appeared, then he takes his calculation from the time Elijah Muhammad paired with Fard. Which is it? It is neither. Farrakhan is essentially telling black people that they only have eight years to decide whether or not to become a Muslim. Farrakhan believes that by the year 2004 America will be destroyed and that those blacks who do not separate themselves from white people before then, will be destroyed along with the white man. We will see that in the year 2000 as well as the year 2004, there will be plenty of white people living in America and America will not have been destroyed.

I'm not asking you if you want to join me. You can if you want to. But if you're in the church you better make the church right cause judgement is going to begin at the so-called house of God.

Farrakhan denies the deity of Christ and makes overt racist statements. He is therefore not in a position to criticize the church.

Farrakhan tries to clean things up a bit. He has already illustrated to us in this speech and in others that he is indeed asking blacks to join him, but he wants us to believe that he's not.

Notice that Farrakhan calls the church "the so-called" house of God. By using this adjective, he is indicating that he does not believe that the church is the actual house of God. Instead, he believes that the Mosque is the House of God and he wants every black person in America to believe the same thing.

I was told I had one more thing to do and then I could come to the wheel again.

Farrakhan did not specify what he meant by this. However, it appears Farrakhan believes that Elijah Muhammad is flying around in space somewhere inside of a wheel and that he has the ability to join him.

If I go, will I see you again? And the book says they saw him going away in a cloud and he returned in like manner in the clouds of heaven having great power. It means he went in a plane that looked like a cloud and he returned in like manner. But I can guarantee you this: that the power of America has to be broken before God will reveal any new world to you lest he would use it to stay here a little longer.

Once again Farrakhan is attributing a Messianic Biblical prophecy to himself. The book of Matthew quotes Jesus as saying that after the seven year tribulation, he, along with his angels, shall come through the clouds to gather his elect. Let's take a look:

> 29 Immediately after the tribulation of those days shall the sun be darkened, and the moon shall not give her light, and the stars shall fall from heaven, and the powers of the heavens shall be shaken:
>
> 3 And then shall appear the sign of the Son of man in heaven: and then shall all the tribes of the earth mourn, and they shall see the Son of man coming in the clouds of heaven with power and great glory.
>
> 31 And he shall send his angels with a great sound of a trumpet, and they shall gather together his elect from the four winds, from

one end of heaven to the other. (Matthew 24:29-31)

The Son of man that the scripture is referring to is Jesus Christ. This fact is confirmed in the following scripture reference:

> 13I saw in the night visions, and, behold, one like the Son of man came with the clouds of heaven, and came to the Ancient of days, and they brought him near before him.
> 14And there was given him dominion, and glory, and a kingdom, that all people, nations, and languages, should serve him: his dominion is an everlasting dominion, which shall not pass away, and his kingdom that which shall not be destroyed. (Daniel 7:13-14)

As previously discussed, we know that Jesus Christ is the one who will have everlasting dominion over all of the earth. "Ancient of days" is a phrase found in the seventh chapter of Daniel that describes God as everlasting.

It is clear from the scriptures quoted, that Jesus Christ will literally return through the clouds at his second coming. The scriptures also tell us that after Jesus' post resurrection ministry, he ascended into heaven in a cloud. Let's take a look:

> 6When they therefore were come together, they asked of him, saying, Lord, wilt thou at his time restore again the kingdom to Israel?
> 7And he said unto them, it is not for you to know the times or the seasons, which the Father hath put in his own power.
> 8But ye shall receive power, after that the Holy Ghost is come upon you: and ye shall be witnesses unto me both in Jerusalem, and in all Judaea, and in Samaria, and unto the uttermost part of the earth.
> 9And when he had spoken these things, while they beheld, he was taken up; and a cloud received him out of their sight.
> 10And while they looked stedfastly toward heaven as he went up, behold, two men stood by them in white apparel;

> [11]Which also said, ye men of Galilee, why stand ye gazing up into heaven? this same Jesus, which is taken up from you into heaven, shall so come in like manner as ye have seen him go into heaven. (Acts 1:6-11)

The book of Acts tells us that Jesus continued to give commandments to the apostles forty days after his resurrection and before his ascension into heaven. The above scripture reference gives indication that Jesus was taken up into a cloud. However, Farrakhan says "he went in a plane that looked like a cloud and he returned in like manner." With subtle implication, the "he" that Farrakhan is referring to is not Jesus Christ, but himself. Farrakhan traveled to Libya in a plane and returned in a plane.

In the preceding excerpt of his speech, Farrakhan says that the cloud was a plane. He has to say this if he wants people to see him as the Messiah. However, Farrakhan has not been lifted up in a cloud into heaven at any time in his life. Furthermore, there were no planes in the days of Jesus. Orville and Wilbur Wright had not yet been born. How then could the ascension cloud spoken of in the book of Acts be a plane? Maybe Farrakhan meant that the cloud was symbolic of a plane. However, the scripture unquestionably indicates that the cloud is literal, both in the event of Jesus' ascension to heaven, as well as in the event of his second coming, which makes Farrakhan's attempt to liken himself to Jesus, futile.

SUMMING UP THE MATTER

Farrakhan's speech at Mosque Maryam can be described as a sequel to his Saviour's Day speech: both speeches expose the real Farrakhan, no smoke screens. At his Saviour's Day speech, Farrakhan confirmed that he believes Fard is God and that the Nation of Islam is the religion for the black man. At Mosque Maryam, Farrakhan alludes to his belief that white people are demons by teaching that white people are unnatural, inferior, doomed, and have the mark of the beast. Instead of applying St. John's visions (cited in the book of Revelation) to the second coming of Christ and the limited future reign of the antichrist, Farrakhan clouds his interpretation of Revelation with racial overtones.

When considering all that has been discussed, a determination must be made as to whether or not Farrakhan is the messenger of God that he claims to be. The following chapter addresses this issue.

CHAPTER SEVEN

FARRAKHAN: CALLED OF GOD OR GUIDED BY SATAN

Farrakhan consistently claims that God is directing his path. However, the god he speaks of is Allah, not the Jehovah God (Yahweh) whom the Bible speaks of. This chapter will give the answers to the following four concerns: Whether or not Farrakhan is a child of God, whether or not Farrakhan is an antichrist, whether or not Farrakhan is a false prophet, and whether or not Farrakhan is a racist. Although some of these concerns have been addressed in previous chapters, the upcoming discussion is specifically targeted to investigate the answers to these questions in detail.

Much of this book has been devoted to identifying who God is. However, a discussion on who Satan is has not yet been presented. Since the ultimate question this chapter deals with is whether or not Farrakhan is called of God or guided by Satan, our discussions in this chapter will begin with an expose on Satan.

Who is Satan?

Before his fall, Satan was a beautiful and anointed cherub angel whose assignment was to cover the throne of God. At first, he was perfect, until he decided to commit sin. Let's take a look:

> 13Thou has been in Eden the garden of God; every precious stone was thy covering, the sardius, topaz, and the diamond, the beryl, the onyx, and the jasper, the sapphire, the emerald, and the carbuncle, and gold: the workmanship of thy tabrets and of thy pipes was prepared in thee in the day that thou wast created.
>
> 14Thou art the anointed cherub that covereth: and I have set thee so: thou wast upon the holy mountain of God; thou hast walked up and down in the midst of the stones of fire.

> [15]Thou was perfect in thy ways from the day that thou wast created, till iniquity was found in thee.
> [16]By the multitude of thy merchandise thy have filled the midst of thee with violence, and thou hast sinned: therefore I will cast thee as profane out of the mountain of God: and I will destroy thee, O covering cherub, from the midst of the stones of fire.
> [17]Thine heart was lifted up because of thy beauty, thou hast corrupted thy wisdom by reason of thy brightness: I will cast thee to the ground, I will lay thee before kings, that they may behold thee. (Ezekiel 28:13-17)

Most Christian religious scholars agree that the above scriptures are referring to Satan. Before Satan lost favor with God, his name was Lucifer, meaning: "Son of the Morning." His purpose was to cover and guard the throne of God. He is depicted as beautiful with precious stones inundated within his body or attire. Verse 16 tells us that God cast Satan from heaven because sin was found in him. Verse 17 tells us that Satan became conceited because of his beauty and began to think too much of himself, which led to his downfall. The following reference explains this further:

> [12]How art thou fallen from heaven, O Lucifer, son of the morning! how art thou cut down to the ground, which didst weaken the nations!
> [13]For thou hast said in thine heart, I will ascend into heaven, I will exalt my throne above the stars of God: I will sit also upon the mount of the congregation, in the sides of the north:
> [14]I will ascend above the heights of the clouds; I will be like the most High.
> [15]Yet thou shalt be brought down to hell, to the sides of the pit. (Isaiah 14:12-15)

Lucifer (Satan) wanted to be like God and therefore set out to overthrow God. However, God, who is all-powerful, cast Lucifer from heaven to earth as punishment for his revolt against him. This account is given in the following scripture reference:

[7]And there was war in heaven. Michael
and his angels fought against the dragon, and
the dragon and his angels fought back. [8]But
he was not strong enough, and they lost their
place in heaven. [9]The great dragon was
hurled down--that ancient serpent called the
devil, or Satan, who leads the whole world
astray. He was hurled to the earth, and his
angels with him.
[10]Then I heard a loud voice in heaven say:

"Now have come the salvation and the
power and the kingdom of our God,
and the authority of his Christ.
For the accuser of our brothers,
who accuses them before our God day
and night,
has been hurled down.
[11]They overcame him
by the blood of the lamb
and by the word of their testimony;
they did not love their lives so much
as to shrink from death.
[12]Therefore rejoice, you heavens
and you who dwell in them!
But woe to the earth and the sea,
because the devil has gone down to
you!
He is filled with fury,
because he knows that his time is
short. (Revelation 12: 7-12)

When Satan (the dragon) revolted against God, there was a war in heaven. Michael (the archangel) and his angels fought against Satan and his angels. Verse 9 above, tells us that Satan lost the battle and was hurled down to earth along with his angels. Satan's angels are those who joined him in his revolt against God. In regards to the dragon, Revelation 12:4 tells us that "his tail drew the third part of the stars of heaven, and did cast them to the earth." Theologians believe that "the third part of the stars" represents a third of the angels of heaven that joined the ranks of Satan. The Bible refers to these angels as demons. It is believed that this great war in heaven took place before the creation of man. When Lucifer decided to fight against God, God no longer called him Lucifer, but called him Satan instead.

Called of God?

The old saying, "misery loves company" greatly applies when we look at the plight of Satan. God's final judgment of Satan is near. Consequently, Satan is going to take as many as he can down with him. The word for "adversary" in the Greek is "Satan." 1st Peter 5:8 tells us that Satan walks around "seeking whom he may devour." Verse 10 of Revelation 12:7-12 above, reveals Satan's hatred for Christians. He accuses them before God day and night. However, verse 11 informs us that those who are Christians have overcome Satan by the blood of the Lamb (Jesus).

It was Satan who introduced sin into the world by lying to Eve and tempting her to sin. Genesis 3:3 tells us that Satan persuaded Eve to eat of the forbidden fruit by convincing her that in doing so, she and Adam would become like gods. Adam and Even did eat of the fruit, but did not become gods. Instead, they were punished by God for doing what he told them not to do. It was also Satan who entered into Judas Iscariot, the man who betrayed Jesus for thirty pieces of silver, and it will be Satan who possesses the antichrist King of times to come (discussed in the previous chapter).

The Bible tells us that Satan, in his quest to persecute people, specifically targets the Jews. Let's take a look:

> 3And there appeared another wonder in heaven; and behold a great red dragon, having seven heads and ten horns, and seven crowns upon his heads.
>
> 4And his tail drew the third part of the stars of heaven, and did cast them to the earth; and the dragon stood before the woman which was ready to be delivered, for to devour her child as soon as it was born.
>
> 5And she brought forth a man child, who was to rule all nations with a rod of iron: and her child was caught up unto God, and to his throne. (Revelation 12:3-5)

The child that the scripture is referring to is Jesus Christ. Jesus is the only one that has been caught up unto God. After his resurrection, he ascended into heaven to be seated at the right hand side of God. The woman that the scripture refers to is Israel. Jesus comes from the line of Israel. He is a Jew. Let's look further:

> 13And when the dragon saw that he was cast unto the earth, he persecuted the woman

> which brought forth the man child. (Revelation 12:13)

Satan is mad at Israel because she gave birth to Jesus and he often persecutes the Jews because of this. The "woman" is symbolic of Israel. To persecute someone is to unjustly and abusively harass them. Farrakhan persecutes the Jews by slandering them. It is with the influence of Satan that he does this.

Is Farrakhan a child of God?

In Farrakhan's eyes, there are only two types of people: white and non-white. In God's eyes there are also only two types of people, but there is a difference in the types: believers and non-believers. The Bible tells us that true believers in Christ are the children of God, whereas those who do not believe in Christ are children of the devil. Let's examine this more closely:

> 5But you know that he appeared so that he
> might take away our sins. And in him is no
> sin. 6No one who lives in him keeps on
> sinning. No one who continues to sin has
> either seen him or known him.
> 7Dear children, do not let anyone lead you
> astray. He who does what is right is righteous,
> just as he is righteous. 8He who does what is
> sinful is of the devil, because the devil has
> been sinning from the beginning. The reason
> the Son of God appeared was to destroy the
> devil's work. 9No one who is born of God will
> continue to sin, because God's seed remains
> in him; he cannot go on sinning, because he
> has been born of God. 1This is how we know
> who the children of God are and who the
> children of the devil are: Anyone who does
> not do what is right is not a child of God; nor
> is anyone who does not love his brother. (1
> John 3:5-10)

Verse 5 is referring to Jesus when speaking of "he" who appeared unto man to take away our sins. We know the scripture is referring to Jesus because there is no other person the Bible refers to as being able to take away sins aside from him.

Called of God?

Verse 6 tells us that anyone who "lives in" Jesus Christ does not keep on sinning, which means that those who confess Christ and live by his word do not sin. However, this is not to say that Christians *never* sin. Instead, it means that Christians do not purpose to practice sin without remorse: they can't just "go on sinning" as verse 9 says, because they will feel convicted to stop. If a Christian sins, he repents of that sin and asks God to deliver him from the urge to commit that particular sin again. People who "keep on sinning" do not do this. They, without conscious, continue to sin. The verse goes on to say that those who continue to sin (who practice sin) do not know Jesus. Let's look a little further into this:

> [2]He that saith, I know him and keepeth not his commandments, is a liar, and the truth is not in him.
> [3]But whoso keepeth his word, in him verily is the love of God perfected: hereby know we that we are in him.
> [4]He that saith he abideth in him ought himself also so to walk, even as he walked. (1 John 2:4-6)

The scriptures tell us that a person who says he knows Jesus and does not keep his commandments is a liar. Verse 3 teaches us that part of abiding by the commandments of God is obeying (keeping) the Word of God. However, Farrakhan perverts the Word of God thereby denying it. One doesn't keep something he denies. Farrakhan does not abide in the Word of God and consequently does not keep the commandments of God. By denying the Word of God and his commandments, Farrakhan, according to scripture, is a liar. Furthermore, as we have seen, Jesus is God. However, Farrakhan denies him as being God. Those who are of God do not deny him.

In Mark 12:29-31 we find Jesus saying that the greatest commandment is that we should love the Lord thy God with all our heart, mind, soul, and strength and that the second greatest commandment is that we should love our neighbors as we love ourselves. As discussed in Chapter Six, neighbors are people who we co-exist with. Therefore, white people are neighbors to black people just as much as black people are neighbors to white people. Farrakhan views white people as doomed demons. Therefore, it is safe to say that he doesn't love them. By not loving them, he is breaking the second greatest commandment given by God. Consequently, he is not keeping a commandment of God. Again, those who do not keep the commandments of God are liars and do not know God. Those who do not know God are not children of God.

Verse 7 and 8 (1John 3:5-10) informs us that those who do what is right are righteous and are of God, and those who sin are of the devil. In the previous chapter we learned that Noah was a righteous man because he acknowledged God and followed his ways. We have deducted that Farrakhan is a liar because he denies Jesus. If he is a liar, then he can not be righteous. If he is not righteous, then he can not be a child of God.

Verse 10 (1John 3:5-10) tells us that there are children of God and children of the devil. Verse 9 tells us that those who continue to practice sin are not born of God. Farrakhan continues to sin by denying the Lordship and deity of Jesus Christ. He is therefore not born of God. If he is not born of God then he is born of the devil. Let's look further:

> 10He that believeth on the Son of God hath the witness in himself: he that believeth not God hath made him a liar; because he believeth not the record that God gave of his Son.
> 11And this is the record, that God hath given to us eternal life, and this life is in his Son.
> 12He that hath the Son hath life; and he that hath not the Son of God hath not life.
> (1 John 5:10-12)

Jesus Christ is the Son of God. Only through belief in him, will one inherit eternal life. However, Farrakhan does not believe that Jesus is who the Bible says he is. He also does not believe in heaven or hell. However, it does appear that he believes that the black race will rule the world eternally.

> 42Jesus said unto them, If God were your Father, ye would love me: for I proceeded forth and came from God; neither came I of myself, but he sent me.
> 43Why do ye not understand my speech? even because ye cannot hear my word.
> 44Ye are of your father the devil, and the lusts of your father ye will do. He was a murderer from the beginning, and abode not in the truth, because there is no truth in him.

> When he speaketh a lie, he speaketh of his own: for he is a liar, and the father of it.
> [45]And because I tell you the truth, ye believe me not.
> [46]Which of you convinceth me of sin? And if I say the truth, why do ye not believe me?
> [47]He that is of God heareth God's words: ye therefore hear them not, because ye are not of God. (St. John 8:42-47)

Farrakhan's entire way of theological thinking is the same as Elijah Muhammad's. Both men believe that one's salvation has to do with one's race. In their estimation, whites are doomed the day they are born simply because they are white. This is why many question whether or not the Nation of Islam had anything to do with the murder of Malcolm X. When Malcolm X began to promote a colorless theology, he was murdered. By promoting a colorless theology, Malcolm X was going against the very core of Black Muslim Theology.

The scriptures quoted in 1st John and St. John tell us that salvation has nothing to do with color, but instead with a belief in Jesus Christ. Verse 47 above, states that those who are of God will hear his words. But Farrakhan has refused to hear the Word of God. Instead he tunes his ear to the words of Fard and Elijah Muhammad. In doing so, and according to the Word of God, Farrakhan excludes himself from being a child of God, thereby making himself a child of the devil.

Some would say that since God made everyone, then everyone is his child. But this is not what the Word of God says. God only honors those as his children who honor him as their Father through a belief in Jesus Christ. Romans 8:14-15 tells us the following: "For as many as are led by the Spirit of God, they are the sons of God. For ye have not received the spirit of bondage again to fear; but ye have received the Spirit of Adoption, whereby we cry, Abba Father." Even though God made everyone, he adopts his children. Those that he adopts in the Spirit are his. Jesus did not bite his tongue when it came to this issue. He taught, without apology, that there are those who are children of God and those who are children of the devil, as the following scripture reference attest to:

> [25]Another parable put he forth unto them, saying, The kingdom of heaven is likened unto a man which sowed good seed in his field:

> 25 But while men slept, his enemy came
> and sowed tares among the wheat, and went
> his way.
> 26 But when the blade was sprung up, and
> brought forth fruit, then appeared the tares
> also.
> 27 So the servants of the householder came
> and said unto him, Sir, didst not thou sow
> good seed in thy field? from whence them
> hath it tares?
> 28 He said unto them, An enemy hath done
> this. The servants said unto him, Wilt thou
> then that we go and gather them up?
> 29 But he said, Nay; lest while ye gather up
> the tares, ye root up also the wheat with
> them.
> 30 Let both grow together until the harvest:
> and in the time of harvest I will say to the
> reapers, Gather ye together first the tares,
> and bind them in bundles to burn them: but
> gather the wheat into my barn. (St. Matthew
> 13:24-30)

Jesus explains his own parable in the scripture reference below:

> 36 Then Jesus sent the multitude away, and
> went into the house: and his disciples came
> unto him saying, Declare unto us the parable
> of the tares of the field.
> 37 He answered and said unto them, He
> that soweth the good seed is the Son of man;
> 38 The field is the world; the good seed are
> the children of the kingdom; but the tares are
> the children of the wicked one:
> 39 The enemy that sowed them is the devil;
> the harvest is the end of the world; and the
> reapers are the angels.
> 40 As therefore the tares are gathered and
> burned in the fire; so shall it be in the end of
> this world.
> 41 The Son of man shall send forth his
> angels, and they shall gather out of his
> kingdom all things that offend, and them
> which do iniquity.

> 42 And shall cast them into a furnace of fire: there shall be wailing and gnashing of teeth. (St. Matthew 13:36-42)

The tares are the children of the wicked one. The wicked one is the devil whose name is Satan. The children of the devil and the children of God live in the world side by side. Satan is the one that sows the tares. In other words, he schools those vulnerable to him thereby bringing them into his fold as his children. However, at the second coming of Christ, the tares will be separated from the children of God and cast into a furnace of fire. The furnace of fire is hell. Because of Farrakhan's great influence in the Christian black community, he is a tare among Christians. With all the evidence brought forth in this discussion, there is no getting around the deduction that Farrakhan is a child of the devil. With this being the case, it stands to reason that he is guided and influenced by Satan.

Is Farrakhan an antichrist?

There was discussion in the previous chapter on the advent of the antichrist's rule during the seven year tribulation. The particular man who fills this role will be the antichrist of antichrists and some biblical scholars believe that he will also be possessed by Satan himself. However, he will not be the only earthly antichrist. There are antichrists who, on a smaller plane, exist today.

The term "anti" is a prefix that means to oppose or to take a different view other than. An antichrist, therefore, is a person who opposes Christ and his teachings. Let's take a more intricate look at how the Word of God defines an antichrist:

> 7 For many deceivers are entered into the world, who confess not that Jesus Christ is come in the flesh. This is a deceiver and an antichrist.
>
> 8 Look to yourselves, that we lose not those things which we have wrought, but that we receive a full reward.
>
> 9 Whosoever transgresseth, and abideth not in the doctrine of Christ, hath not God. He that abideth in the doctrine of Christ, he hath both the Father and the Son. (2 John 7-9)

Verse 7 above, describes an antichrist as one who does not confess that Jesus Christ came in the flesh. Of course, everyone who is naturally born is born with flesh. Therefore, this verse must mean something else. 1st Timothy 3:16 says the following: "And without controversy great is the mystery of godliness: God was manifest in the flesh, justified in the Spirit, seen of angels, preached unto the Gentiles, believed on in the world, received up into glory." We know that the scripture is speaking of none other than Jesus, because throughout the Bible, Jesus is the only person described with all of these qualities. God was manifest (he came in) the flesh through the body of Jesus Christ. St. John 1:1 tell us that: "In the beginning was the Word, and the Word was with God, and the Word was God." Then the 14th verse of that same chapter says: "And the Word was made flesh, and dwelt among us, (and we beheld his glory, the glory as of the only begotten of the Father,) full of grace and truth."

Moreover, Jesus Christ is the only person in the Bible ever described as God's "only begotten." Therefore, if the Word that was made flesh was the "only begotten," then the Word must have been Jesus. Furthermore, if the Word was God and Jesus was the Word, then Jesus must be God who came in the flesh.

Farrakhan does not believe that Jesus Christ came in the flesh. Instead, he believes that Fard Muhammad came in the flesh. Because of this belief, according to 2nd John 7, as well as other scriptures, Farrakhan fits the description of an antichrist and a deceiver (a liar).

Verse 9 of 2John above, tells us that those who do not abide in the doctrine of Christ, do not have God. As we have seen in the four previous chapters, Farrakhan does not abide in the doctrine of Christ, which the following points attest to:

a) Farrakhan gives praise to Allah, but Psalms 106:1 tells us to praise the Lord, not Allah.

b) Farrakhan does not believe in the resurrection of Jesus Christ but instead believes in the resurrection of the black man's mind. However, Romans 10:9 says: 'that if thou shalt confess with thy mouth the Lord Jesus, and shalt believe in thine heart that God raised him from the dead, thou shalt be saved." The Bible teaches that belief in the resurrection of Jesus is part of what saves souls.

c) Farrakhan believes in evolution, but Genesis 1:1 tells us that: "In the beginning God created the heaven and the earth." The earth was created, it did not evolve.

d) Farrakhan's day of atonement is not the day Jesus was crucified, but instead the day of the Million Man March. However, Romans 5:10-11 says the following:

> [10]For if, when we were enemies we were reconciled to God by the death of his Son,

> much more, being reconciled, we shall be saved by his life.
> [11]And not only so, but we also joy in God through our Lord Jesus Christ, whom we have now received the atonement.

The only atonement man has received is that which was given to him by the blood of Jesus for the remission of sins.

e) Farrakhan believes that Fard is the Saviour and believes him to be God incarnate as indicated by clauses 12 and 13 of the Nation of Islam's doctrinal statement (found in any Final Call Newspaper) which says "We believe that Allah (God) appeared in the person of Master W. Fard Muhammad, July 1930; the long-awaited 'Messiah' of the Christians and the 'Mahdi' of the Muslims. We believe further and lastly that Allah is God and besides HIM there is no God and he will bring about a universal government of peace wherein we all can live in peace together."

However, the following scripture references teach us that there is no God besides Jehovah Yahweh who represents himself in three persons: The Father, Son, and Holy Ghost:

> [6]Thus saith the Lord the King of Israel, and his redeemer the Lord of hosts: I am the first, and I am the last; and beside me there is no God. (Isaiah 44:6)

> [13]I am Alpha and Omega, the beginning and the end, the first and the last.
> [14]Blessed are they that do his commandments, that they may have right to the tree of life, and may enter in through the gates into the city.
> [15]For without are dogs, and sorcerers, and whoremongers, and murderers, and idolaters, and whosoever loveth and maketh a lie.
> [16]I Jesus have sent mine angel to testify unto you these things in the churches. I am the root and the offspring of David, and the bright and morning star. (Revelation 22:13-16)

> [29]And Jesus answered him, The first of all the commandments is, Hear O Israel; The Lord our God is one Lord: (Mark 12:29)

Called of God?

The scriptures just cited tell us that there is only one God, the first and the last, who appeared in the person of Jesus Christ and besides Him there is no other God. However, the Nation of Islam says that Allah is God who appeared in the person of Fard Muhammad and besides Him there is no other God. The Nation of Islam is in error.

As we have seen, St. John teaches us that Jesus is God incarnate. Furthermore, the Bible teaches that there is only one Saviour of whom is Jesus, not Fard. Isaiah 43:11 says the following: "I, even I, am the Lord; and beside me there is no Saviour." God is speaking here and describes himself as Lord and Saviour. St. John 4:42 describes Jesus as being the "Saviour of the world." Titus 2:11-13 says the following:

> 11For the grace of God that bringeth salvation hath appeared to all men,
> 12Teaching us that denying ungodliness and worldly lusts, we should live soberly, righteously, and godly, in this present world;
> 13Looking for that blessed hope, and the glorious appearing of the great God and our Saviour Jesus Christ.

God says that there is no Saviour besides him. Jesus is defined as Lord and Saviour. Therefore, again, Jesus must be God. In verse 13 above, Jesus is described as God and Saviour who will appear again (second coming). There is no indication anywhere in the Bible that there ever was or will ever be another Saviour besides Jesus Christ. Wallace Fard is not the Saviour nor is he God in the flesh, as Farrakhan believes and teaches.

f) Farrakhan teaches that it is a mistake to worship Jesus and that to do so makes one powerless. However, as we have seen before, Jesus himself tells us to worship him and to worship him only (Matthew 4:10).

g) Farrakhan has also said that Elijah Muhammad was the Messiah. As we have seen, neither Elijah Muhammad nor Wallace Fard is the Messiah.

h) Farrakhan continuously compares himself to Jesus and considers himself a type of Jesus and a type of Messiah. By doing so, he has formed his own trinity: Wallace Fard, Elijah Muhammad, and Louis Farrakhan. Satan has done the same: The beast, the false prophet, and the antichrist. However, there is only one Godly Trinity: The Father, The Son, and The Holy Ghost. Ephesians 4:5-6 tells us that there is only one Lord, one faith, one baptism and one God. No one else besides Jesus is Jesus. Farrakhan is not Jesus. He is not a type of Jesus. He is not a reproduction, duplication, or facsimile of Jesus. He is merely, Louis Farrakhan.

i) Farrakhan believes that a new gospel is coming. However, as we have seen, Galatians 1:6-9 tells us that those who preach another gospel besides the one of Jesus Christ will be cursed because they are perverting the gospel of Christ.

In looking at all of the above points, it is clear that Farrakhan teaches "another gospel" in place of the gospel of Jesus Christ. Therefore, he does not abide in the gospel of Christ and is therefore cursed and "hath not God."

1st John 2:21-23 informs us that those who deny that Jesus is the Christ is also denying God. Let's take a look:

> 21I have not written unto you because ye know not the truth, but because ye know it, and that no lie is of the truth.
> 22Who is a liar but he that denieth that Jesus is the Christ? He is antichrist, that denieth the Father and the Son.
> 23Whoesoever denieth the Son, the same hath not the Father: but he that acknowledgeth the Son hath the Father also.

By denying that Jesus is the only Saviour for mankind, Farrakhan has, in essence, denied God and denied that Jesus is the Christ. He also teaches a different gospel other than the gospel of Christ. In looking at all the aforementioned points of this discussion, there is no question that Farrakhan is indeed an antichrist.

Is Farrakhan a false prophet?

A false prophet is a person that teaches false doctrine and heresies but claims that these teachings are the teachings of God. A false prophet is also a person that predicts the future incorrectly but claims that his or her prediction came from God. Let's take a look, for a moment, at the latter:

> 14Then the Lord said unto me, The prophets prophesy lies in my name: I sent them not, neither have I commanded them neither spake unto them: they prophesy unto you a false vision and divination, and a thing of nought, and the deceit of their heart.

> [15] Therefore thus saith the Lord concerning the prophets that prophesy in my name, and I sent them not, yet they say, Sword and famine shall not be in this land; By sword and famine shall those prophets be consumed. (Jeremiah 14:14-15)

Jeremiah was a prophet of God. Earlier verses (not quoted) in chapter 14 of Jeremiah tells us that the nation of Israel had angered God once again by turning away from him. As punishment, God threatened them with famine and death by the sword. Jeremiah complained to God, telling him that certain men who called themselves prophets of God were telling Israel the opposite of what God had told them: that they would not suffer from famine or the sword. God told Jeremiah that the prophesies from these certain men, who called themselves prophets of God, were false and that he (God) had never spoke to them, nor did he send them to prophesy. Because these men used God's name to give false prophesy, God cursed their land (the land in which the false prophets lived) with famine and with the sword.

When looking at Farrakhan's speech at Mosque Maryam, we see that Farrakhan prophesied that the Islamic people would be the ruler of the next world. However, as we have seen, the Bible teaches that Jesus will rule the next world. Jesus is not Islamic. Therefore, Farrakhan's prophesy that Islamic people will rule the next world is a false one.

Farrakhan has also prophesied that all the white people on earth will be destroyed by the year 2004. He also believes that America will be destroyed at that time. He has stated that God will be the one responsible for the destruction. This will not happen. It is a false prophecy. White people will still be walking around on the earth in the year 2004 and America will still be standing.

The New Testament adds more meaning to the description of a false prophet. Let's take a look:

> [15]Beware of false prophets which come to you in sheep's clothing, but inwardly they are ravening wolves.
>
> [16]Ye shall know them by their fruits. Do men gather grapes of thorns, or figs of thistles?
>
> [17]Even so every good tree bringeth forth good fruit: but a corrupt tree bringeth forth evil fruit.

> [18]A good tree cannot bring forth evil fruit, neither can a corrupt tree bring forth good fruit.
> [19]Every tree that bringeth not forth good fruit is hewn down, and cast into the fire.
> [20]Wherefore by their fruits ye shall know them. (Matthew 7:15-20)

According to the Word of God, false prophets come in sheep's clothing. In other words, they either appear to be Christians when they are not, say they are Christians when they are not, or try to convince others that they uphold the teachings of the Bible when in essence they do not. Farrakhan falls into the latter category. His aim is to convince unstudied Christians that Muslims and Christians worship the same God and that the Bible and the Koran basically say the same thing. This makes him a false prophet in sheep's clothing. When taking into consideration all that has been discussed in this book, we know that Muslims and Christians do not worship the same God. Not only does Farrakhan attempt to convince Christians and non-Christians alike that the Bible and the Koran compliment each other, but he is often invited to preach in church after church, as if he were a true prophet of God. Unfortunately, many Christians believe that he is. They are blinded by their impression of the outer man and thus can not see Farrakhan for what he really stands for.

The Word of God tells us that we will know a false prophet by his fruits. What a person produces on earth, when it comes to his works for God, is compared to fruit in the Bible. Fruit either ripens or rots. It's either good or bad. A man's work is either good or bad. Verse 17 above, tells us that if a man is corrupt, he will bring forth evil fruit. Farrakhan has no doubt corrupted the Word of God and is therefore bringing forth evil fruit when he preaches or speaks.

> [1]But there were also false prophets among the people, just as there will be false teachers among you. They will secretly introduce destructive heresies, even denying the sovereign Lord who bought them--bringing
> swift destruction on themselves. [2]Many will
> follow their shameful ways and will bring the
> way of truth into disrepute. [3]In their greed
> these teachers will exploit you with stories they have made up. Their condemnation has long been hanging over them, and their

> destruction has not been sleeping. (2 Peter 2:1-3)

Peter compares false prophets with false teachers. False teachers "introduce destructive heresies." Heresy is any opinion, doctrine, or train of thought that contradicts the teachings of the Bible. There can be no doubt, when looking at the whole of what Farrakhan says, that his teachings contradict those of the Bible. He introduces destructive heresies when he denies the deity of Christ and encourages his audiences to worship his false god: Fard. His heresies are destructive because those who worship Fard as God instead of Jesus, put their souls in the path of everlasting damnation.

Verse 2 above, tells us that many will follow the ways of a false prophet thereby discrediting the Word of God. The "many" that the scripture is referring to are Christians. Peter is addressing himself to believers. Ephesians 4:14 gives believers this warning: "That we henceforth be no more children, tossed to and fro, and carried about with every wind of doctrine, by the sleight of men, and cunning craftiness, whereby they lie in wait to deceive." This tells us that, by the cunning craftiness of a false prophet, Christians can unknowingly embrace false teaching. When this happens, the Word of God is disgraced because it is being mixed with heretical rhetoric from a false prophet upheld by Christians who should know better.

The scripture reference goes on to inform us that false prophets have a tendency to exploit their audiences with made-up stories. Farrakhan makes up a lot of stories when it comes to white people and Jews. Remember, he believes in and upholds the false teachings of Elijah Muhammad, who said that the tribe of Shabazz evolved from an explosion sixty trillion years ago because of the unsuccessful attempt of a god-scientist (who belonged to a team of twenty-four god-scientists, one of which created the white man 6000 years ago) to kill all of mankind. There is no proof that these god-scientists ever existed. They are fictional characters in Elijah Muhammad's made-up stories; stories that Farrakhan also tells. However, many black people, because of the non-healing of their festering sore, will easily follow a man who labels whites as inferior, as does Farrakhan. Not only will they follow Farrakhan, but they will also give money toward his "cause." In this sense, they are being exploited.

Verse 3 (of Peter, above) explains the reason behind the exploitative ways of the false prophet: greed. A person can be greedy when it comes to almost anything. Many people are greedy when it comes to money and power. They want all the money and power they can get. Farrakhan is willing to accept money from Khadafy despite the fact that the American government considers him a terrorist. Farrakhan collected money from the Million Man March. He has talked about a three year economic plan for black people. However, he has been talking about the plan and collecting money to implement it for much longer than three years. Some black people are beginning to question where the money is going. But not enough black people question Farrakhan, and certainly not enough Christians. One reason is because many high profile black people speak well of Farrakhan. The Bible warned us about this trait of the false prophet. Let's take a look:

> 26Woe unto you, when all men shall speak well of you! for so did their fathers to the false prophets. (Luke 6:26)

The Bible teaches that false prophets will be spoken well of by many people.

> 17Now I beseech you, brethren, mark them which cause divisions and offences contrary to the doctrine which ye have learned; and avoid them.
> 18For they that are such serve not our Lord Jesus Christ, but their own belly; and by good words and fair speeches deceive the hearts of the simple. (Romans 16:17-18)

Farrakhan deceives the hearts by "good words and fair speeches." "Good words" is more literally translated as "fair speech" in the Greek with the colloquial term being: "smooth talk." Farrakhan is a very articulate man. His speeches can be very captivating and inviting to many African-Americans because he portrays himself as one who is attempting to bolster the self esteem of the black race. In public, he is always immaculately dressed and smiles many times while addressing an audience. Farrakhan appeals to the intellectual and the heart broken. Many blacks are pulled in by his smooth talk and charming demeanor and consequently succumb to his "fair speech." However, verse 18 goes on to tell us that those who are easily persuaded by the likes of Farrakhan are simple minded. Verse 17 instructs us to avoid men who do not serve Jesus Christ but instead cause “divisions and offenses contrary to the doctrine” of Christ. Such a man is Farrakhan. He is offensive to the doctrine of Christ. Therefore, we are to avoid him. However, we can not avoid Farrakhan and follow him to Washington at the same time. "Avoid" means to "keep away from." It is evident that Farrakhan is a false prophet. The Bible instructs us to keep away from false prophets. Therefore, the Bible is instructing us to keep away from Farrakhan.

Is Farrakhan a racist?

There is a difference between racism and prejudice. We have all been prejudiced in our thinking at some time or another when it comes to people of other races. We may not have even been aware that we were thinking or behaving in a prejudiced manner until someone pointed it out to us. In order to think in a prejudiced way, one must accept preconceived notions about a particular group or race of people that are usually stereotypical or false. Racist thoughts are different from prejudiced thoughts in that racist thoughts encompass the belief that one race is by nature superior to another. When we look at the way Farrakhan thinks about white people, there is no getting around the fact that he sees them as inferior to black people. He sees white people as doomed demons that were created by a "god-scientist."

Farrakhan believes that the color of a white man's skin is unnatural thereby characterizing the Caucasian race as mutants. He believes that God will destroy the entire white race by the year 2004. Farrakhan says that white people are at the root of all the lies and murders worldwide. This train of thought does nothing but reflect a superior attitude of the person relaying the thought. If a white man were to say these same things about black people, Farrakhan as well as most black people, would be quick to call that white man a racist. Remarkably, these things are no less racist in content when said by Farrakhan about the white race. Therefore, one can only conclude that Farrakhan is indeed, a racist.

SUMMING UP THE MATTER

We have conclusive evidence that, according to the Word of God (The Bible), Farrakhan is an antichrist, a false prophet, and a racist. With this being so, it stands to reason that he is not a child of God. As we have seen, those who are not children of God are children of the devil. A person has a biological father and then a spiritual father. Those who are children of God, have God as their spiritual Father. Those who are children of the devil have Satan as their spiritual father. When writing about these things, the apostles were very straightforward. They did not bite their tongues. Therefore, neither can we. Farrakhan is a child of the devil. His spiritual father is Satan. Farrakhan says that he is called of God to do God's work. However, he can not truly be called to do the work of God if he is not born of God and he is not born of God if he does not acknowledge Jesus as Lord and Saviour. Since Farrakhan is a child of the devil, he is not guided by God in the things that he says and does, but instead is guided by his spiritual father: Satan.

THE EPILOGUE: To American Blacks

There is no question that we, as black people, have been mistreated at the hands of many white people since our African ancestors arrived in America as kidnapped prisoners who were forced into slavery at the onset of the seventeenth century. Aside from the atrocities of slavery, there continues to be residual effects of racism and discrimination that haunt America. These take the form of monstrous acts such as southern black church burnings, the Central Intelligence Agency's involvement of the deliberate planting of drugs into black neighborhoods, the government's infamous experiment on black men stricken with syphilis, and so on. In the latter case, the men were given the false impression that they were being treated for the disease. They were instead being given placebos as medication so that the government could study the effects of the disease.

In 1997, President Bill Clinton made a public apology on behalf of the American government for the last offence cited. However, one wonders whether or not black people would have ever heard a such an apology if the truth had never been uncovered. Just as a public apology was made to blacks concerning the syphilis scandal, another public apology from the government needs to be made on a wider scale when it comes to the issue of slavery, as well as issues surrounding previous Jim Crow laws, segregation laws, discriminatory practices and the historical accounts of the non-prosecution of murderous angry white mobs.

To even speak of such things strikes a dissonant chord in the hearts of most black people (and some white people). However, this does not give us any justification, as a people, to put our faith in a man who is not only an antichrist and a false prophet, but a racist as well. Fighting racism with racism only makes for more racism.

In order to understand how Farrakhan is being guided by Satan and his demons, we must digress for a moment and take a more in-depth look at how Satan operates. 1Peter 5:8 describes Satan as a roaring lion seeking to devour people. St. John 8:44 tells us that Satan is a murderer and the father of lies. When we look at the book of Job, we see that Satan will do anything to get people to turn from God. Let's take a look:

> 6One day the angels came to present themselves before the Lord, and Satan also came with them. 7The Lord said to Satan, "Where have you come from?"

> Satan answered the Lord, "From roaming through the earth and going back and forth in it."
>
> [8]Then the Lord said to Satan, "Have you considered my servant Job? There is no one on earth like him; he is blameless and upright, a man who fears God and shuns evil."
>
> [9]"Does Job fear God for nothing?" Satan replied. [10] "Have you not put a hedge around him and his household and everything he has? You have blessed the work of his hands, so that his flocks and herds are spread throughout the land.
>
> [11]But stretch out your hand and strike everything he has, and he will surely curse you to your face.
>
> [12]The Lord said to Satan, "Very well, then, everything he has is in your hands, but on the man himself do not lay a finger." (Job 1:6-12)

Satan went to God looking to get into mischief. God allowed Satan to test Job. Satan has no power unless God allows him to have it. People are tempted to do wrong by Satan and his demons. However, people have control over whether or not they will succumb to temptation. At any rate, God gave Satan the go-ahead to destroy everything Job had. Satan felt that Job loved and revered the Lord only because God blessed Job with a good life and many things. Satan felt that if God took these things away from Job that Job would curse God and speak against him. In other words, Satan tried to convince God that Job's faithfulness to him (God) was conditional. By the time Satan was finished doing his dirty work, Job's servants and sheep were consumed by fire and his children were killed. However, despite Job's grief, he continued to worship the Lord. But Satan didn't give up, as the following scripture reference attests to:

> [1]On another day the angels came to present themselves before the Lord, and Satan also came with them to present himself before him.
>
> [2]And the Lord said to Satan, "Where have you come from?"
>
> Satan answered the Lord, "From roaming through the earth and going back and forth in it."

Epilogue

> [3]Then the Lord said to Satan, "Have you considered my servant Job? There is no one on earth like him; he is blameless and upright, a man who fears God and shuns evil. And he still maintains his integrity, though you incited me against him to ruin him without any reason."
>
> [4]"Skin for skin!" Satan replied. "A man will give all he has for his own life. [5]But stretch out your hand and strike his flesh and bones and he will surely curse you to your face."
>
> [6]The Lord said to Satan, "Very well, then, he is in your hands; but you must spare his life."
>
> [7]So Satan went out from the presence of the Lord and afflicted Job with painful sores from the soles of his feet to the top of his head. [8]Then Job took a piece of broken pottery and scraped himself with it as he sat among the ashes.
>
> [9]His wife said to him, "Are you still holding on to your integrity? Curse God and die!"
>
> [10]He replied, "You are talking like a foolish woman. Shall we accept good from God, and not trouble?"
>
> In all this, Job did not sin in what he said. (Job 2:1-10)

Job held on to his integrity and did not curse God. However, the book of Job tells us that his suffering was so great that he cursed the day he was born and wished he had died in the womb. The scriptures also go on to inform us that one of Job's friends tried to convince him that he brought his suffering on himself by some wrongdoing. However, Job denied any wrongdoing. He had not brought his suffering upon himself. Despite Job's misery and the poor counsel he received from his wife and friends, Job maintained his steadfastness in the Lord. Therefore God blessed him with more than he had before. Job 42:12-13 says, "The Lord blessed the latter part of Job's life more than the first. He had fourteen thousand sheep, six thousand camels, a thousand yoke of oxen and a thousand donkeys. And he also had seven sons and three daughters." Verse 15 of the same chapter goes on to say that "Nowhere in all the land were there found women as beautiful as Job's daughters, and their father granted them an inheritance along with their brothers."

Epilogue

Through the historical account of Job, the Bible gives us one of many lessons on how Satan and his demons operate. Satan's primary goal is to turn people away from God. If he is not successful at doing so, he will then attempt to destroy the reputation of those who believe in God in order to turn other people from God. Satan tried to destroy Job's reputation.

Satan wanted Job to curse God and turn away from him. In order to try to get Job to turn from God, Satan needed to determine the right "buttons to push." All of us have "buttons" that, when pushed, increase the probability that we may do something that we would not normally do. At first, Satan destroyed everything Job had, including members of his family. However, he soon discovered that, despite these traumas, Job's "buttons" had not been pushed to the point of cursing God. A frustrated Satan then obtained permission to push more of Job's buttons. This time Satan took away Job's health by tormenting him with festering sores. Although, Job did not curse God, Satan managed to bring Job to the point where he wished he were dead. However, God blessed Job tremendously in the end for not turning against him in the midst of adversity.

The same tactics that Satan used against Job are the same tactics he uses against people today. Satan and his demons attack people individually or they attack groups of people. It is easy for Satan to attack a group of people when the people within the group have similar "buttons" that can be pushed. Although we, as black people in America, are markedly different from one another on an individual basis, we have similar "buttons" that when pushed, cause many of us to behave in ways we might not otherwise behave. Our "buttons" are similar because we have suffered similar injustices. Consequently, our buttons are pushed when we come across anything that symbolizes racism or serves it. Racism and discrimination, has plagued black people with a psychological festering sore that has never really completely healed. Therefore, anyone who pushes the buttons of racism and discrimination, has, in essence, for many blacks, knocked the scab off the sore. This is why many of us rioted in California when the Rodney King verdict was announced. Of course, there is no justification for random acts of violence. However, the point is that the buttons of racial inequality in the American judicial system were pushed once more. Consequently the scab was snatched off of the sore, it began to again fester, and several of us did something that we would never have normally done: rioted.

Our psychological sores are akin to Job's physical sores. Farrakhan is a master at pushing the necessary buttons that embitter blacks toward whites. He often reminds us of what was once a brutal slavery system in America and causes us to remember the civil rights injustices that have been upheld by the government throughout the years. After pushing these particular buttons and reopening the sore, Farrakhan cleverly suggests his solution to it all: Solidarity of American blacks by a meticulous and methodical ingratiating of us into the Nation of Islam. He is so good at what he does, that even Christian blacks are fooled by his charisma for they have had their scabs snatched away as well. Consequently, we have Christian blacks who actually believe that those who follow the teachings of Jesus worship the same God as those who follow the teachings of Farrakhan. They believe it because they want to believe it and they want to believe it because their festering sore is pulsating and they see Farrakhan as the person who can stop the bleeding. What they don't see is that Farrakhan has designed things so that he is seen as the leader of the American black community who has a plan to heal all wounds. And what they don't see is his ultimate plan to encourage all African-Americans to become Black Muslims.

Those of us who are Christians blacks and have been influenced by Farrakhan, don't usually go to the point of turning against Jesus, but many of us embrace Farrakhan. By doing so, we have embraced the Nation of Islam. However, as Christians, we can not afford to put our ethnicity above our spirituality. We can not sacrifice or compromise the latter for the former. It certainly behooves us to continue in the struggle for civil rights, however, this does not justify an association with a man who is clearly an antichrist and whose purpose is to recruit for the Nation of Islam. As a matter of fact, when we look at the second book of John 10-11, we see that God makes it very clear that we are not to associate with the likes of Farrakhan. The scripture reads, "If there come any unto you, and bring not this doctrine, receive him not into your house, neither bid him God speed: For he that biddeth him God speed is partaker of his evil deeds."

Those of us who are Christians are commanded not to receive anyone into our houses who brings us another doctrine besides the doctrine of Christ. The scripture goes on to tell us that we should not even wish them "God speed." The New International Version translates "God Speed" more specifically as "welcome." We are not to welcome anyone who delivers false teaching. In other words, we are not to be "chummy" with people who preach and teach another gospel. If this is the case, then what justification do Christians have in following or supporting Farrakhan? Farrakhan preaches another gospel other than that of Jesus Christ. Therefore, if those of us who are Christians are mandated not to invite Farrakhan to our houses, then it stands to reason that we should not invite him to speak in the pulpit of *God's house* either! Accordingly, we should not follow him to Washington or any other place where he speaks. How can we say that it's all right to follow Farrakhan to Washington and support his efforts there, when God has instructed us not to invite him into our homes? If we are not to invite him into our homes, then we are not to invite him into our hearts either because in doing so we are "partaker of his evil deeds." Clearly then, we can not invite him to speak in our churches. However, many church leaders have done so, thus going against God's word.

As we have seen, it was Farrakhan's main intention to secure an audience for the purposes of promoting the Nation of Islam rather than for the purpose of solidifying more unity amongst American blacks. It has been estimated that 98% of his audience at the Million Man March were of some denomination of the Christian faith. This means that, by Nation of Islam estimates, one million American black men (most of whom were Christians) went to Washington to support a man who delivered a message that was heavily tainted with Black Muslim theology. Thus, we can only conclude that this phenomenon, was designed and executed, not by God, but by demonic forces.

Those of us who are Christians can not allow ourselves to get caught up in the rhetoric of Farrakhan, because in doing so, we not only open ourselves up to the teachings of Black Muslim theology, but we might also unintentionally sway others to follow him who are not saved. If we embrace and support Farrakhan, our unsaved family members, friends, and associates may begin to do so also, depending on the amount of influence we have over them. Many Christians have stated that they can support Farrakhan's message of black unity without supporting the man himself. However, there are three problems that arise with the belief that one can do this:

Problem 1: Farrakhan has made it quite clear that he does not want to be separated from his message. As we have seen, in his Million Man March speech, Farrakhan stated that he was aware that many had "tried to distance the beauty of this idea from the person through who the idea and the call was made." Christian black people were among the many, who wanted to identify with the theme of black unity, but did not want to identify with Farrakhan. We can not identify with his message without identifying with him because essentially it is indeed Farrakhan's message that we are listening to and no-one else's. Even Farrakhan himself insinuated that we can't have it both ways.

Farrakhan went on to say that those who attempted to separate him from his message were either mistaken or did so maliciously. "Mistake" and "malice" are negative words, not positive ones. Consequently, by describing those, as mistaken or malicious, who purposed to separate him from his message, Farrakhan, basically chastised them and did so within ten minutes of the onset of his speech. Apparently, because his ultimate goal is to get as many blacks as he can to join the Nation of Islam, this separation of man and message was something that

Farrakhan wanted to discourage right away. The job of enticing blacks to join the "Nation" proves more difficult for Farrakhan if most of his audience tries to separate what he says from who he is. In order to carry out his plan to propagate his theology, Farrakhan must first get blacks to identify with him. He does this by establishing a comradeship, through his speeches, between he and those blacks who are angry with white people as a whole.

Once we, as black people begin identifying with Farrakhan, then the likelihood that we will listen to him increases. Once we begin listening, then the likelihood that we may become Black Muslims also increases if we have no firm foundation in Christ. Case in point: Reverend Benjamin Chavis, because of his association with Farrakhan, his willingness to give an open ear to Farrakhan's message, and his basic anger towards white people, became a Black Muslim in February of 1997. He is no longer a Christian and is now referred to as Minister Benjamin Chavis Muhammad. Benjamin Chavis wasn't able to listen to the message of black unity and disregard the messenger. He listened to Farrakhan's message of black unity and *joined* the messenger. The possibility of this very kind of occurrence is the reason behind why this book was written. We can not afford to turn a blind eye to who Farrakhan really is and what he really stands for.

Problem 2: For those of us who are Christians, it is naive for us to think that we can support Farrakhan without influencing unsaved people to do the same, which may very possibly lead to them joining the "Nation." We should remember that sometimes the only "Bible" a person will ever read is our lives and the way in which we live it. As Christians, we may be able to beam in on the black unity part of Farrakhan's messages and throw out the rest, but not every one is able to do this. If Farrakhan can influence people like Ben Chavis, who was a minister that preached the Word of God, then he can most certainly influence those who do not know God's word. When a Christian supports Farrakhan, his or her behavior is analogous to a person carrying a virus that they are immune to or may be minimally affected by. Although the person carrying the virus is immune, the virus is still contagious and those who are not immune to it might catch it. As Christians, we need to make sure that we don't carry the virus of Farrakhan's false doctrines and racist teachings to those unbelievers or unlearned Christians who are not immune.

Problem 3: Many Christians believe that Farrakhan is only preaching a message of black unity and nothing more. They have not investigated the things that he teaches. They have overlooked his indirect suggestions and subliminal messages. However, in looking at the history and teachings of the Nation of Islam as we did in Chapter One, as well as looking at the content of the four speeches that have been discussed in Chapters Three through Six, there is little question that the majority of what Farrakhan teaches is more so a lesson on the doctrines of the Nation of Islam rather than a lesson on how we, as black people, can become more unified amongst ourselves. Consequently, those who support Farrakhan are, in essence, supporting teachings of false doctrine and racism.

Farrakhan's message to the black man is the same as Elijah Muhammad's message to the black man: separation of the races, denouncement of the Christian religion, and belief that all blacks are Muslim by nature and should become Black Muslims. However, I have another message to the black man in America that entails the following:

a) The influence of Farrakhan and the Nation of Islam in the black community have put black Americans in great spiritual jeopardy. As we have seen, the only way to God is through a belief in Jesus Christ as Lord and Saviour. To believe anything that contradicts this is to be, according to the Word of God, condemned to hell. However, Farrakhan wants us to believe in those things that would send us to hell.
b) This life is only temporary, but life after death is forever. Therefore, my concern is for the salvation of "my people" because salvation in Jesus Christ promises eternal life in the Kingdom of God. The Million Man March was nothing more than a catalyst used by Farrakhan to gain a larger audience for induction into the "Nation." Therefore, on October 16, 1995, an estimated million American black men listened with open hearts to what Farrakhan had to say, thereby increasing the odds that they would possibly consider joining the ranks of the Nation of Islam and by doing so risk loosing their souls.
c) Jesus Christ died on the cross as the ultimate sacrificial lamb for all of mankind. His resurrection is proof that he is who he said he is. Christianity is not just for the white man but it is for everyone, Jew and Gentile alike. It is the only true religion.
d) The Bible has not been tampered with. However, the devil would like for us to believe that it has been tampered with in order to sway us from it.
e) White people are human beings just like us. They are not devils. However, demons do exist and the devil is very real. Satan is our adversary along with his demons. He is the enemy that we should always contend to fight against. As black people, sometimes we tend to forget that there are as many white people whose ancestors fought against slavery as there are those who fought in favor of it. Not only this, but if we look back far enough, many of our ancestors were not only slaves but

slave masters as well. We must try to remember these things when we experience any ill feelings against the white race.

f) I can not begin to speculate as to why God allowed slavery in America. He has his reasons, just as he had his reasons for allowing Job to suffer. However, what we should focus on is that the same God who allowed slavery, had it abolished.

Farrakhan has joined forces with Khadafy to promote Islam worldwide. Both men realize that each of them do not wholeheartedly support the doctrinal teachings of the other. However, they both believe that they can promote the basics of Islam together. Muslims believe in the Jihad. The Jihad is the doctrine of "holy war" which is taught in the Hadith. Jihad is the act of forcing non-Muslims to convert to Islam. This act of force can include threat of death. There are places in the Middle East where the building of churches is absolutely forbidden. Furthermore, Muslim countries are the only countries that continue to practice slavery. Those who are enslaved in Muslim countries are Christians. In some Muslim countries, death penalties have been instituted for turning away from Islam. The Jihad, slavery, and the death penalty are just some of the things that Farrakhan supports by consorting with Khadafy.

Malcolm X, Benjamin Chavis Muhammad, Elijah Muhammad, and Farrakhan were all raised in Christian homes. Some might wonder how they strayed so far from away from the Word of God. The following scriptures explain what may have led these men away from the truth:

> 19When any one heareth the word of the kingdom, and understandeth it not, then cometh the wicked one, and catcheth away that which was sown in his heart. This is he which received seed by the wayside.
>
> 20But he that received the seed into stony places, the same is he that heareth the word, and anon with joy receiveth it;
>
> 21Yet hath he not root in himself, but dureth for a while: for when tribulation or persecution ariseth because of the word, by and by he is offended.
>
> 22He also that received seed among the thorns is he that heareth the word; and the care of this world, and the deceitfulness of riches, choke the word, and he becometh unfruitful.
>
> 23But he that received seed into the good ground is he that heareth the word, and

> understandeth it, which also beareth fruit, and bringeth forth, some an hundredfold, some sixty, some thirty. (Matthew 13:19-23)

Verse 19 tells us that there are those who hear the Word of God but do not initially understand it. Before they get the understanding, the devil comes along and snatches away the little bit of understanding the person may have had. Therefore, the person is left to their own understanding. From this comes false doctrine. 2Timothy 2:15 tells us to "study to shew thyself approved unto God." Proverbs 3:5 tells us to "trust the Lord with all thine heart; and lean not unto thine own understanding." In order to understand the Bible the way God intends for us to understand it, we must study it. Otherwise, we will begin to create our own interpretation and understanding of scripture and fall away from sound doctrine.

Verses 20 and 21 tell us that there are those who hear the Word of God and receive it with joy but only until they are persecuted for their beliefs. Once they are persecuted, they become offended by the Word of God and inevitably turn from God. However, Matthew 5:10 says, "Blessed are they which are persecuted for righteousness' sake: for theirs is the kingdom of heaven."

Verse 22 tells us that there are those who hear the Word of God but are so wrapped up in the affairs of life and monetary ambitions that they end up not serving God but instead serving only themselves.

Verse 23 tells us that there are those who hear the Word of God, understand it, live righteously, serve God, and bring others to Christ in the process.

It is not clear what category Malcolm, Chavis, and Elijah Muhammad fit into. However, it appears that Farrakhan fits into the category described in verse 19. Farrakhan has his own understanding of the scriptures that leads him to pervert their meaning. Throughout all of his speeches, Farrakhan quotes from the Bible substantially more often than he quotes from the Koran. There is no question, therefore, that he has studied the Bible. The wicked one (the devil) has snatched away the understanding of the scriptures from Farrakhan's heart. However, Farrakhan has allowed Satan to do so by not studying the Word of God as it should be studied. Farrakhan entices Christians to listen to him because he quotes more from the Bible than he does from the Koran. However, he twists the meaning of the scriptures.

It is my plea that we don't fall into the same trap that Farrakhan has fallen into. We must study the Word of God continuously so that we will not be, as Ephesians 4:14 puts it: "carried about with every wind of doctrine, by the sleight of men, and cunning craftiness, whereby they lie in wait to deceive."

Epilogue

I do not hate Mr. Farrakhan, nor do I hate the members of the Nation of Islam. I love them all with the love of the Lord. However, as a Christian, I can not stand by and idly watch as one million black men are duped into listening to the teachings of Nation of Islam theology in the name of black unity and civil liberty. There are too many souls at stake. With this said, I will leave you with the following scripture reference to consider: this is one in which Paul the apostle, is speaking to Timothy (a preacher). Paul said this to Timothy shortly before Paul was executed for preaching the gospel:

> 1 I charge thee therefore before God, and
> the Lord Jesus Christ, who shall judge the
> quick and the dead at his appearing and his
> kingdom;
> 2 Preach the word; be instant in season, out
> of season; reprove, rebuke, exhort with all
> longsuffering and doctrine.
> 3 For the time will come when they will not
> endure sound doctrine; but after their own lusts
> shall they heap to themselves teachers, having
> itching ears;
> 4 And they shall turn away their ears from
> the truth, and shall be turned unto fables.
> 5 But watch thou in all things, endure
> afflictions, do the work of an evangelist, make
> full proof of thy ministry.
> 6 For I am now ready to be offered, and the
> time of my departure is at hand.
> 7 I have fought a good fight, I have finished
> my course, I have kept the faith:
> 8 Henceforth there is laid up for me a crown
> of righteousness, which the Lord, the righteous
> judge, shall give me at that day: and not to me
> only, but unto all them also that love his
> appearing. (2 Timothy 4:1-8)

Peace be with you.

BIBLIOGRAPHY

Adams, Moody. *Farrakhan, Islam & the Religion that is Raping America,* The Moody Adams Evangelistic Association,. 1996

Arberry, Authur J. *The Koran Interpreted*, New York, Collier Books Macmillan Publishing Co., 1955

Butler, Trent C. *Holman Bible Dictionary*. Nashville Tennessee, Holman Bible Publishers, 1991

Holy Bible, The *New International Version.* Grand Rapids Michigan, Zondervan Publishing House, 1984

Holy Bible, The *King James Version*

Koran, The. New York, Ivy Books published by Ballantine Books First Ballantine Books edition, 1993

Lincoln, Eric C. *The Black Muslims in America*, Trenton New Jersey, Africa World Press, Inc. William B. Eerdmans Publishing Co., Third Edition, 1994

Miller, William M. *A Christian's Response to Islam*, Wheaton Illinois, Tyndale House Publishers Inc., 1976

Morey, Robert. *The Islamic Invasion*, Eugene Oregon, Harvest House Publishers, 1992

Moyer, Elgin S. *Who was Who in Church History*, New Canaan Connecticut, Keats Publishing, Inc., 1974

Muhammad, Elijah. *Message To The Blackman in America*, Chicago Illinois, Muhammad's Temple No.2, 1965

Roberts, J. M. *History of The World*, New York, Oxford University Press, 1993

Smith, Jerome. *Treasury of Scripture Knowledge*, Nashville Tennessee, Thomas Nelson Publishers, 1992

White, James. *The King James Only Controversy*, Minneapolis Minnesota, Bethany House Publishers,1984

NAME INDEX

Abraham
60-61, 65, 112, 136
Ali, Noble Drew 2, 3
Allah 8, 14, 15
Aton 66, 67
Bibliander, Theodor 32
Caedmon 30
Chavis, Benjamin
79-81, 109, 207, 210
Christ, Jesus
39, 40, 41-45, 143
144
Clinton, Bill 201
El Shaddai 14
El Elyon 14
El Berith 14
El Roi 14
Erasmus 30
Esau 62
Fard, Wallace
5, 9, 19, 49, 78
82, 87, 90, 98, 105
118, 192-193
Farrakhan, Louis 11, 56-57
Garvey, Marcus 3, 4, 113
God (see Yahweh)
Isaac 62, 184
Iscariot, Judas 42
Jacob 62
Jerome 30
Habakkuk 92-94
Haley, Alex 111
Ham 7, 22
Hinckelman, Abraham 32
Immanuel (see Christ, Jesus)
Kariem, Muhammad
(see Muhammad, Elijah)
Khadafy, Muammar
1, 73, 82-84, 107-110
113-117, 133, 139-140
King James V1 29
King, Martin Luther 129
Melchizedek 42
Muhammad (570 A.D.)
8, 9, 18
Muhammad (see below)
Muhammad, Elijah
2, 9-12, 15, 21, 53
81, 106-107, 118
124-125, 142, 151,
172-173, 178, 208
Muhammad, Fard
(see Fard, Wallace)
5, 9, 10, 11, 12, 15,
21, 53
Muhummad, Jalil 81
Muhammad, Tynetta
77-79
Nebuchadnezzar 34
Pilate, Pontius 44, 140
Plummer, Glenn 141
Poole, Elijah (see
Muhammad, Elijah)
Retenensis, Robert 32
Rodwell, J.M. 32
Ryer, Sieur Du 32
Shabazz, Malcolm X
(see X, Malcolm)
Shem 7, 22
Tyndale, William 30
Walcott, Eugene (see
Farrakhan, Louis)
Wycliffe, John 30
Yahweh 8
Yakub 12
Malcolm 10, 113